John Miller

Seeing is Believing

For Michael Truscott who
has shared so much of it
with me

He who binds himself a joy,
Does the winged life destroy;
He who kisses the joy as it flies,
Lives in Eternity's sunrise.

William Blake 1757-1827
'Eternity'

John Miller

Seeing is Believing

Edited conversations with

Heather Corbett

Truran

ISBN 1 85022 153 7 (hardback)
ISBN 1 85022 154 5 (paperback)

Published in 2001 by Truran,
Croft Prince, Mount Hawke, Truro, Cornwall TR4 8EE

Designed by Peter Bennett, St Ives, Cornwall
Printed in Cornwall by Rowe the Printers, Hayle
Main text set in Helvetica Neue

Every effort has been made to thank the owners of the paintings reproduced;
those unknown please accept our thanks

Photography credits

John Bartlett (**JB**)
Bob Berry (**BB**)
Simon Cook (**SC**)
David Cornwell (**DC**)
Stephen Cornwell (**SnC**)
Ander Gunn (**AG**)
David Howarth (**DH**)
Murray King Images (**MK**)
Michael Truscott (**MT**)
Andrew Whatley (**AW**)
Unattributed photographs are from the Miller album

Foreword by Gary Rhodes

It was the year of 1994 that our friendship was born. The last programme of my first full BBC television programme was to be set in Cornwall, a part of the country that I had never experienced. Our producer, Gabrielle, had established a long term loving relationship with this corner of the West Country; it also held so many different culinary features that the two reasons just walked together so naturally.

There's a feeling that runs through you when arriving here, along with a feeling that you're greeted with, very much like that of the wonderful textural surroundings, with the completed relationship becoming long term almost instantly. It's probably these features that drew, excited and kept John and Michael for the past forty years.

We met, talked and an instant respect for one another's beliefs was found. I was to be cooking mackerel; John was to be painting mackerel. The two were married very quickly – cooking and painting – working with textures, consistencies, knowing when enough 'seasoning' has been added just to lift and not spoil the finished results.

Looking back on this first encounter, finishing with just a few minutes of television, still makes a big impression in my memory. It was to be a quick piece of filming, adding another scene to an already quite full programme. Instead a day passed and my mind was blossoming on an educational trip of one man's works.

It is within the following pages that a similar trip can be taken. The story tells how painting and styles have changed over the years – looking back at many that he no longer appreciates, and as John explains, were 'far too energetic', but with that all carrying an honest statement of how he felt and where he was in life.

The learning process was about developing and moving with the times; each new thought approached carefully, creating space for the work's natural progression – allowing the main ingredients to remain the most predominant with soft garnishes to accompany. John loves to experience the joy of discovering new colours, very much as I do with new flavours, both happily finding their way onto the palate – sharing his thoughts, style and concepts with us, the viewers, as well as other artists.

Collecting Miller paintings has been for pure enjoyment, his natural feeling of celebration sitting on the wall, each carrying its own personality and identity. As a family we have been encaptured by this man: not just his works, but the man himself – his warmth – his feelings – his honesty – thank you John.

After reading and seeing comes the believing.

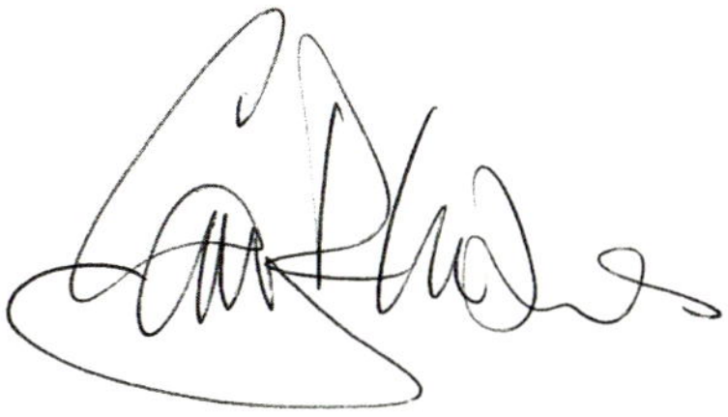

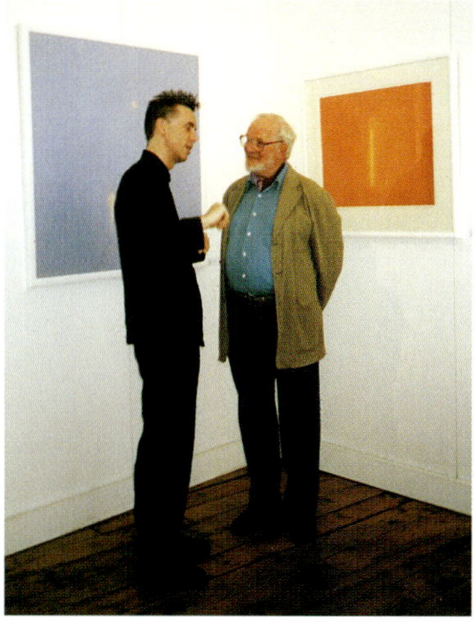

▲ **John Miller and Gary Rhodes at the White Gallery, Hove**
2000
AW

Introduction

I have known John Miller for a long time and over the years we have had many informal discussions about his life and work. It gradually dawned upon both of us that John wanted to make a more formal statement. His imminent seventieth birthday provided the stimuli for us to endeavour to put something together. But of course he wanted to paint not write.

This book therefore is the result of taped conversations that took place between John and myself in his studio during the summer and autumn of 2000. The text was then edited and the final draft was agreed between John and myself after further discussions.

John's rich and colourful life has given him a storehouse of experiences and anecdotes that many novelists would envy and we were inevitably swamped with material. Though we had started with a framework for the book we found that we had to discipline ourselves to create stricter parameters.

The text was important but so were the pictures and we were anxious to print as many as possible – not just for their sheer impact but also John was very keen to show a retrospective view of his work; he has after all been painting for over 50 years. He wanted to show where he had come from and how he had developed.

It is very easy for authors and even easier for editors to allow their authors to pontificate; I hope we have avoided this and that the book will delight John's countless admirers and give them a further insight into a remarkable man and his remarkable paintings.

Heather Corbett
Cornwall March 2001

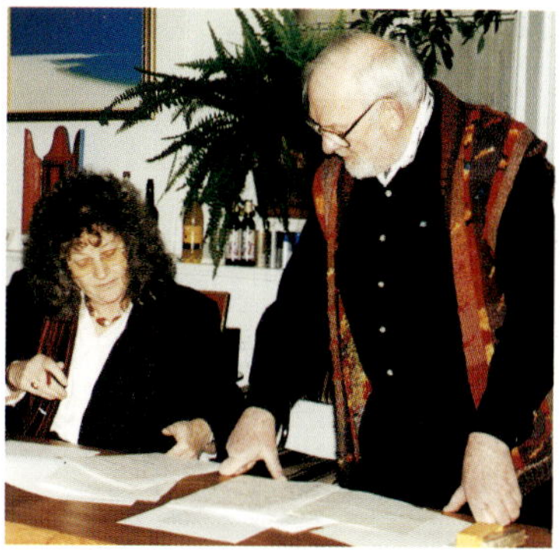

▲ **John Miller and Heather Corbett**
2001

◀ **Summer Sandspur**
2000 gouche 25x25

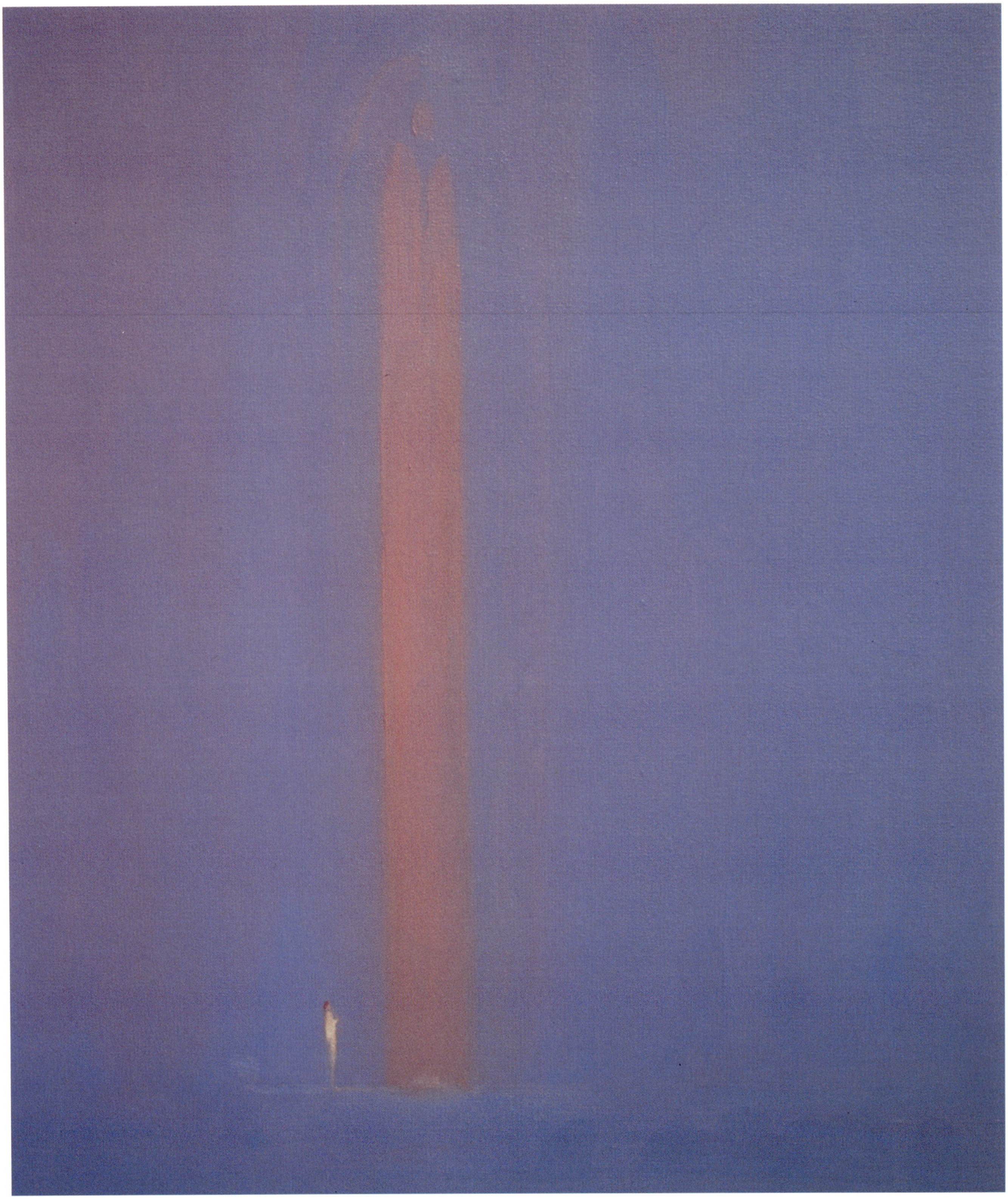

Artist's statement

Very few days pass when I am not
brought swiftly out of myself by something beautiful:

The flash of sunlight on a Cornish beach;
The juxtaposition of two colours in the landscape;
The tenderness, momentarily overheard, in a mother's voice;
The glimpse of eternity in the eyes of a dying friend;
The smell of new-mown hay;
The feel of a summer breeze upon my cheeks;
The breath of a curious cow upon my neck when drawing in a field;
The colours where sea and sand meet caught in a backward glance;
The adventure into infinity when sea and sky become one
And the timeless moment when the sun hangs poised above the dawn horizon.

All these experiences, often uninvited, are very precious
Like the love and laughter of friends.

Painting is my way of celebrating them.
Valuing them
Enshrining them
Sharing them.

It is also an act of gratitude.

Because:
Having seen and known the good and evil in myself
And, at times, in others
I have also known
The beautiful has always been there for the finding.

Now I make plain and simple
Statements which can,
Hopefully,
Go straight to the heart.

John Miller February 2001

◀ **Figure in Mauve Interior**
2000 75x70
MT

Beaches

My childhood memories are of beaches and sunshine. We went on family holidays and weekends to the south coast – Brighton, Eastbourne, Bexhill, Hastings, Worthing, Winchelsea and Rye. I have vivid memories of the sparkle of the sun on the sea and the myriad colours of the beach.

Sometimes my father hired a rowing boat and took me fishing. He loved fishing and patiently taught me the skills as his father had taught him. I can remember the thrill of being on the open sea – off the shore and alone in the vast expanse of blue and how good it was to be there with my father.

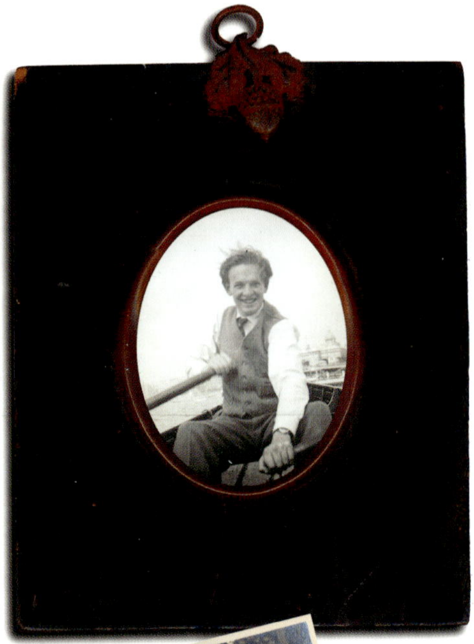

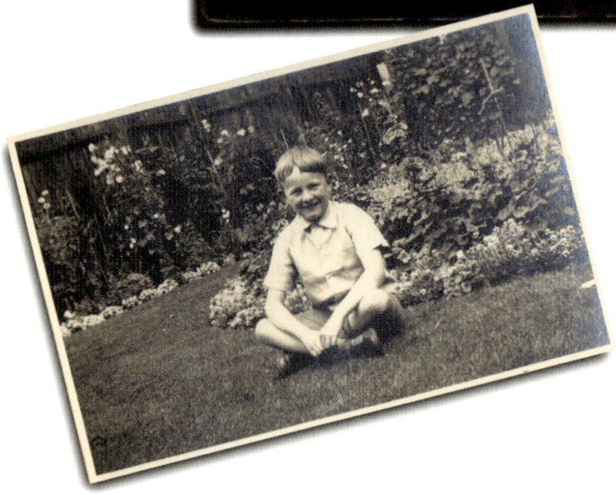

▲ **Eastbourne**
July 1949

▲ **Aged 6 or 7 in the garden at home**

War

When the Second World War began in 1939 I was eight years old. The beaches were soon covered in barbed wire and tank traps and we were no longer able to visit them. I remember feeling that something very special had been taken away – something irreplaceable.

The outbreak of war coincided with my beginning school. My parents sent me to St Joseph's College, Beulah Hill which was run by a Roman Catholic order called the De la Salle Brothers. We were not Catholics but an uncle had been educated there.

The school was almost immediately evacuated to Cuckfield, Haywards Heath in Sussex. Most of us were billeted in private houses and a large house was given over to classrooms. I went with a boy called Peter to live with Miss White in her cottage on the outskirts of Ansty. She had been a nanny to the Napier family.

Although there were parks and commons near my home in London this was my first real experience of rural England. My memory is of a kaleidoscope of colours combined with the buzz and fizz of a hot summer's day. I can recall lying beneath a tree and looking at the blue sky and white clouds through the colours of the leaves and branches in and out of shade. Even now that memory stirs a sensation of utter bliss. But as for all young people life wasn't always blissful.

My father, an architect with the London County Council, was co-opted into Heavy Rescue and stationed at Deptford and Woolwich, which, being dockland became prime targets when the bombing began. We saw him only when he came on leave. I missed him a lot.

Mother came to visit me at Ansty whenever she could. There were restrictions on travel. She brought me lead soldiers and models. Peter and I made earthworks in the little kitchen garden and went to war with our model soldiers and tanks. As with most little boys there were occasions when we misbehaved and incurred the wrath of n'aunt's White (as she became known). She proved to be a fierce adversary but a fair one. After the war my family adopted her – as they did countless people – and she often accompanied us on holidays to the West Country.

I suppose because the early part of the war took place in Europe and there appeared to be no imminent danger of invasion the school returned to London. Underground shelters had been constructed and the school buildings were shored up with massive balks of timber against the possibility of bombing.

I will always be grateful for the education that I received from the brothers. Over and above the academic curriculum we were shown a set of values for life. The brothers lived a rigorous day, rising at 5.30 am and praying the monastic offices through the day as well as teaching. It was a severe life for them but they were not severe with the pupils. Of course we were caned if we misbehaved, but in those days everyone was caned.

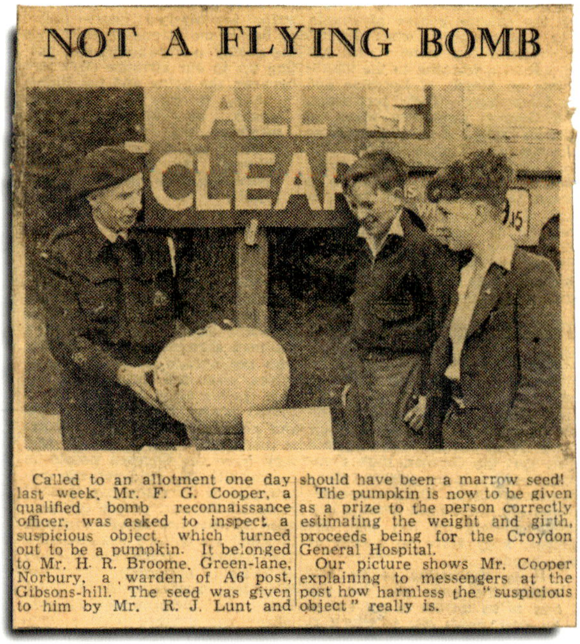

NOT A FLYING BOMB

Called to an allotment one day last week, Mr. F. G. Cooper, a qualified bomb reconnaissance officer, was asked to inspect a suspicious object, which turned out to be a pumpkin. It belonged to Mr. H. R. Broome, Green-lane, Norbury, a warden of A6 post, Gibsons-hill. The seed was given to him by Mr. R. J. Lunt and should have been a marrow seed!

The pumpkin is now to be given as a prize to the person correctly estimating the weight and girth, proceeds being for the Croydon General Hospital.

Our picture shows Mr. Cooper explaining to messengers at the post how harmless the "suspicious object" really is.

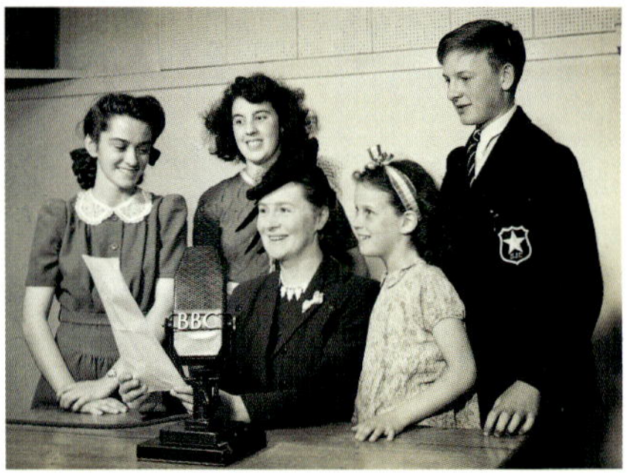

▲ **John Miller (middle) as a messenger boy for the ARP**

▲ **Station WLW Mailbag Club, London Chapter**
John Miller broadcasts to Cincinnati USA
1945

I became fascinated by the life of the spirit and was encouraged by one of the brothers to explore the mystics: St John of the Cross, St Theresa and Dame Julian of Norwich. He took some of us to lectures on the mystics at King's College London. All that opened the spirituality in me, inevitably forever, because once that part of oneself has been enlivened it can never be put back to sleep. It was then that I began to experience the oneness of time and space and the whole of creation.

Some years later, when I was peering over a vast sea of suburbia in a state of both wonderment and confusion because of the good and evil I had seen in myself and others during those war years, it was as though everything was gathered into a ball of light which I knew at once to be absolute love.

During the war I was amongst other things a messenger boy for the ARP. South London often got the bombs intended for central London and the docks when they were dropped too early or jettisoned by a damaged aircraft eager to turn and limp home. I suppose there were no walkie-talkies in those days which is why we were sent off on our bicycles in our tin hats inscribed with 'M', to 'incidents' to keep the wardens and rescue workers on site in touch with the central ARP post.

Looking back on those days I realise that, as we get older, we are less able to endure the emotional and physical shocks we can take in our stride when young. I simply couldn't do now the things I did then. For example: assisting to extricate the dead and nearly dead from a bombed building. On one occasion I threw down my bicycle and leaped behind a low front garden wall in time to avoid the bullets from a Heinkel bomber which was spraying the street as it passed over only two or three hundred feet above the ground. It left a United Dairies' horse dead in the shafts and several people badly injured and dead in its wake, including children. On another occasion I looked up at a damaged bomber creeping home just above the rooftops and the pilot waved!

There were of course countless happy times. My father had taught me carpentry and I made sledges and on one occasion I constructed a tank on a set of pram wheels big enough to get into and hurtle down a hill on the common. It seemed that every shed, workshop and garage had someone working in it for the war effort. I became involved with an old man who made parts on his lathe for the gliders which were to be used for the invasion of Europe. I took these parts on my bicycle to an enormous building where I was able to glimpse the massive gliders that were being made. I observed they were made from wooden struts covered with canvas. With the aid of wood salvaged from bomb sites and brown paper I constructed my own glider and launched myself from a nearby hill. The air pressure tore open the brown paper and I plunged to the ground – with no ill effects thanks to very long grass. Talking with Michael Finn at a luncheon for his eightieth birthday exhibition at the Newlyn Art Gallery, I learned he had piloted a Dakota which towed gliders like those I had seen being made.

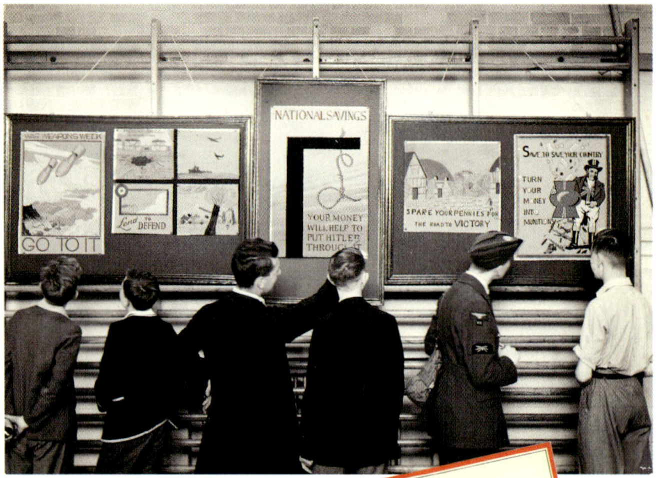

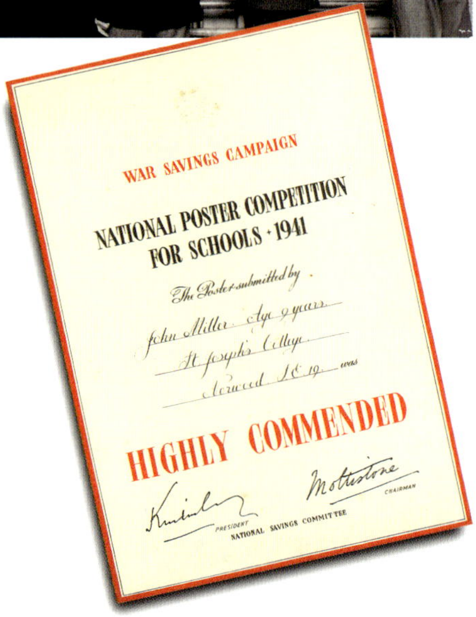

WAR SAVINGS CAMPAIGN

NATIONAL POSTER COMPETITION FOR SCHOOLS · 1941

The Poster submitted by

John Miller Age 9 years
St Joseph's College
Norwood SE 19 was

HIGHLY COMMENDED

PRESIDENT NATIONAL SAVINGS COMMITTEE CHAIRMAN

▲ **Poster 'Spare your pennies for the road to victory'**
for a National Savings competition on display at school
1941

▲ **National Savings poster competition certificate**
1941

▶ **'Children's Newspaper' letter**
1947

▶ **'Children's Newspaper' consolation prize certificate**
1947

I was a maker

Reflecting upon those early years when I was absorbing countless impressions which would later be celebrated in paint, I was then more a maker than a painter. However I did paint a poster for a war savings competition. The idea was my mother's. Mother was full of ideas and very creative. She wrote poetry and was extremely perceptive. Had she lived in today's world she would probably have been a writer. Her idea for the poster was to lay down pennies like paving slabs to form a pathway to 'victory' in the distance. It was Mother who first took me to the opera. We saw 'La Bohème' and 'Madame Butterfly'. She also took me to operettas like 'The Desert Song', 'Rose Marie' as well as the D'Oyly Carte productions of the 'Mikado' and the 'Pirates of Penzance.' She played the piano and we used to sing the songs from the shows at home. I even had a go at 'Vesti la guibba' from Pagliacci!

My maternal grandmother lived near us and took me to films. On one of those occasions when we left the cinema in Croydon I looked up and saw aeroplanes in the sky and puffs of smoke. 'Look,' I said, 'It's an air raid.' 'No,' said my grandmother, 'It's just a practice.' In fact we were watching one of the first raids on Britain when Croydon airport was dive bombed by Stukas.

Looking back, those war years were more about activity than about sitting down to draw or paint. After the war I did manage to pass in art for my matriculation with a pretty limpid still life. I also cycled around Sussex in the school holidays and made drawings of pubs which I tried to sell to the landlords for a few shillings.

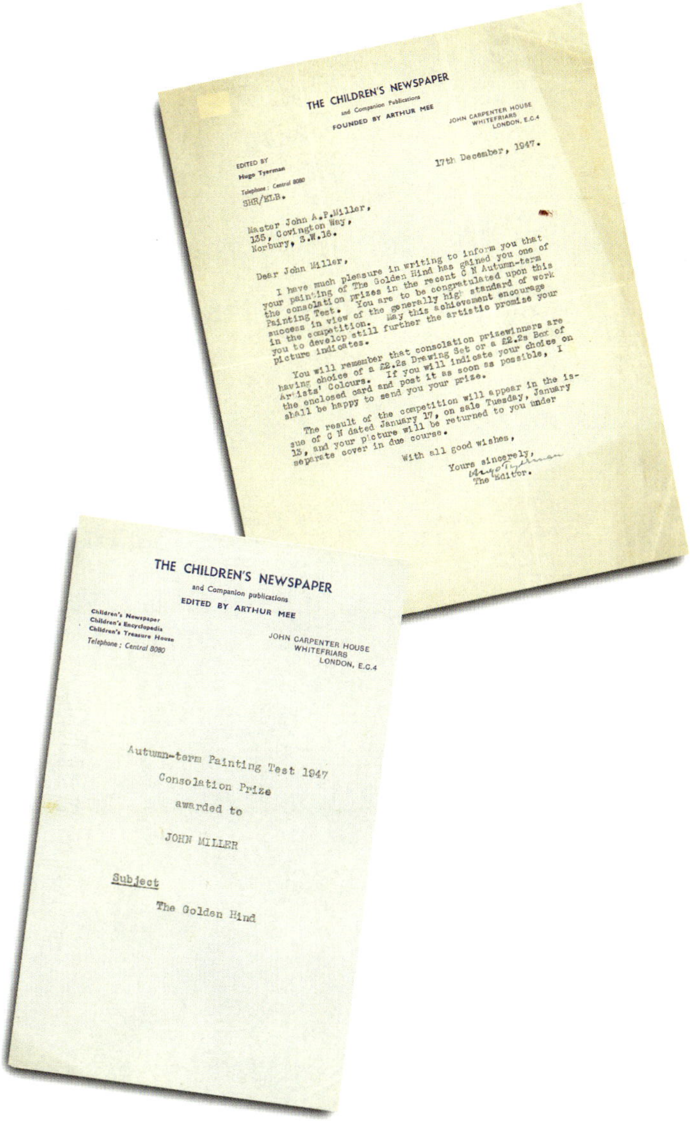

THE CHILDREN'S NEWSPAPER
and Companion Publications
FOUNDED BY ARTHUR MEE

JOHN CARPENTER HOUSE
WHITEFRIARS
LONDON, E.C.4

EDITED BY
Hugo Tyerman
Telephone: Central 8080

SHR/ELB.

17th December, 1947.

Master John A.P.Miller,
135, Covington Way,
Norbury, S.W.16.

Dear John Miller,

I have much pleasure in writing to inform you that your painting of The Golden Hind has gained you one of the consolation prizes in the recent C N Autumn-term Painting Test. You are to be congratulated upon this success in view of the generally high standard of work in the competition. May this achievement encourage you to develop still further the artistic promise your picture indicates.

You will remember that consolation prizewinners are having choice of a £2.2s Drawing Set or a £2.2s Box of Artists' Colours. If you will indicate your choice on the enclosed card and post it as soon as possible, I shall be happy to send you your prize.

The result of the competition will appear in the issue of C N dated January 17, on sale Tuesday, January 13, and your picture will be returned to you under separate cover in due course.

With all good wishes,

Yours sincerely,
Hugo Tyerman
The Editor.

THE CHILDREN'S NEWSPAPER
and Companion publications
EDITED BY ARTHUR MEE

Children's Newspaper
Children's Encyclopedia
Children's Treasure House
Telephone: Central 8080

JOHN CARPENTER HOUSE
WHITEFRIARS
LONDON, E.C.4

Autumn-term Painting Test 1947
Consolation Prize
awarded to
JOHN MILLER

Subject
The Golden Hind

Watercolours

One of the most important lessons was at kindergarten long before the war where we were taught by two stern ladies how to make water colour washes. That is a skill which has never left me. In 1975, the art historian who saved the late Turners, Kenneth Clarke sent me a letter of admiration for a watercolour of Venice he had seen in a friend's house. He sent with it a copy of his autobiography 'Another Part of the Wood' which I found fascinating and informative.

Atonement

One day towards the end of the war my father took us to the cinema where we saw the first pictures of Belsen on the newsreel. I was so horrified by what I saw that I felt obliged to take upon myself the whole of the collective guilt and decided to set out upon a path of atonement. The most obvious path was that of the monk but my father wisely insisted I wait until I was twenty-one before becoming a Catholic. I was allowed to visit the noviciate for a while and this experience coupled with the one overlooking the suburbs of London showed me that I had first to take upon myself the responsibility for my own life before attempting to live it for a cause – however worthy. In that way I might one day discover the real route of atonement.

First I went to art school for a term and then into the theatre before I was called up into the army for National Service.

Crucifix
When Lord St Levan decided to strip the church on St Michael's Mount and return it to its medieval simplicity I found myself being the 'on the spot man' for the architect John Phillips with whom I had worked at Milner and Craze. Lord St Levan told me his search for a suitable medieval crucifix was proving difficult and on one occasion I asked Lady St Levan if she thought it would be appropriate to volunteer to make one. She immediately replied in the affirmative. I first made a model from clay suspended on wire arranged between three nails. One night it collapsed leaving the arms out-stretched in a gesture of welcoming embrace and I knew that to be the way it had to be carved. As I worked on the final carving I contemplated the terrible death by crucifixion. I recalled a man from Auschwitz concentration camp saying, 'After so much suffering how could one depict the suffering of one man.' I knew then I had to try to show the vulnerability of absolute love over and above pain.

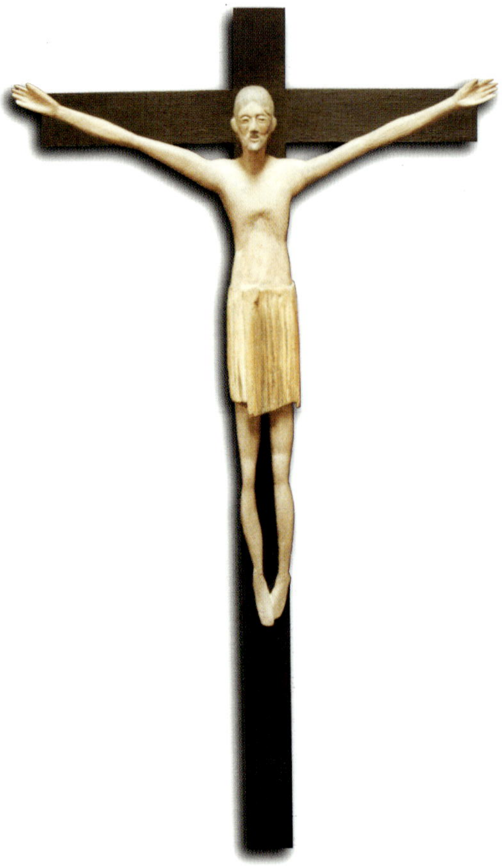

▲ **Crucifix for St Michael's Mount Church**
1987 wood approx 75x70
MT

Theatre

Having enjoyed acting Shakespeare at school, when I left, I worked a season at Derby Little Theatre both acting and working on the sets. I got some quite meaty parts like Peter Trofimov in 'The Cherry Orchard' and a few good reviews. I had learned a lot about acting from one of the brothers at school who produced a Shakespeare play every year in which I had taken part and worked on the scenery. Before leaving for the army I had painted seven historical settings for an exhibition 'Derbyshire Homes Through Three Centuries' in Derby Museum organised by Lady Lothian in aid of the British Red Cross Society.

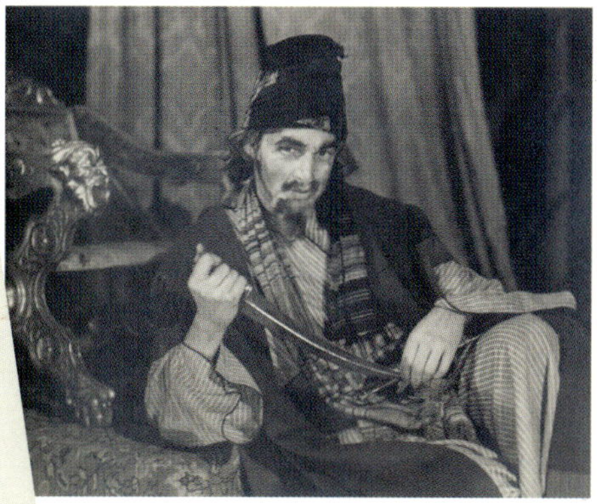

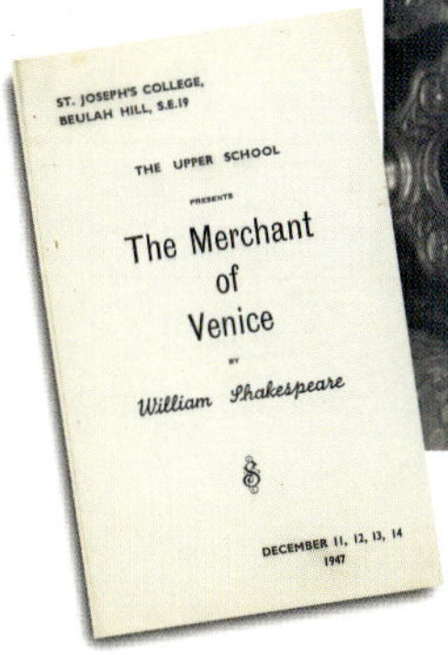

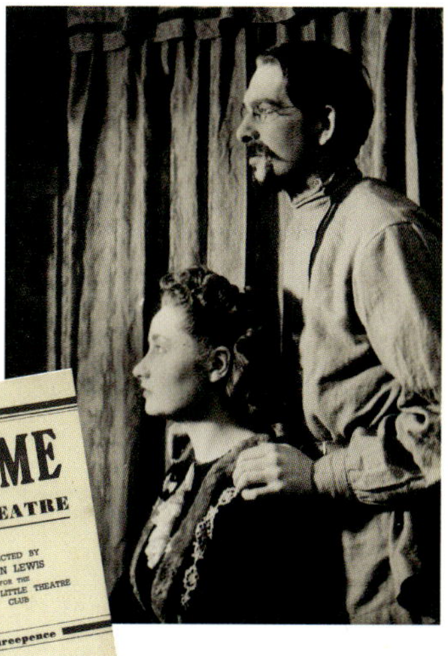

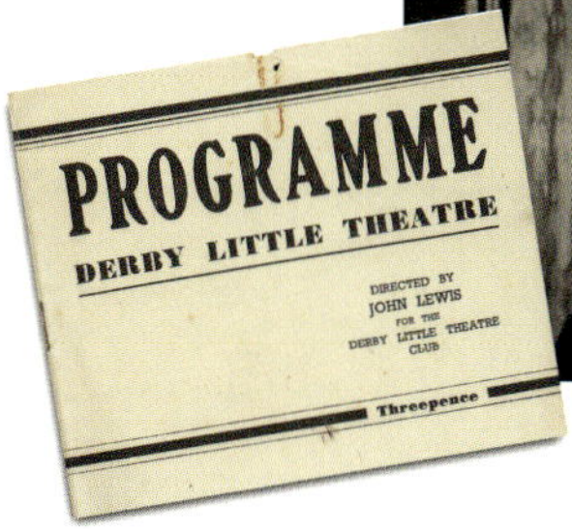

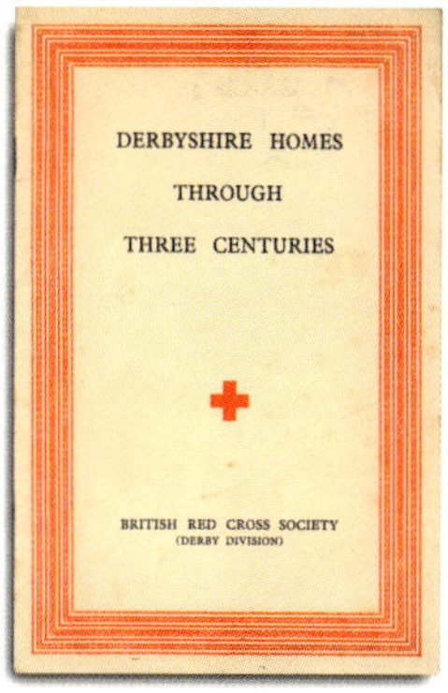

▲ **As Shylock in the school production of 'The Merchant of Venice'**
1947

▲ **'Merchant of Venice' programme**

▲ **As Trofimov in 'The Cherry Orchard' at Derby Little Theatre**
1949

▲ **Programme for Derby Little Theatre**

▲ **Catalogue for 'Derbyshire Homes Through Three Centuries' exhibition at Derby Museum**
1949

Army

I reported to barracks in Aldershot on 3rd November 1949 and on 5th November I walked into the education centre at the barracks hoping to find some sort of sanity in what had become a strangely mad world. To my amazement there in the 'London Illustrated News' were pictures of the seven settings all now appropriately furnished with pieces from many of the fine houses in Derby: Renishaw and Chatsworth to name only two. I turned to someone nearby and said, 'Look I did those.' He wasn't interested. I think he was seeking his own link with a saner past.

I soon began to enjoy the challenge of the army and got a real kick from completing the assault courses and perfecting the drill. I began to learn the value of discipline and team-work. At the end of the basic training I was put up for a commission and managed to pass the three-day selection board. I was not a natural leader but I think my talent for making things helped because I often found myself leading our team through the physical tests such as crossing a river with three spars half its width and a piece of rope.

I found officer training school very tough. 'I call you sir and you call me sir but I'm the biggest sir here'– the regimental sergeant major was 'Bully' Britton – made famous by playing himself in a film about the Coldstream Guards. His voice echoed across the enormous parade ground and everyone was scared stiff of him, especially the junior officers. Every day was an extraordinary experience which I wouldn't have missed. I grew to love it. I met people from all walks of life and learned so much – most of which I have never forgotten.

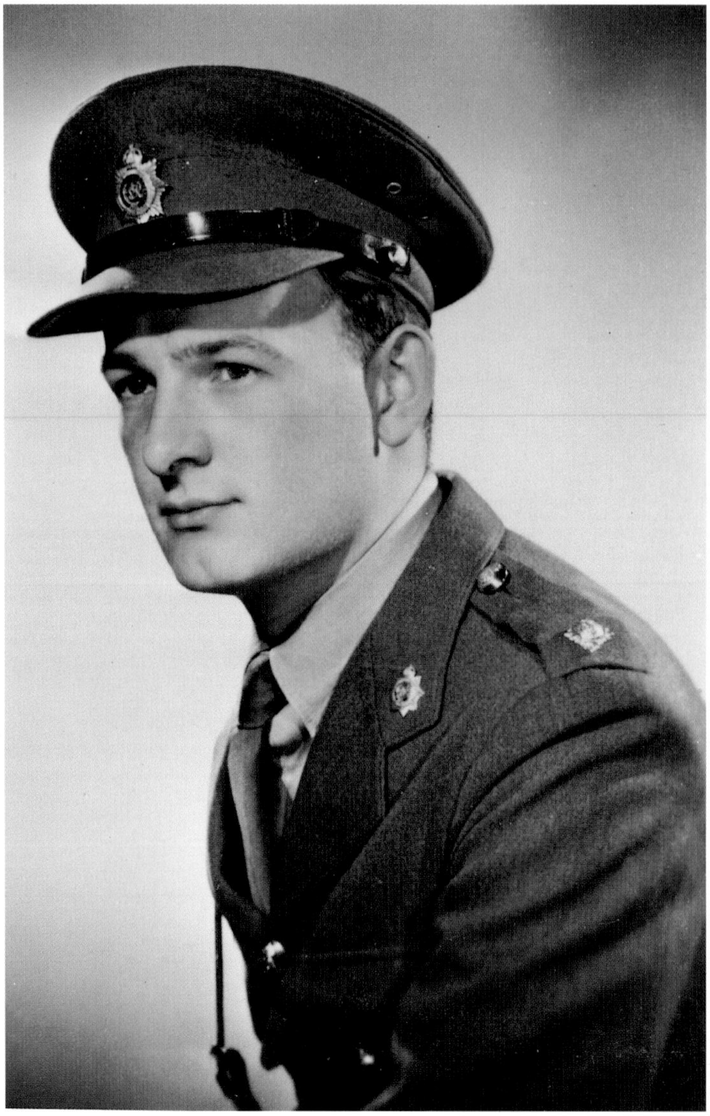

▲ **Officer Miller**
1950

▶ **In hospital in Malta**
1951

Malta

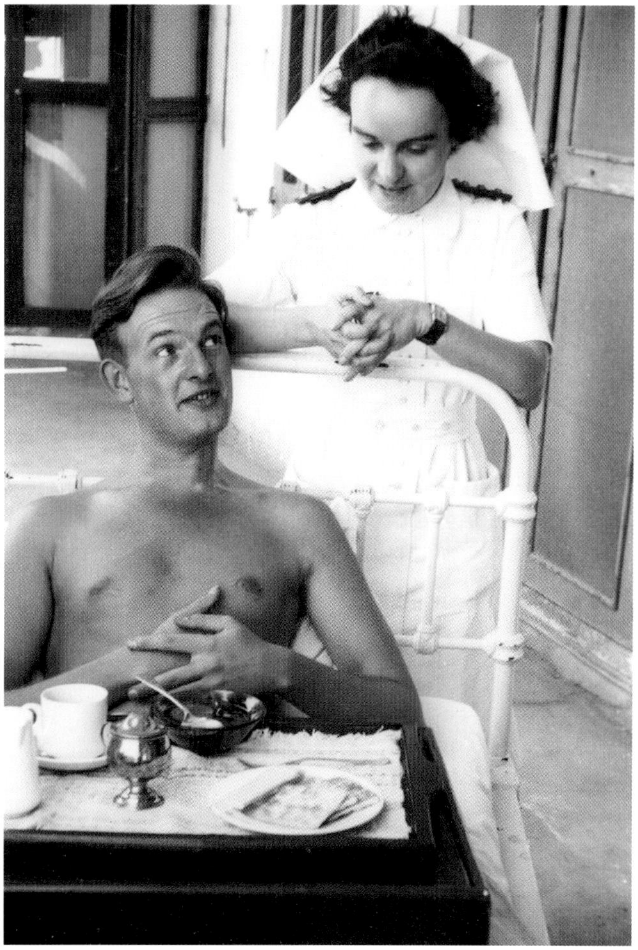

I was posted to Malta with a pip and a stick. The brothers ran a teacher training college there and lived in St Julian's Bay near my mess so I was able to see them quite a lot.

When the colonel asked me what my sports were. I said 'Sailing', having spent a week with a friend in a canoe on the Thames. 'Splendid' he replied 'Officer in charge of the yacht basin.' Not knowing anything about boats or sailing I put up a notice requesting anyone interested in sailing to report to me. Fortunately Corporal Pegg from Southampton came along. He knew boats inside out and taught me to sail. One of the boats we had to maintain was 'Bluebottle' which belonged to Prince Philip who was captain of a frigate based in Valetta.

I was immediately entranced by the light in Malta and the range of changing colours through the seasons and began to make water-colours again. I even managed to purchase some oil colours and painted on cardboard. Things were still very scarce following the war and Malta had been heavily bombed.

Through Brother Anselm with whom I still correspond, I took part in a play in aid of the Malta Playing Fields Association founded by Prince Philip, whose letter of appreciation I still have. That play and a mess pantomime were the only acting I did during army service.

Then during an exercise I sustained some severe injuries. I spent months in the military hospital at Mtarfa with visits to the naval hospital for operations. Following one of these I came very close to death and was gently told this by one of the sisters. I can remember regretting all the beautiful things about this world I had failed to appreciate; the love my parents had bestowed which I had taken for granted; the friendship people had given which I had also taken for granted and the sheer beauty of creation which I now began to value in retrospect. I wished I could walk through an English field just once more and run for and leap onto a moving bus again.

As I began to recover I felt obliged to celebrate all the things I had taken for granted and ensure that I remained more aware of them in the future. It seemed that unless I did this it would be a betrayal of all those who had been deprived of the beauty of this world, and their lives, in places like Belsen.

There was a balcony outside my hospital room and they began to push my bed onto this. From there I could see the domes of Mdina across the valley and away in the distance the sea and Valetta Harbour. It was a tremendous gift. It was then that I began to paint with a purpose and explored ways of painting colour, light and space for the first time. I think it was in that hospital that the painter in me began to wake up. It was to prove a very long process of awakening.

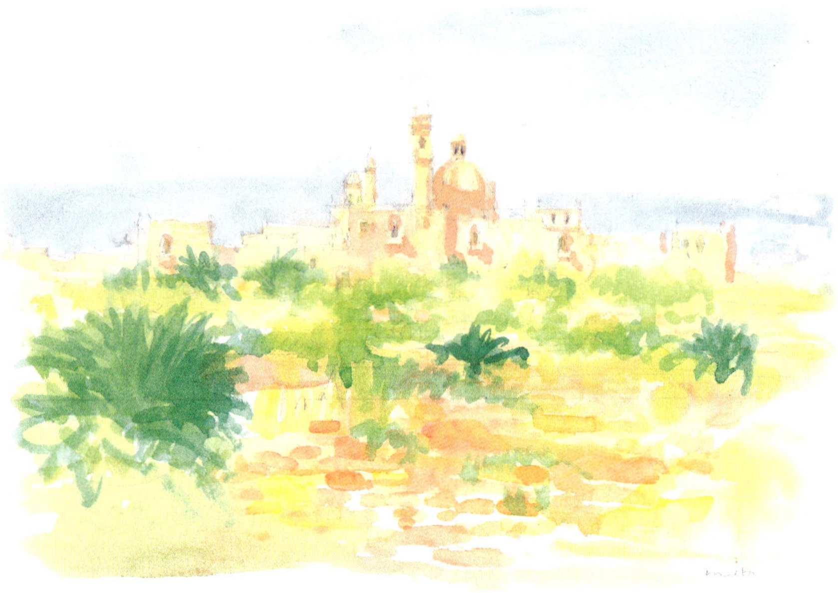

▲ **Sketch of a village church with characteristic dome on a return visit to Malta in the early 1980s**

Although I painted at school I don't really know why I went on to art school – I was more a maker than a painter. Whether I was making a glider or making a painting I was simply fulfilling an urge to create.

In the last fifteen or twenty years I have drawn upon a lifetime of experiences and really begun to celebrate with paint. Painting has become a way of writing poetry, a way of creating psalms, rather than just the making of images. Nevertheless there always was a glimmer of what was eventually to emerge.

I left Malta in a hospital ship which collected me on its way back to England from Korea. I heard first hand accounts of the war in Korea and of hand to hand fighting with an enemy so different to us. Most of the servicemen were between eighteen and twenty – a tender age to be subjected to such savagery in a far-off land.

Architecture

I went back into the world of acting playing small parts in the theatre and even smaller parts in the Ealing comedies. I did land a season in a TV programme called 'Kaleidoscope' at Lime Grove but it began to dawn upon me that I really wasn't star material. One of the art directors at Denham Studios suggested I study architecture which would qualify me for the job of designing film and TV sets. My father introduced me to a former colleague called Romilly B Craze who took me into his practice. At the same time I studied at Regent Street School of Architecture in the evenings for the first five years and full time for the remaining two years.

I soon realised I had embarked on an amazing and exciting journey of discovery. The course covered the study of art, music, social and religious history and science in addition to the study of building techniques and design.

As I worked for a firm of church architects this brought me in close touch with the medieval and classical buildings they were restoring following bomb damage. I began to learn about time and space in relation to human scale. I learned the way the Egyptians, Greeks and Romans approached this. I learned about the relationship of materials to design and came to appreciate the extraordinary vision and invention of the human race – and I marvelled.

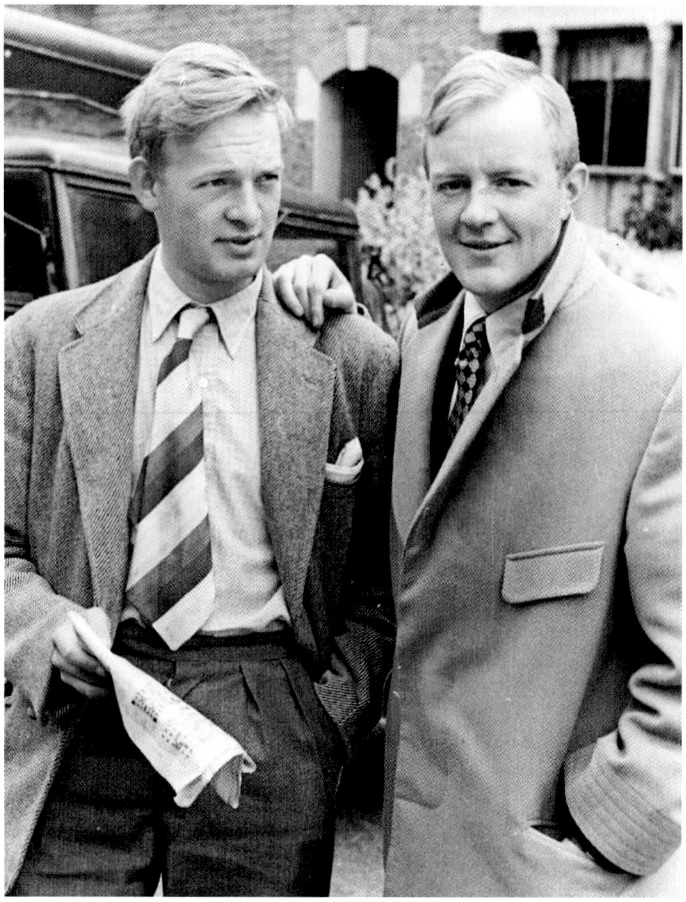

▲ **John (left) as a film stand-in earning £30 a day with actor Peter Reynolds**

▶ **The artist with one of his Van Gogh look alike paintings**
June 1948

▶ **Selling paintings at Hyde Park**
about 1948

Van Gogh

I went to the Van Gogh exhibition at the Tate Gallery at a time when England was still shrouded in grey. Everything including furniture and clothes was 'utility' and drab. Van Gogh's visionary celebrations opened my eyes to the way colour can describe space. I began to paint very bad Van Gogh lookalikes. But another seed had been sown.

I was taken by a remarkable old lady I had met by chance called Edith Williams, who lived in a room lined with books. She was a follower of George Bernard Shaw and admired his socialist principles. She had been a schoolteacher in the East End of London and regularly marched her young pupils (who had shaven heads to prevent lice) to the theatres of the West End where they went in the penny gods and saw the great classical plays. She marched me to Charing Cross Road where we busked to raise enough cash to go to the theatre. I wore her son's degree gown and we sang melodies from Noel Coward and the London shows. She led me into exciting adventures of the mind and spirit – she was undoubtedly my university.

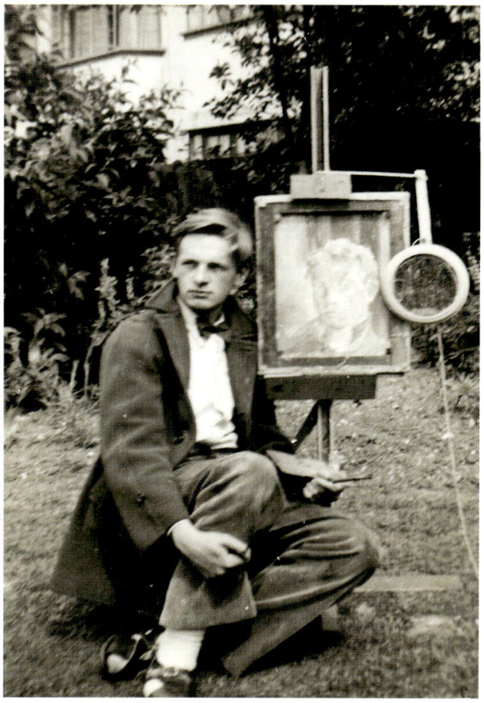

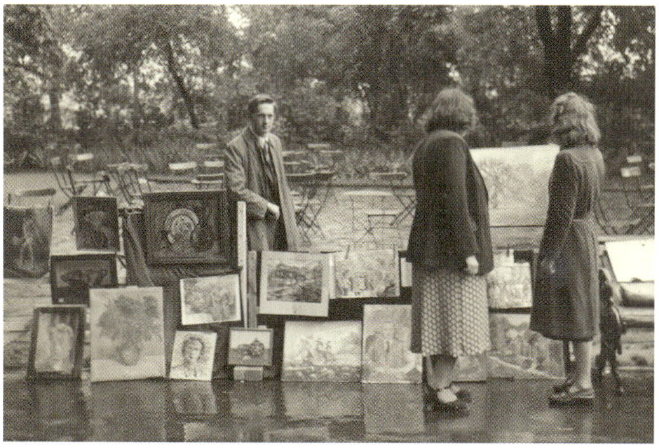

Perspective

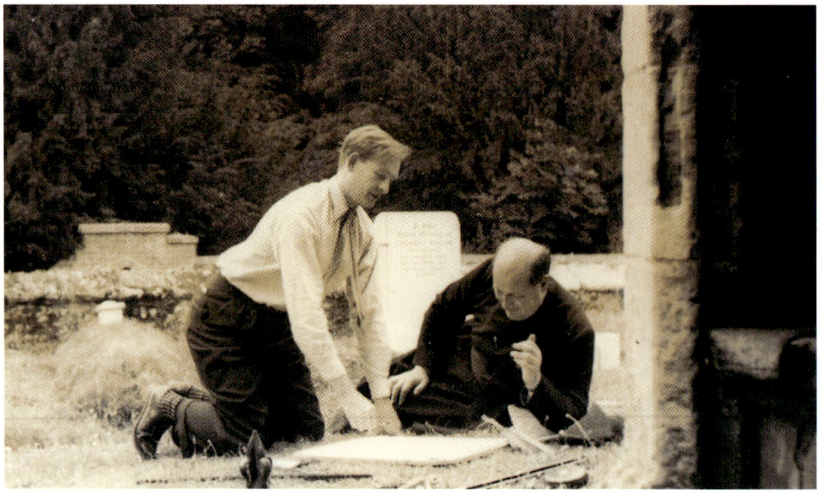

I had learned how to set up mechanical perspectives of proposed buildings by a complicated means of projection from the plans. A viewpoint is chosen and the result is an almost photographic representation of how the building will look from that viewpoint. There is a danger that this sort of exercise can deprive one of actually experiencing space. I think it may have something to do with our need to possess everything, to get it under our belt. We think if we know how it works we own it, but this doesn't always mean we experience it.

One morning recently I was sitting on the balcony overlooking Mount's Bay and watched a yacht leave the harbour and sail towards St Michael's Mount. At a certain distance it fitted neatly into a small triangle of rigging at the top of the mast of a similar yacht still in the harbour. I was fascinated and astounded by this. I knew that this phenomenon could be quite easily explained but I didn't want to engage in that. As the yacht travelled away and became small enough to fit into the top triangle of rigging of the stationary yacht I knew that I had received a revelation of time and space which had a significance beyond analysis.

▲ **At Walsingham surveying the church**
1953

▶ **John painting in the flat in Adam and Eve Mews, London**
1955

Milner and Craze had designed the Anglican shrine at Walsingham, Norfolk and this became one of my office jobs. I designed a new gatehouse, hostel and shop which entailed frequent visits. On one occasion a parish priest from Birmingham for whom I had designed and decorated a new pulpit asked one of his pilgrims to help me by holding the end of my tape for a survey. This was Michael Truscott who was a great help although we hardly spoke a word.

Michael wrote to me later and told me he was planning to enter a religious order. He had been told to train as a nurse before joining so that he could work in the mission fields. When I took a room in the house of a friend in Adam and Eve Mews, Kensington it coincided with Michael's year in London working in a specialist field of nursing. He was able to arrange to take a room in the same house. Through our attraction to monastic life we discovered a common yearning for a spiritual dimension which formed the basis of a friendship that continues to grow. In fact Michael never joined his religious order but went to wash up at a very trendy restaurant called 'La Popote' and ended up being the manager.

In our search for ways of extending our range of consciousness we read Colin Wilson's 'The Outsider' and 'Religion and the Rebel' alongside 'Waters of Silence' by Thomas Merton, the Trappist monk whose 'Seeds of Contemplation' remains a favourite of mine. We were fired in our search by the dictum of Socrates that an unexamined life is not worth living.

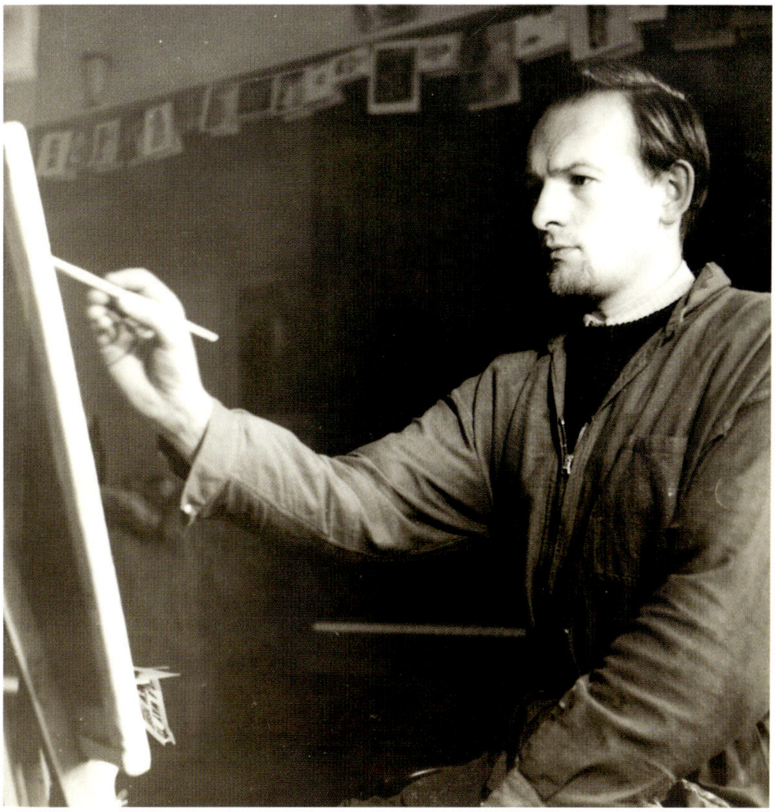

We moved from Adam and Eve Mews to the crypt of St John's, Holland Road, London in quarters prepared for a Benedictine monk whose abbot found the place too damp. In our mid-twenties damp was the least of my worries – although I may be paying for it now! The rent of £4 entailed some church duties when the verger was otherwise engaged. One of these was ringing the bell at midday for the Angelus which sometimes meant rushing home from work during the lunch hour.

At that time F C Happold's remarkably accessible book 'Mysticism' had just been published and this with his later book 'Prayer and Meditation' opened up for us a whole world of spiritual growth. We found in the 'Upanishads', the 'Bhagavad Gita' and the 'Tao' along with the Christian mystics the depth of wonder in the human spirit – a wonder which reflected our own awe for the complexity and beauty of creation. It was a tremendously exciting time which laid the foundations of a lifetime of wonder and spiritual yearning. Now I am more able to understand T S Eliot's plea that old men should be explorers.

Through a friend in the architect's office, Ronald Leask, we were introduced to Gurdjieff work, which is a system of physical and spiritual exercises to enhance awareness and understanding. Whilst working in the centre in Kingston upon Thames an Indonesian called Pak Subud came with a spiritual exercise which was entirely intuitive unlike the Gurdjieff work which was about working upon oneself.

▶ **Michael with the old Austin Seven which carried John and Michael to Cornwall**

▶ **L'Elixir restaurant publicity card**

L'Elixir

We met Robin and Sylvia Tee at the centre and the four of us decided to open a coffee bar and restaurant on Richmond Hill called l'Exilir. As Sylvia couldn't cook Mother and Michael devised some delicious menus with the help of Escoffier. Then Albert who was also practising the Subud exercises gave up a very prestigious job at the Cavendish Street Lyons Corner House to join us.

It was a very exciting project with a lot of fun and a lot of heartache, but it couldn't provide a livelihood for so many people and so Michael and I left and headed for South-West Cornwall in our 1937 Austin Seven and about twenty-seven pounds in our pockets.

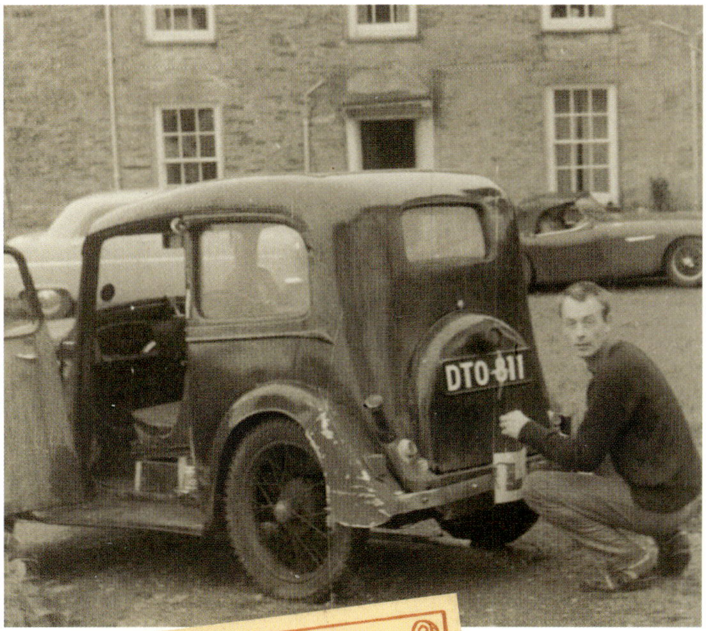

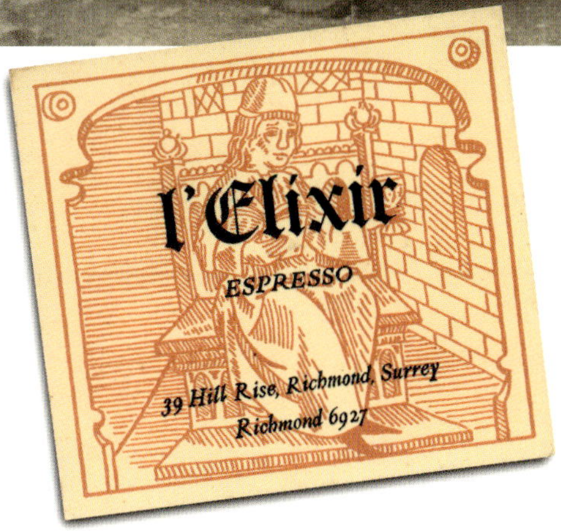

Cornwall

I had visited Cornwall to measure the screen at St Buryan Church for an architectural exam and had become enraptured with the place. Fortunately an actor friend, Richard Lorrimer, allowed us to stay in his rented cottage at Tregiffian near Lamorna, which he only used when 'resting'. The rent was six shillings a week and we lived there until we found a thatched cottage at Treen which was twenty shillings a week – in advance.

Pak Subud told us of a number of people in Cornwall who were eager to learn more about his exercises and this brought us in touch with some artists, including Grace Hocking and Ithell Colquhoun, as well as a few interested people from many walks of life. There is no doubt the exercises contributed to the growth of the inner life and a more balanced life in general. They are 'spiritual' rather than 'religious' allowing one to continue in one's own religious faith. When people began to organise it all we found ourselves drifting away but the value of it remains.

The first few years in Cornwall were more about survival than painting. We carried out quinquennial church surveys for local architects. The surveys were a way of keeping parishes and the diocese in touch with the condition of the buildings every five years and ensuring that important maintenance was carried out. It took us all over South-West Cornwall and by then I always carried a sketchbook.

▲ **St Michael's Mount**
Watercolour

When we moved from the temporary accommodation at Tregiffian to Treen I painted Logan Rock and the surrounding landscape and Michael made mosaics – having made the mosaic tables for 'l'Exilir'. In the first year we earned something like four hundred pounds. A girl in Woolworths was earning about three pounds ten shillings a week at that time so really we weren't doing too badly.

Next, on the advice of a friend, we borrowed a large sum of money and opened a guest house for artists on Escalls Cliff, near Sennen, overlooking the Atlantic. We were beginning to define our lives by limiting the clientele to artists.

First exhibition

In 1960 I had my first exhibition in Causewayhead, Penzance with Commander England. He called the exhibition 'Reason Painting' which was the last thing my work should have been called because I work intuitively. He decided it was a 'catchy' title so that was that.

The paintings were mainly of cliffs, because the structure and solidity of the granite cliffs in relation to the fluidity and yet enormous power of the sea fascinated me. It was all so different from the south coast resorts of my childhood. The blue I use now was there even then. The paintings were mainly blue and white which was put on with a palette knife because the cliffs became near white in the sunlight and were textured. Ever since my days in the Mediterranean I have nearly always painted the sunlight – or misty sunlight.

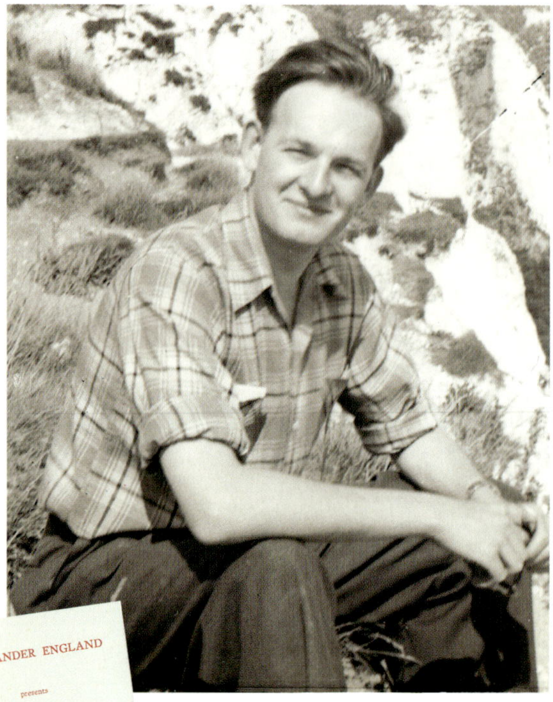

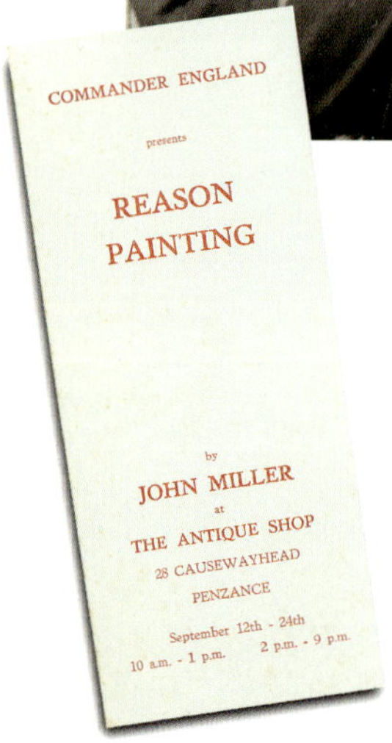

COMMANDER ENGLAND
presents
REASON
PAINTING
by
JOHN MILLER
at
THE ANTIQUE SHOP
28 CAUSEWAYHEAD
PENZANCE
September 12th - 24th
10 a.m. - 1 p.m. 2 p.m. - 9 p.m.

▲ **By the cliffs at Treen**
About 1960

▲ **'Reason Painting' catalogue**
1960

▶ **Kunstars exhibition catalogue**
1963

▶ **Ostend Painters exchange exhibition catalogue**
1963

▶ **Catalogue for Newlyn Society of Artists exhibition in London**

We sold a few of the paintings from that little exhibition – I remember delivering one of Gurnard's Head to a doctor who lived in Yeovil. 'Now how much was it again?' the purchaser asked. 'Eighteen pounds,' I replied. He got out of the easy chair in which he was sitting, lifted the seat, exposed a mass of notes and counted out eighty pounds. 'I'm terribly sorry,' I said 'I'm afraid it's only eighteen pounds.'

Michael went to work for Commander England in his antique shop during the 'off-season' months and when we sold 'Trelogan', the guesthouse on Escalls Cliff, we opened an antique shop with a gallery on the first floor and accommodation above that at 5 Chapel Street, Penzance, now a bookshop.

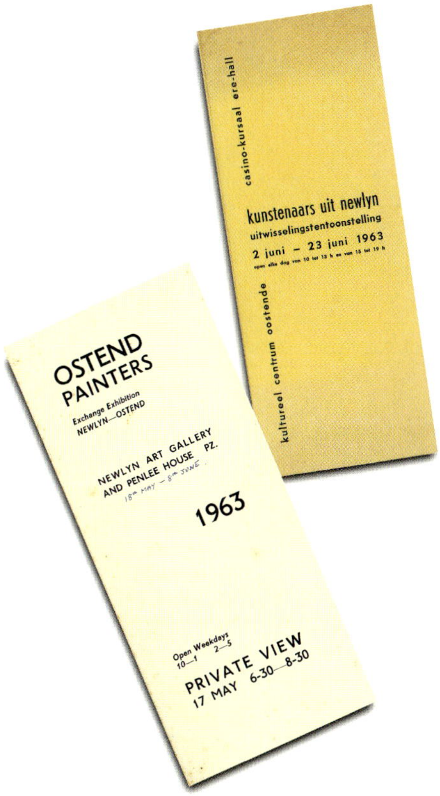

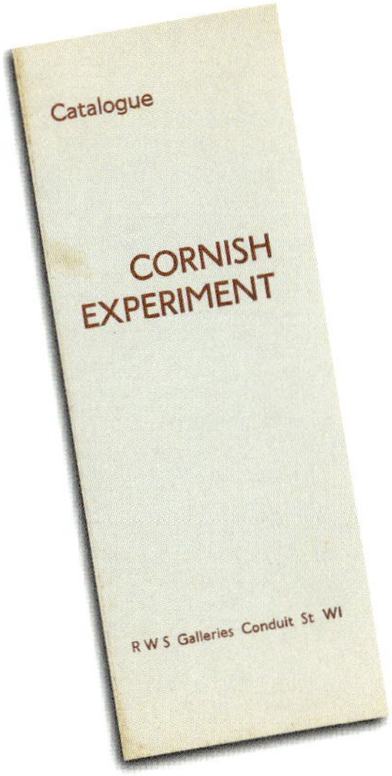

Sancreed

Between 1960 and 1964 when we purchased Sancreed House we bought and sold a number of different properties and engaged in all kinds of activities in order to survive. Much of that is told in my earlier book 'Leave Tomorrow Behind'.

In 1961 Michael Canney and Peter Lanyon suggested I apply for membership of the Newlyn Society of Artists. When Peter Lanyon first saw my paintings of the cliffs and the sea he said 'They're not great but they're interesting.' Then he turned to me and said 'You are layering paint over paint - you must make paint move through paint' which was marvellous advice.

The Society was very vital and was composed of an extraordinarily eclectic collection of artists: Charles Simpson, Dod Procter and Alethea Garstin were still showing alongside people like Peter Lanyon and Alan Davie who had acquired a studio at Crean, near Porthcurno. Michael Canney introduced me to a number of painters and sculptors and I met many more through the society. I found people with whom I could discuss painting for the first time. The society, because it had to sustain itself with only a pitiful grant from the Arts' Council, worked very closely together. The committee that selected paintings for exhibition hung them and if the gallery needed a lick of paint we did it ourselves. We gave our paintings, sculpture and pottery for a Christmas auction, conducted by Michael Newman of W H Lane, to raise funds for the gallery and often ended up buying each other's work! Amongst the members at that time were Charles Breaker, Derek Guthrie, Bouverie and Inez Hoyton, Rose Hilton, Jeremy Le Grice, Margo Maeckelberge,

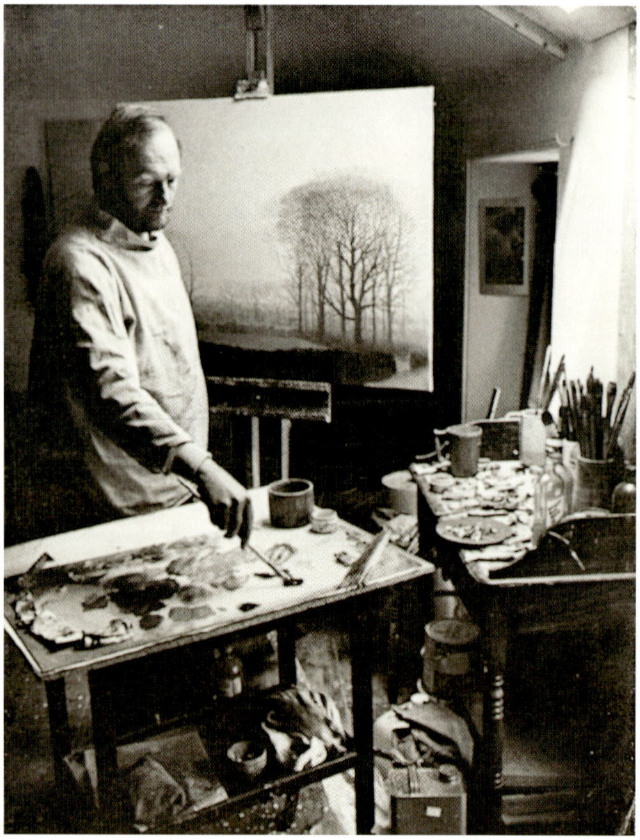

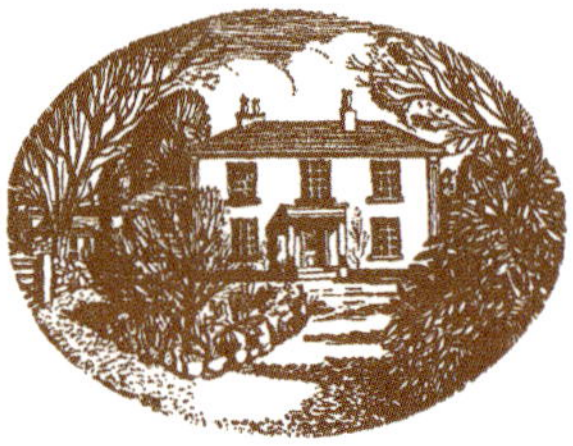

▲ **The studio at Sancreed**
John with a 'tree painting'
1965
AG

▲ **Sancreed letterhead**

▶ **'en plein air'**
1983
BB

Marjorie Mort, Jack Pender, Biddy Picard, Mary Stork, Ken Symonds, John Tunnard, Rosemary Tunstall-Behrens and Giles Auty, who later became an art critic. I have work by quite a number of them.

The society organised exhibitions in other parts of Britain and sometimes abroad and also exchanged exhibitions with other societies. Picture sales in those days were poor – very few people bought original art. I was closely associated with the society between 1961 and 1974. In 1970 the total sales at Newlyn were about eight hundred pounds. My own sales amounted to something in that region from commercial galleries. Sales were not a priority and most of us either taught or did other jobs to provide an income.

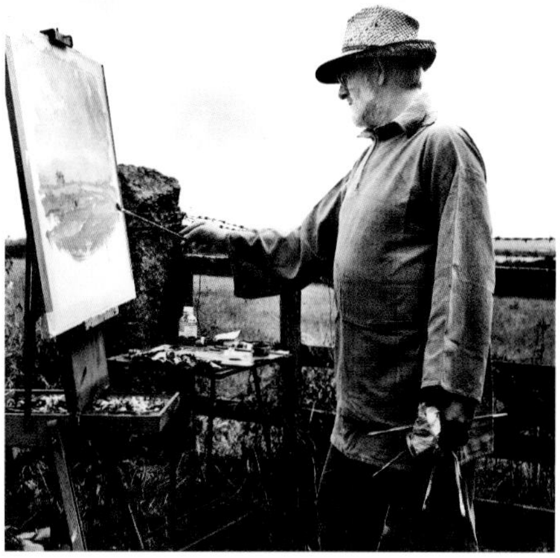

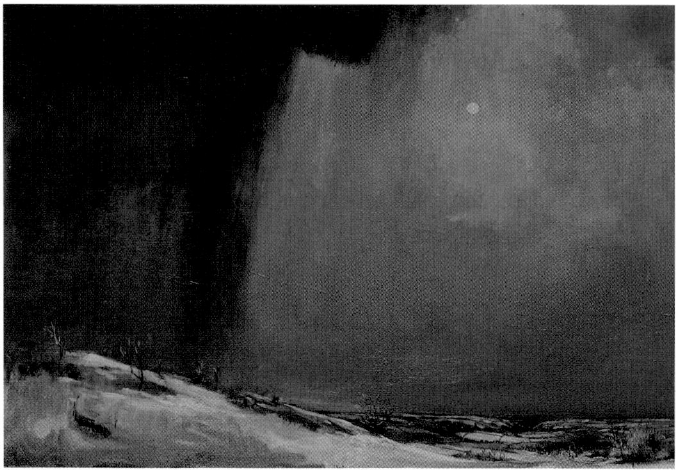

▲ **Morning at Newlyn Harbour**
1974 oil on canvas
MT

▲ **Snowstorm over the Beacon**
1973 oil on canvas
MT

▶ **Tree painting**
oil on canvas
MT

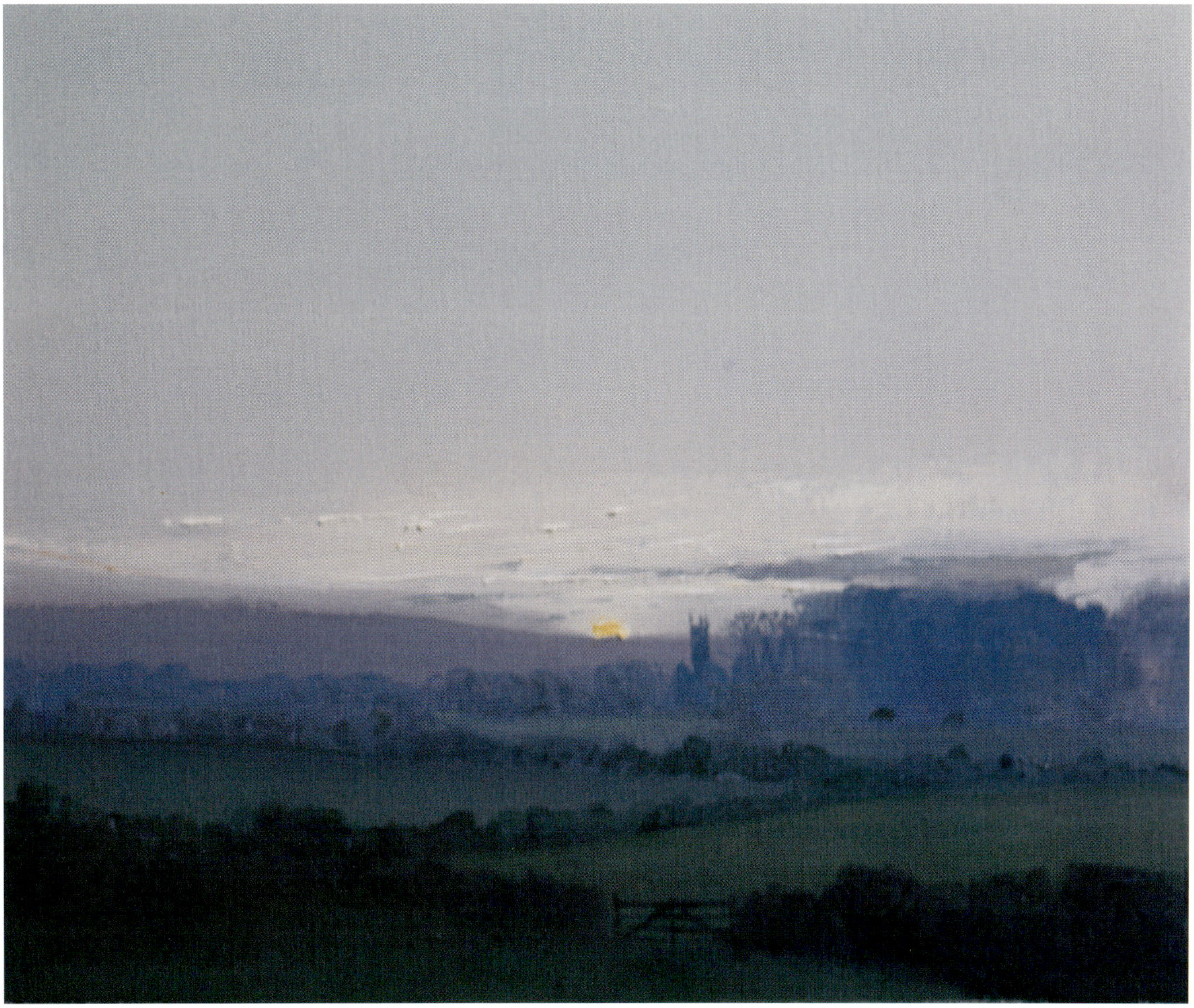

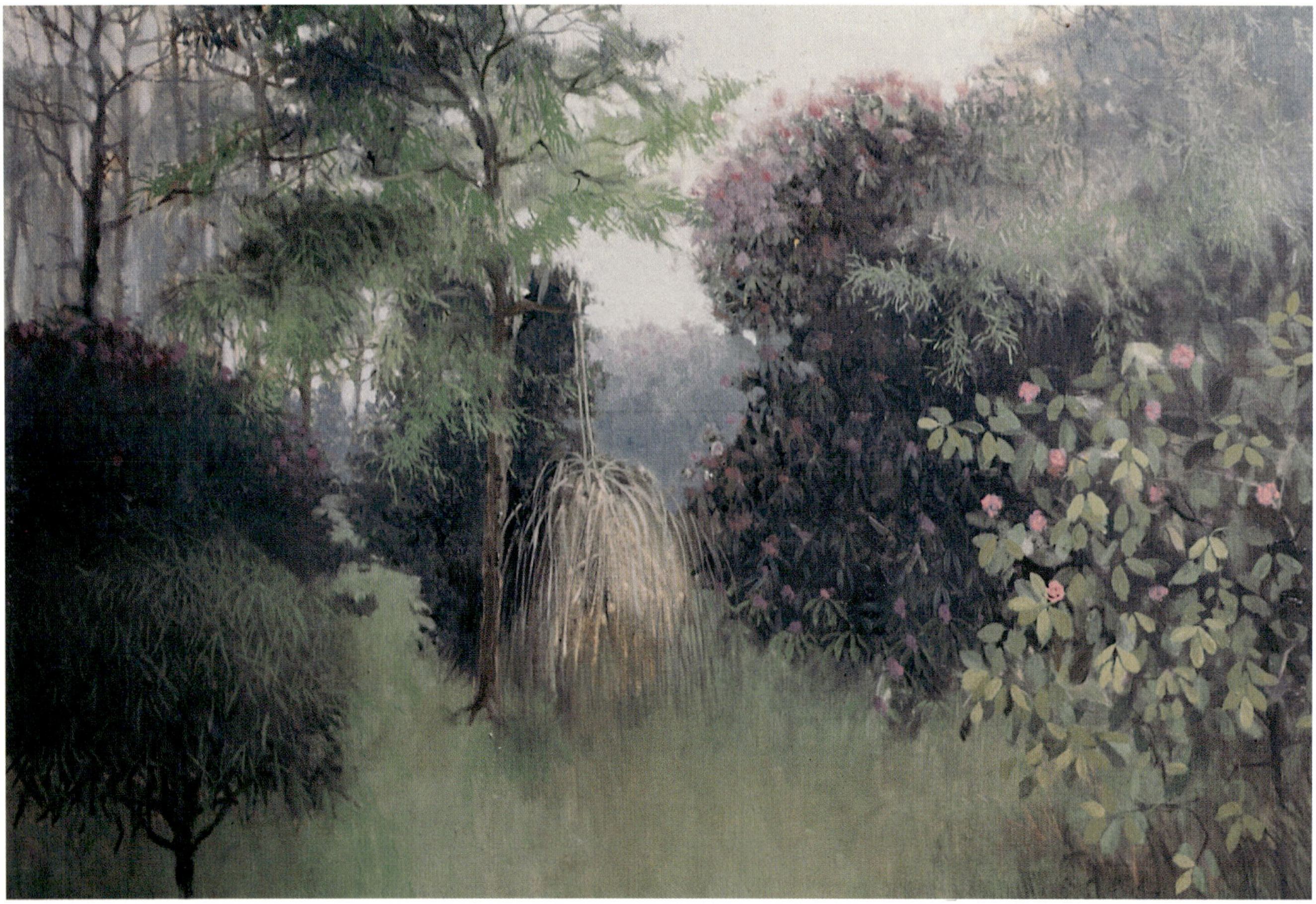

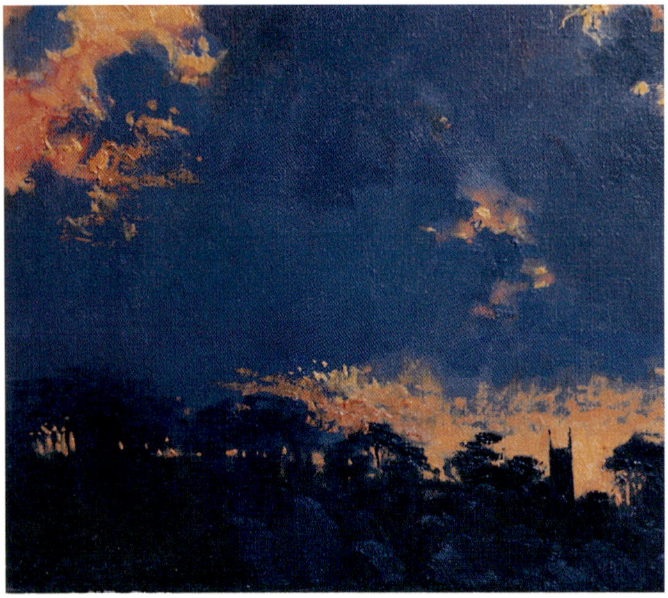

▲ **Sancreed Garden**
oil on canvas
MT

◀ **November Afternoon**
oil on canvas 41x51
MT

▶ **St Michael's Mount**
early 1970s oil on canvas
MT

▶ **Painting at Sancreed**
MK

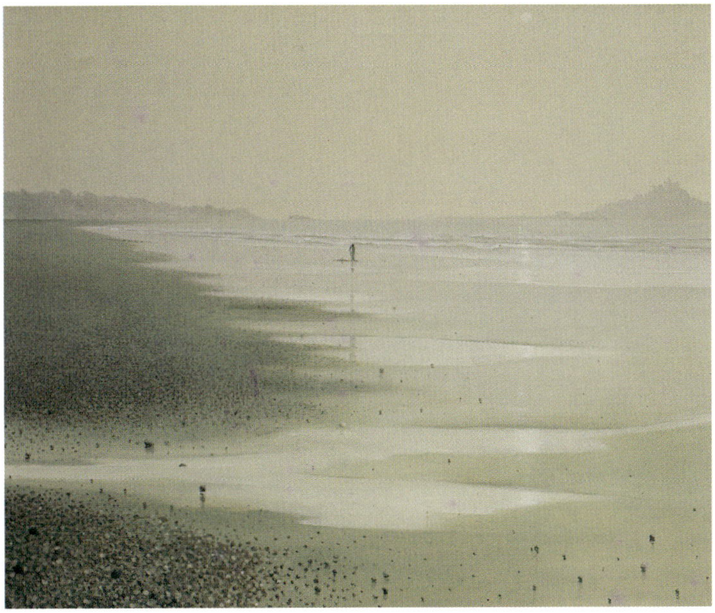

Cyprus

In1974 John and Ella Halkes who ran the Orion Gallery in Penzance invited me to show there which realised something like £2300. Mother, Michael and I went for our first holiday abroad since moving to Cornwall. We rented an apartment in Kyrenia, Cyprus thinking it would be far from the madding crowd and met no less than eleven people we knew as well as quite a number we didn't know. I soon became gathered up into that dazzling Mediterranean light and filled a number of sketchbooks with coded marks – how do you draw light? Making marks is enormously satisfying. It is what I like most about drawing – making marks.

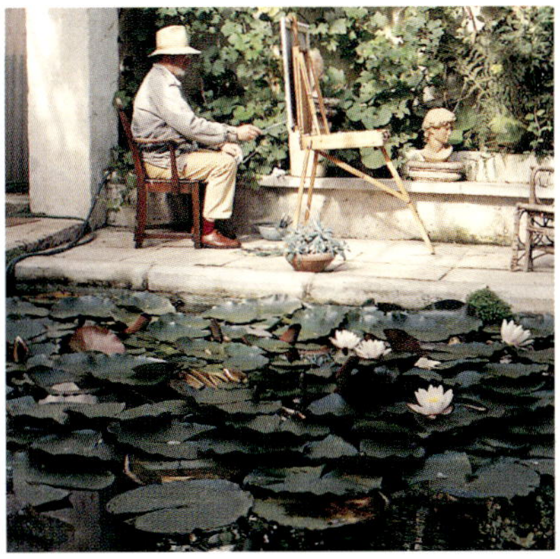

38 **Venice**

We met Marika Hanbury-Tenison in Cyprus who, later with her husband Robin, became a close friend. Robin and Marika took us to Venice in 1975 for a long weekend. They shared with us their own special love for the place, which enriched our visit over and above the riches to be found at every step and around each corner. We returned in 1979 to find the city floating in hazy sunlight with the domes of Santa Maria della Salute shimmering through the mists. Those visits were an inspiration and although I fortified them with subsequent visits the immediate impact will never be the same. Marika said she'd buy me a sketchbook from the famous paper shop in Venice, where this amazingly dignified old lady makes you draw in her big drawing album to see if you're worthy of buying one of their sketch books and there was Graham Sutherland's drawing above mine. I did a little drawing of Sancreed Church and she allowed Marika to buy, at an exorbitant price, a sketchbook for me. Years later, when I went back to Venice for a month with Robin, strangely enough, after Marika died, I went to the same shop again and I said 'I'd like to buy a drawing book please.' 'Ah' she said, looking as if she was going to refuse. I said, 'Give me your big book. That's my drawing'. Then she sold me a sketchbook. Venice was a wonderful experience – it became a magical city for me. Brothertons sold the Venice paintings and so did David Messum.

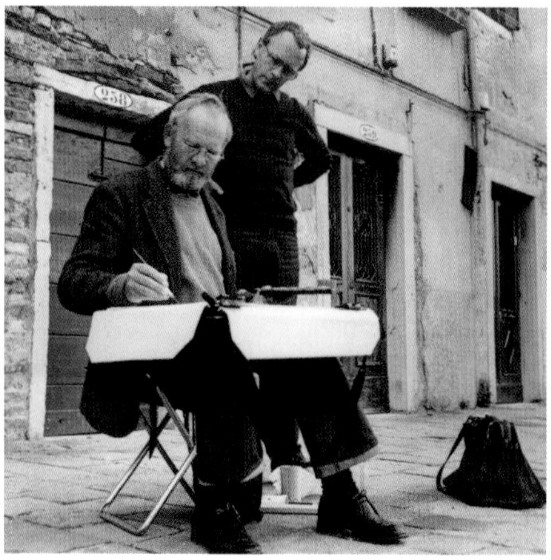

▲ **Venice John Miller and Michael Truscott**
1983
SnC

▶ **Santa Maria della Salute**
1992 oil on canvas 75x70
MT

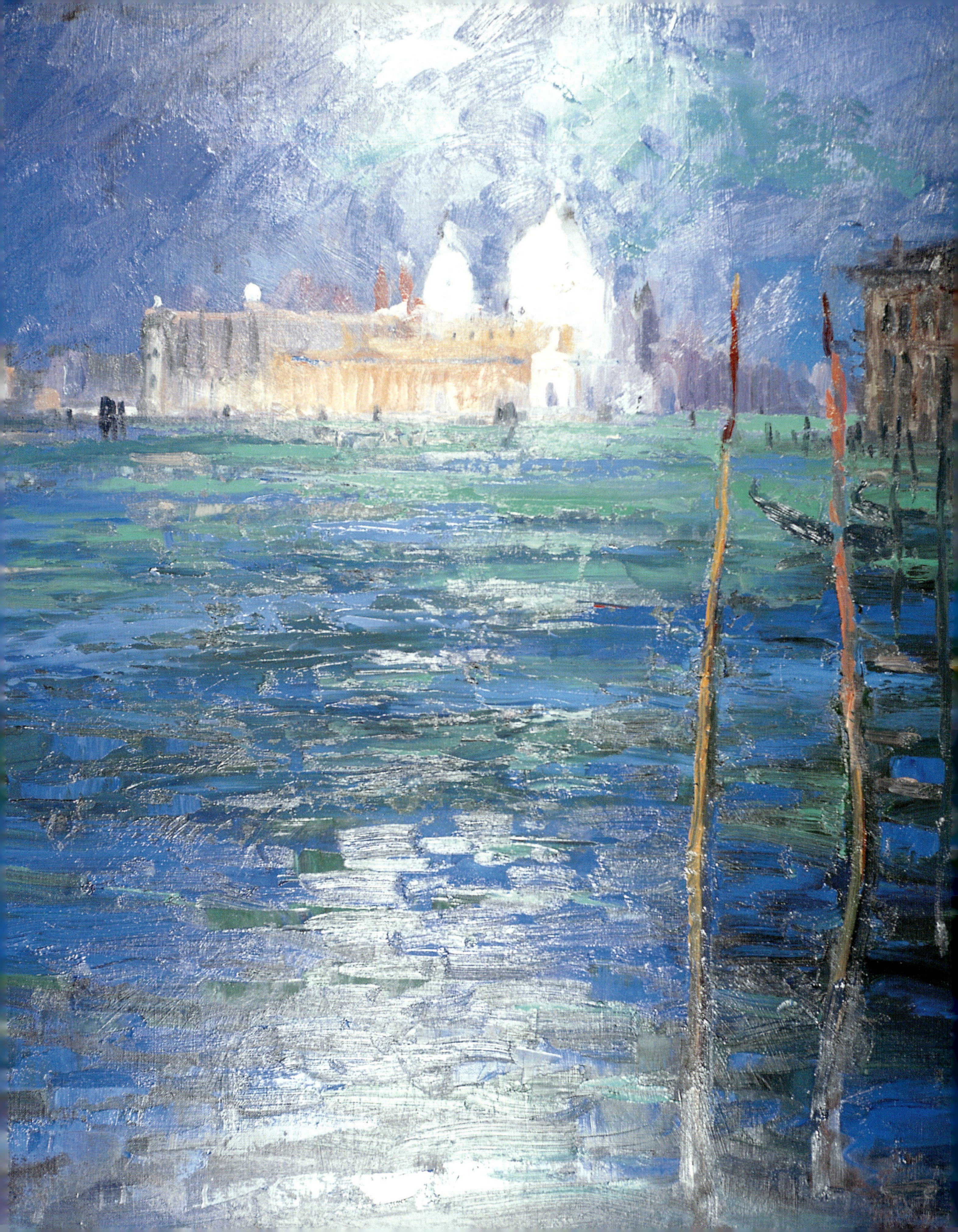

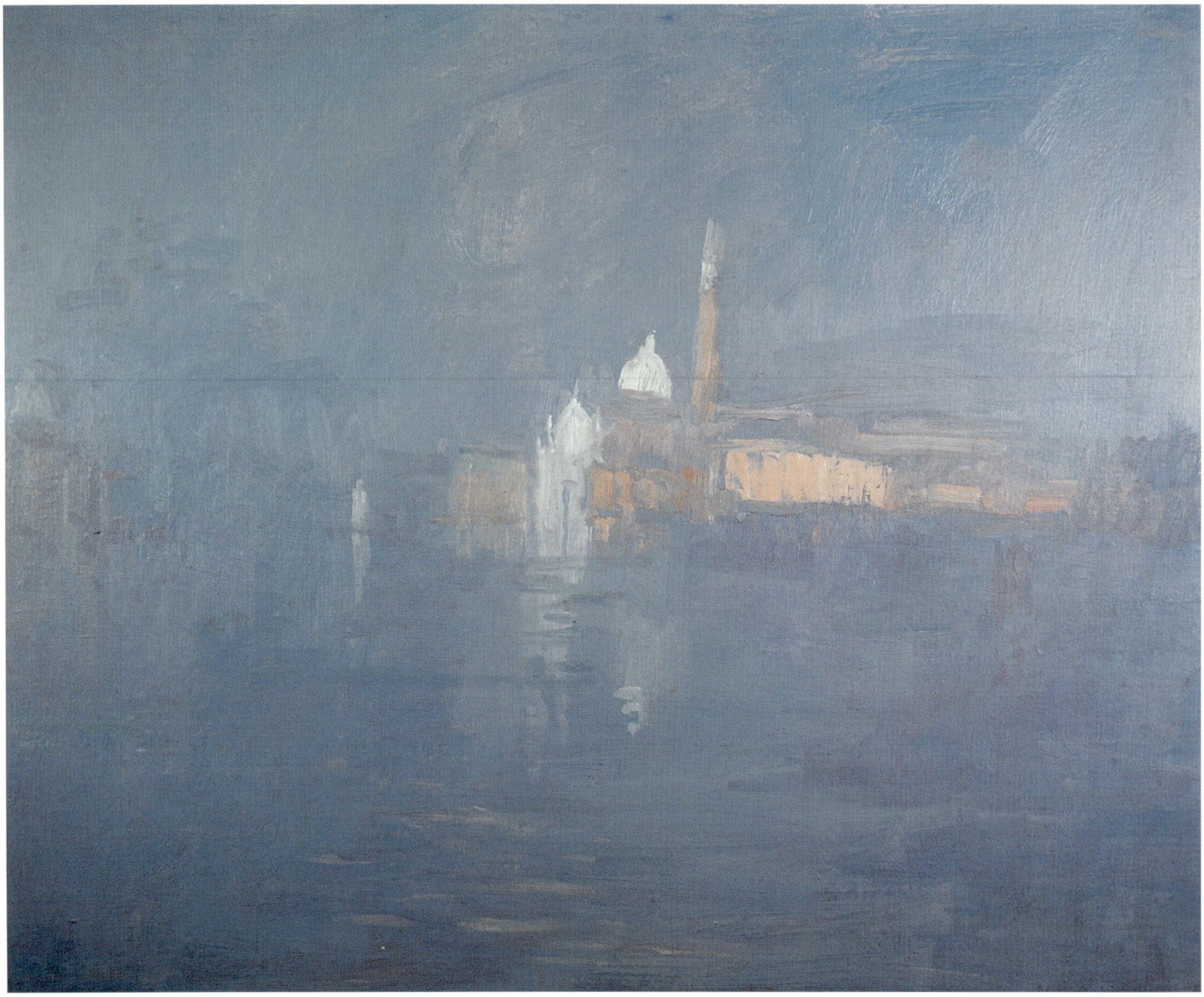

▲ **San Giorgio in Mist**
1992 oil on canvas 66x75
MT

▶ **San Giorgio, Venice, in Winter Light**
1992 oil on canvas
MT

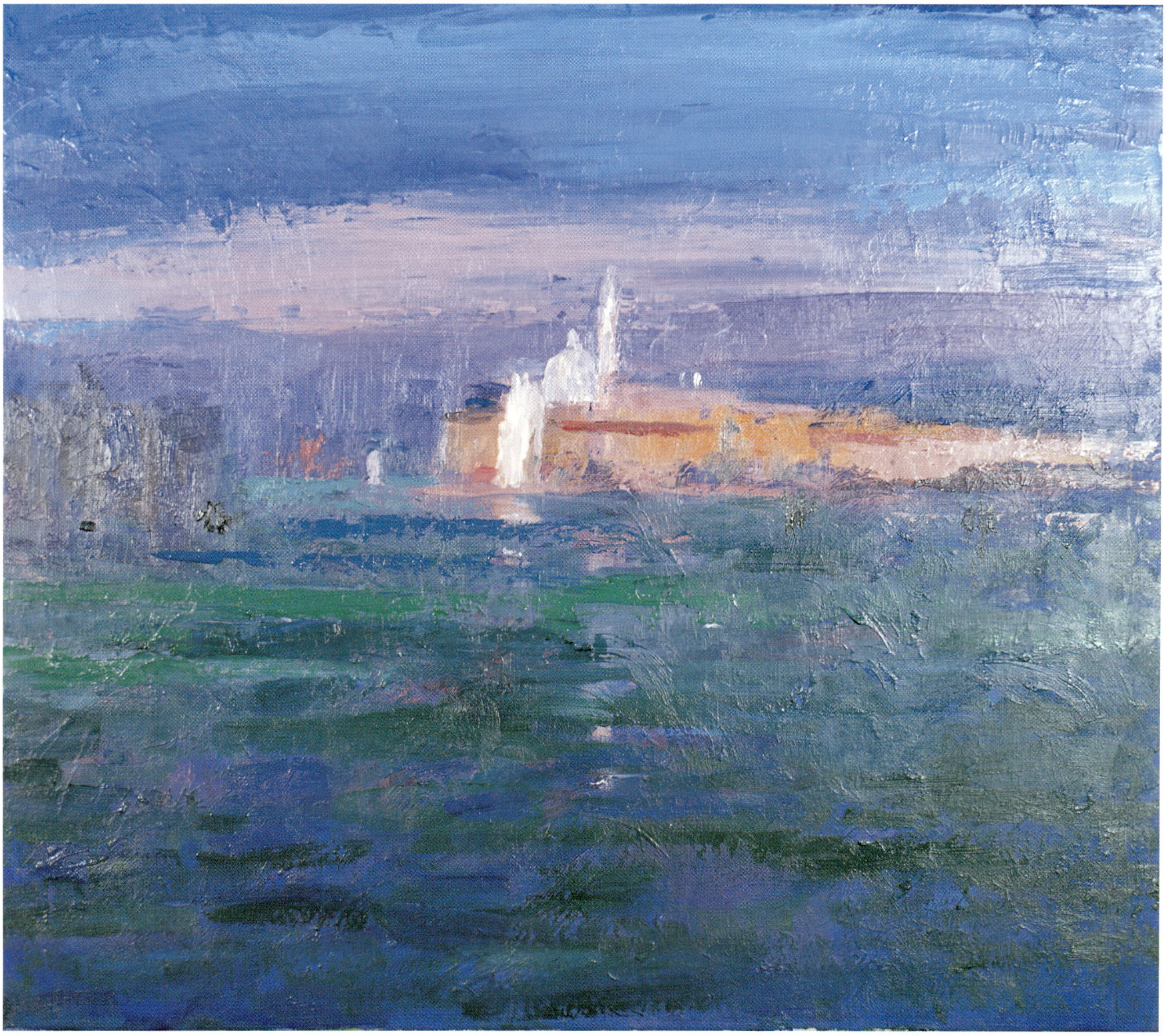

When I joined David Messum in 1982 I had shown with the Anthony Fortesque Gallery, London in 1975, through an introduction by Marika and with Brothertons, Walton Street, London between 1976 and 1981. I had also shown in New York, Miami, Vancouver and a number of galleries in Europe.

David had recently coined the phrase 'British Impressions' which caught on. When we met I was painting the bare trees around Sancreed. I was exploring a particular kind of space. It was almost Gothic space – that distance through bare trees which could be infinity. I had just begun to leave out the trees and explore space, space, space, when I was confronted with a notion of 'impressionism' which I saw as more closely associated with 'expressionism'.

There are some actors who hide behind a role and others who bring their personalities into it – Guinness and Olivier are good examples – so it is with painters. I wanted the painting to speak for itself, unlike the work of the 'expressionists'.

I have a high regard for the ideas of the French Impressionists and in particular Monet's late paintings of waterlilies and Venice. They move me in the same way as Turner's late paintings do, like 'Norham Castle' and the last Venice paintings. But then what about Rembrandt's last portraits – filled with such insight and compassion?

I firmly believe that discipline can lead to a breakthrough and it can also generate passion, although not necessarily overtly. An example of this is the work of the Italian Quattrocento painter, Piero della Francesca whose work is very disciplined and refined, yet enormously passionate.

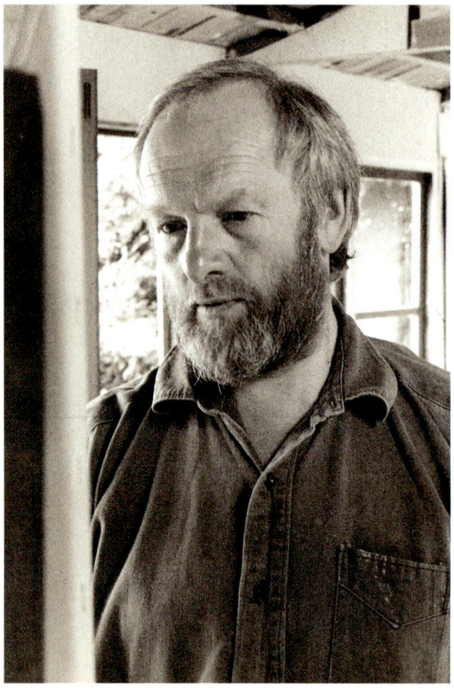

▲ **John at Sancreed**
About 1980
DC

▶ **Santa Maria della Salute**
1984 oil on canvas
MT

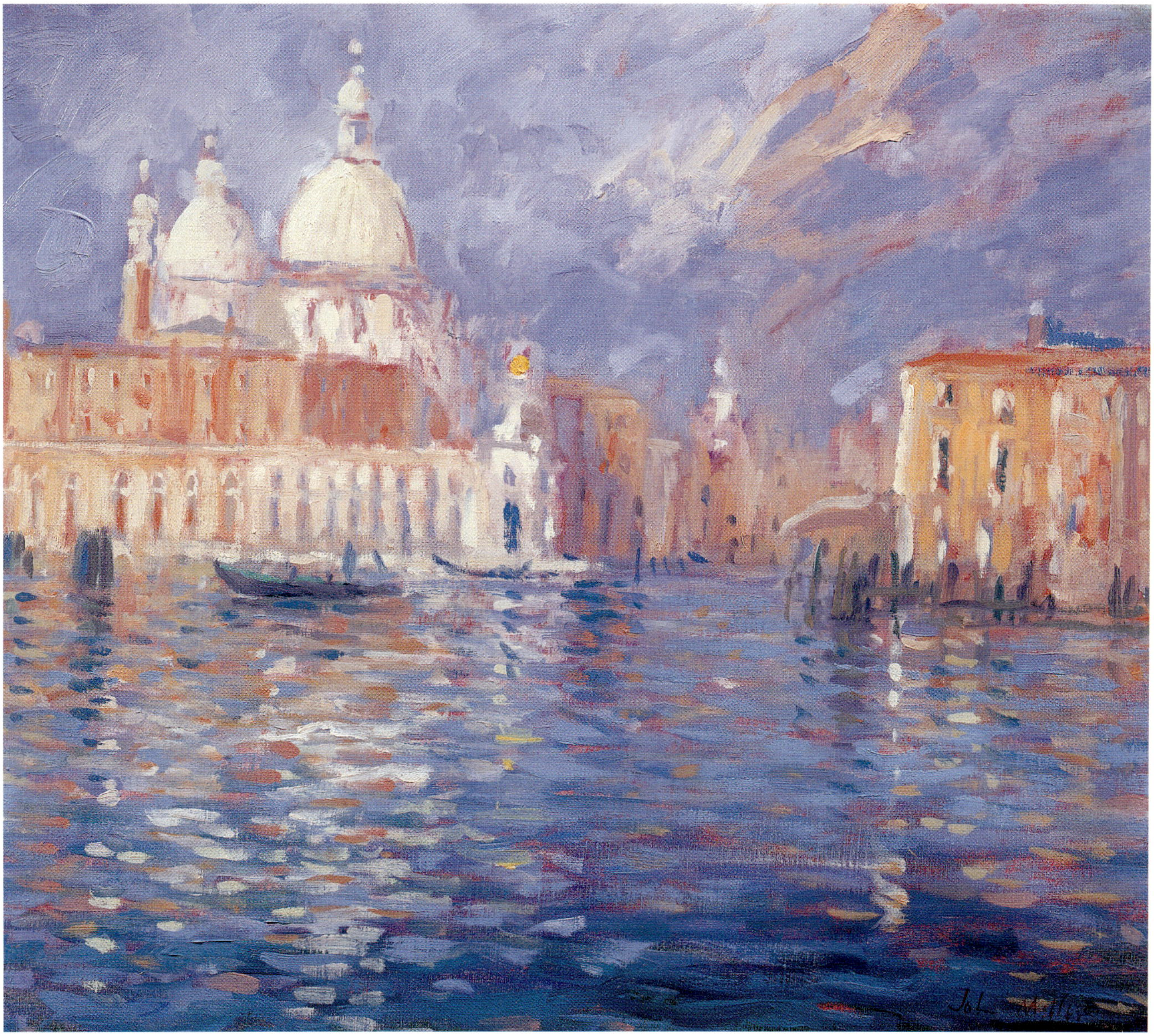

Travel

In the 1970s and 1980s I travelled a lot in Europe and around the Mediterranean. When Michael and Madeleine Canney moved from Somerset to live within the walls of a very beautiful hill town in Tuscany I went there to visit them. They took me to some marvellous places and we saw much very moving art. Michael was working on his geometric assemblies so different from my landscape studies. Each of us was able to appreciate the work of the other and we enjoyed a good friendship. Michael was underrated in his lifetime and I am so pleased to hear from Madeleine that his work is now going into public collections. I returned with a collection of English 'Euston Road School' post-impressionist, images of Tuscany which were later exhibited at Searcy's, London.

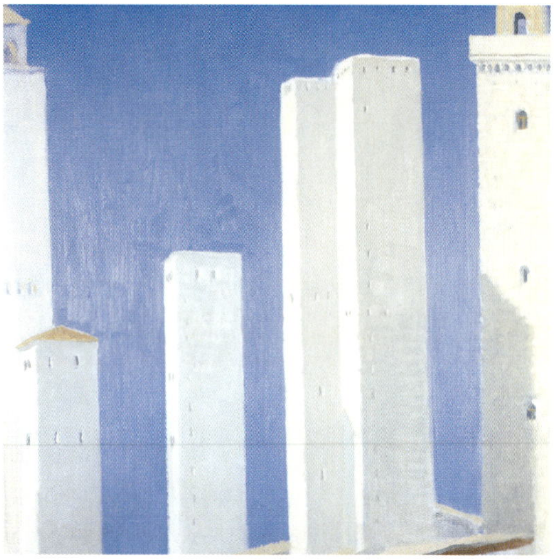

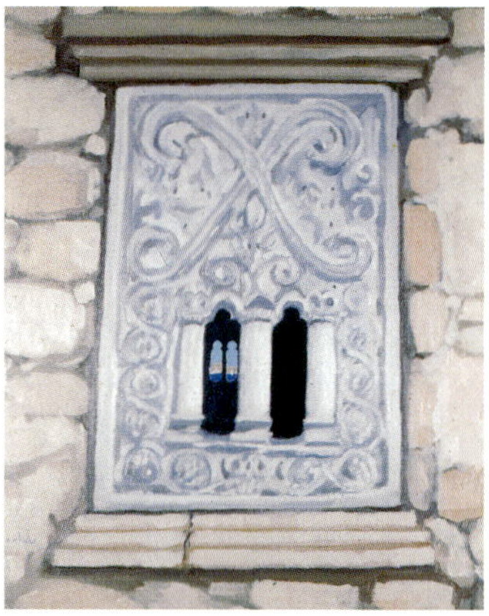

▲ **San Gimignano, Tuscany**
oil on canvas
MT

▲ **Small Church Window in Crete**
1986 oil on canvas
MT

▶ **Paraportiani 5**
1986 oil on canvas 45x45
MT

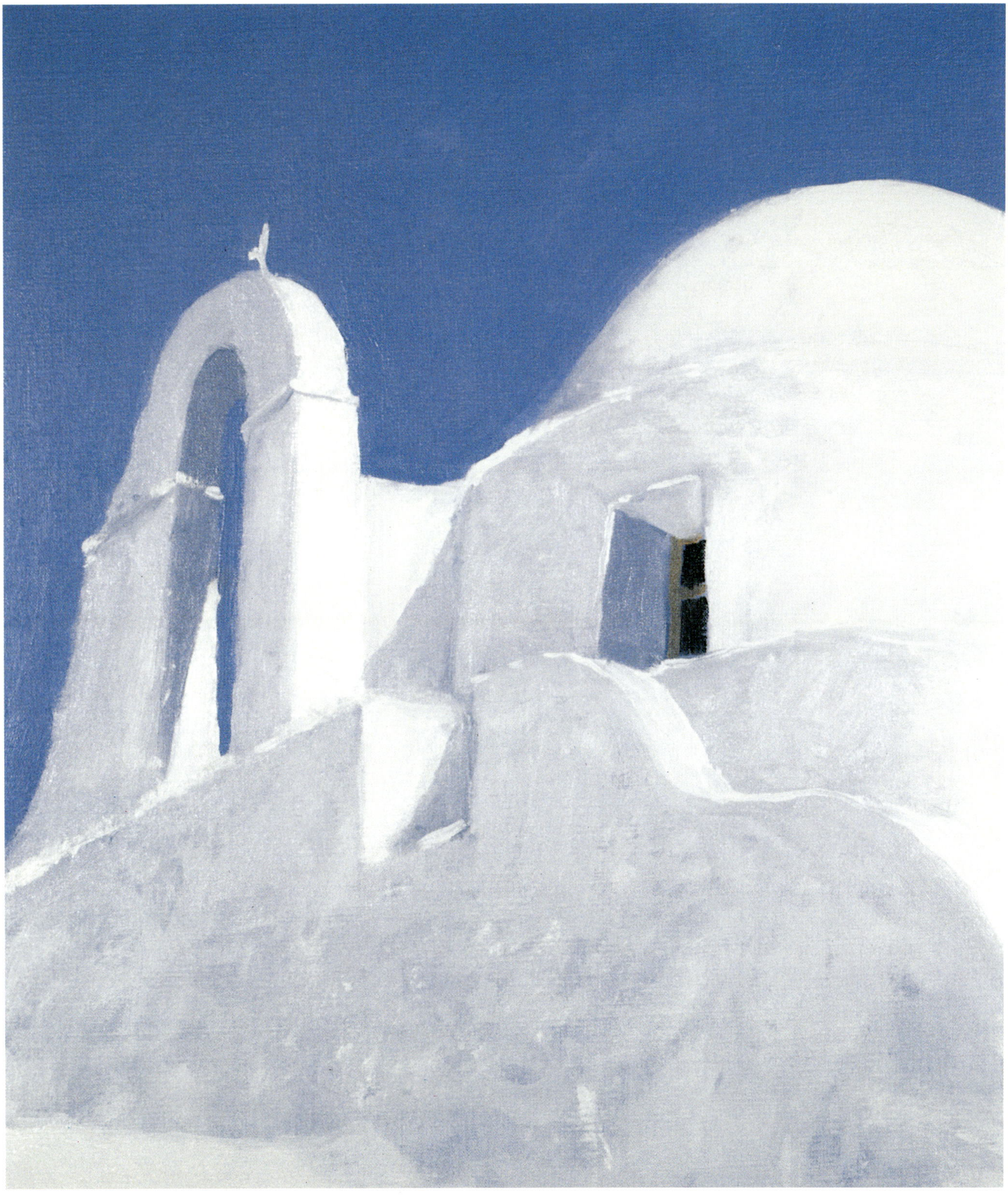

Seeing the sky

I returned to Mykonos where David Cornwell (John le Carré) had taken me in 1980 when researching his novel 'The Little Drummer Girl' and went on to stay in Crete. It was at that time that I first experienced the tactile quality of a very deep blue sky – especially with the white dome of an orthodox church set against it. It appeared like a velvet backdrop that I could touch and I began to understand the philosophy of Gauguin and Matisse when they abandoned all forms of three dimensional trickery for the flat surface of a two dimensional canvas. That was another enormous leap.

Although I experienced the dance of colour on these islands I also saw the need for a discipline and centred that on one particular church in Mykonos which I drew and painted over and over again – the Paraportiani Church of the Fishermen. I was beginning to acknowledge my own vision which until now I had seen only fleetingly. My studies of the Paraportiani would later enable me to paint the beaches.

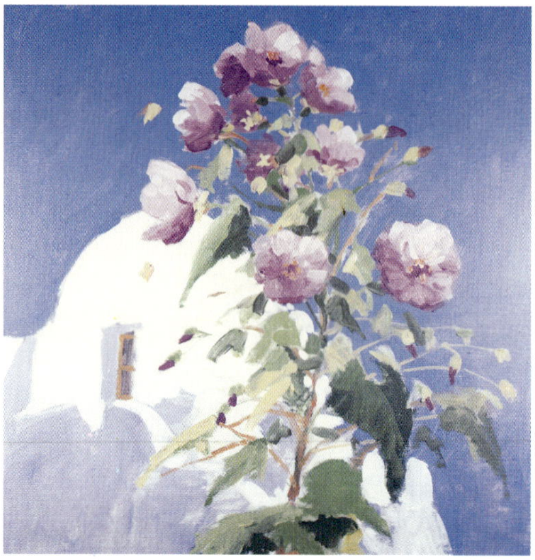

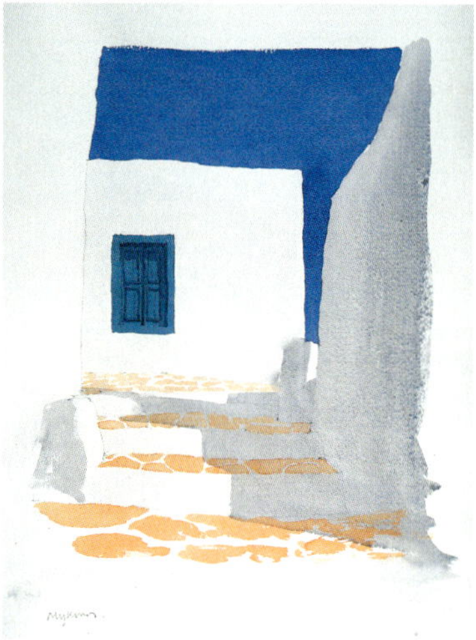

▲ **Dome and Flowers**
1986 oil on canvas 60x60
MT

▲ **Mykonos**
1986 watercolour 25x25
MT

▶ **Gondola Poles Venice**
1992 oil on canvas 55x75
MT

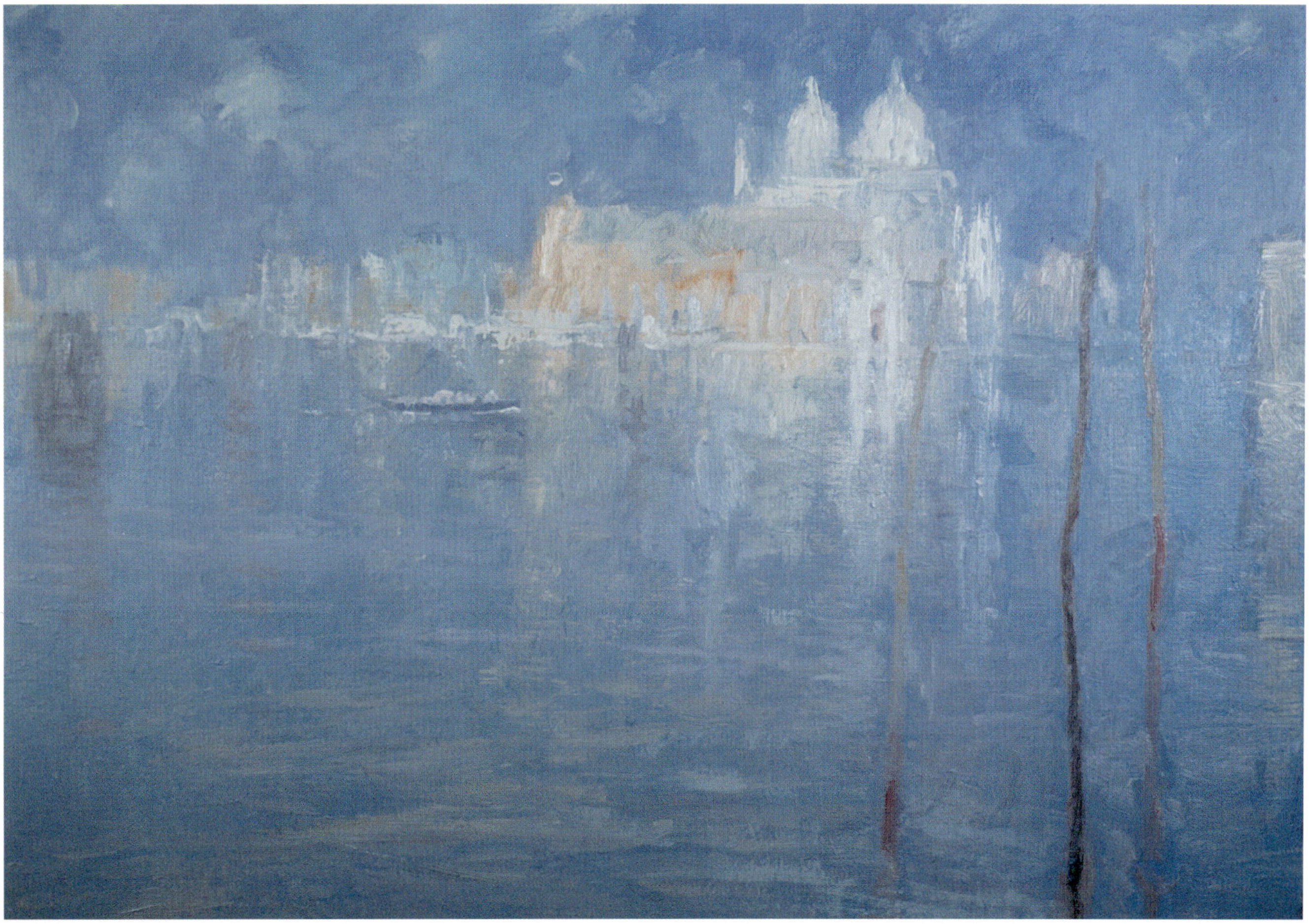

The revelation of a two dimensional world of colour which occurred on the Greek Islands also enabled me to paint the garden at Sancreed when my mother became ill. I used to push her into the garden and there I felt a tremendous energy. It was to do with the need to give her support when her own energy was declining. Looking back on some of those garden paintings, I don't like them at all. They were far too energetic. But they were about the situation I was in. I couldn't go out. I couldn't leave her. We did have nurses after a while but at that time we were looking after her ourselves. When she went into the nursing home, the work formalised much more with landscapes that started to find planes of direction and intense colour but that middle period of the gardens was a frenetic period – a period of coming to terms with the fact that Mother was dying.

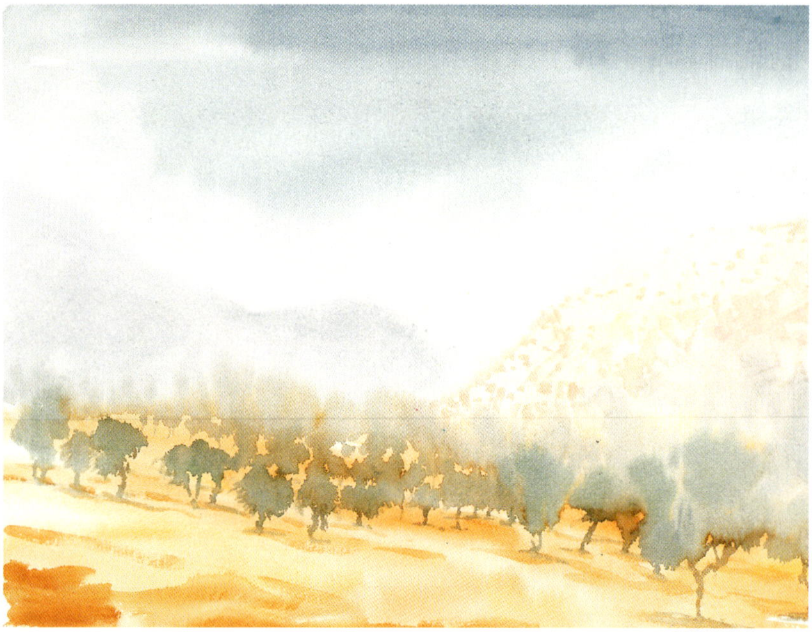

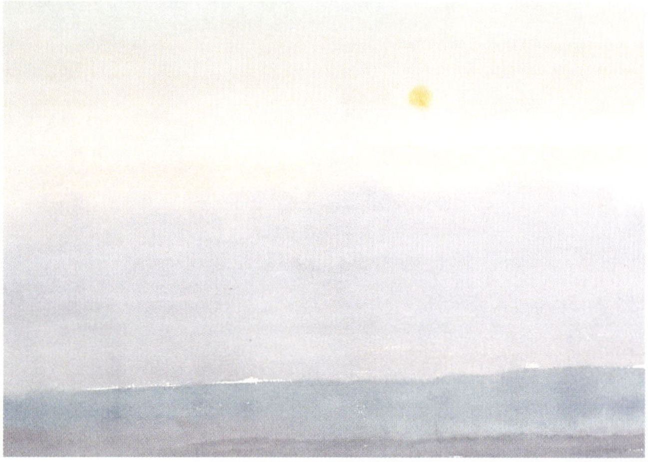

▲ **In the Mountains, Crete**
watercolour
MT

▲ **Evening with Moon 7.30pm**
1985 watercolour study
MT

▶ **Mother**
1988 May watercolour

Interior landscapes

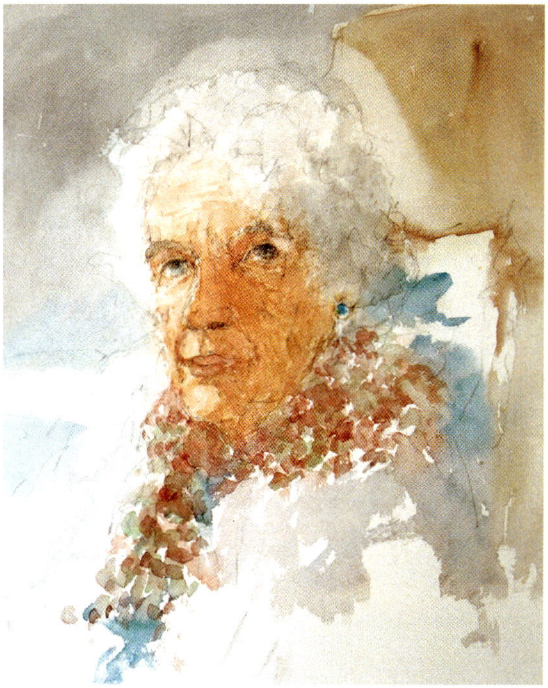

After Mother died came the interior landscapes – they came from the colour I'd found looking at two-dimensional skies linked with the experience of death. These became great slabs of colour in which there were hints of spaces within massive chambers and a tiny figure. Whilst working on these I found a figure I had made in clay following my father's death with great similarities to those which occupied the interior landscapes.

When my father died soon after they moved into the Coach House at Sancreed in 1966, Mother crossed the drive and threw stones up at my bedroom window to attract my attention in the middle of the night. Father had had a heart attack. We called the doctor who said 'We can't do anything about it.' He just gave him morphine and helped him. I knew Father was dying but I thought if he can survive until sunrise, he will live. My whole energy was about keeping him alive until sunlight. I have an almost pagan notion that through our energy we can keep people alive, so that all goes into the painting. It always does, whether you want it to or not.

The interior landscapes and the figure I made following my father's death were, in retrospect, intuitive representations of the journey of the soul. Following a long period of paralysis my mother smiled at each one of us before departing in the most beautiful way.

Paintings change

The paintings change as my life changes and I think that's all right. I used to say to myself, 'Just look at the different stuff I've done over the years and look at that of Karl Weschke for example. You can recognise the work of fifty years ago as his.' Now I don't mind being seemingly inconsistent because I think my work has always been an honest statement of where I was in life. It is not so much that the work has changed, but that my perceptions have changed.

I think as an artist you are in the paintings, but you don't deliberately put yourself in them; that is something I can't do. But the paintings inevitably reflect your life and you see life the way you are at the moment and so you represent life and your observations, your feelings about life, that way. I have questioned myself deeply about this and I've been questioned within the art world. They like somebody who's recognisable pretty well from beginning to end. Although, having said that, Picasso's style changed dramatically over his life and early Monet, is not like the Monet of the 'Water Lilies'. I don't know who to believe is right. Tim Hubbard addressed this when he first came to Sancreed to interview me for a BBC radio programme in the late 1980s. He also asked me why I never appear to paint the harsher side of life and my answer then was, as it would be now, that I could too easily wallow and less easily celebrate if I allowed myself to sink into that viewpoint.

▲ **The Estuary on a Summer's Day**
2000 oil on canvas 92x86
SC

Turner

The early Turners don't touch me but his colour beginnings and his interiors at Petworth are wonderful. I worshipped Turner at one time and I'm sure it's where my own interior landscapes come from because you can see thin windows with little figures against them. They're not the same at all as mine, but they are about a space in a room with a light beyond and an occupant. I'd like to think that, maybe I'm pushing that idea around. In a sense I have always painted in the way of Turner. I have always drawn upon a visual experience. However abstract the work may have become it remains perceptual rather than conceptual.

Van Gogh wrote to his brother 'Now that nature is so beautiful, I am totally unaware of myself.' Similarly St Augustine saw men climb mountains and look out and forget themselves. I think that's true and that's of course, what we're painting – we are reflecting what we see and sharing it with others.

Working at painting

Currently there are a number of my paintings on display in a hospital in Devon. I wanted to create an ambience so that as people passed through they were brought for a moment into a different and peaceful state of mind before churning on. They're such busy places, hospitals. If the busy people can be given something, as they pass, that is marvellous. A large beach painting has been hanging in the hospital since 1994 and the response of patients, staff and visitors has helped the development of the new series.

The project was very exciting because I saw my work developing in unexpected ways. I wanted to create this ambience and painted one misty sunrise which is a very orange painting and very wide – six foot by four foot. There are spaces at each end of this corridor that size and then they're 40 inches high and 30 inches wide between windows, so you've got windows to combat. I worked on a similar theme for the dining room of the Abbey Hotel, Penzance, for my friends Jean and Michael Cox.

▶ **Sunrise of Wonder 1**
oil on canvas 122x163
sc

I was thinking about infinity. In the desert, you get a black line at the edge of desert sometimes which is the line of infinity. That is the beyond. It is not a blue line, it's a black line. I was thinking about that so I got some French black which I have in powder colour – it's pure pigment – and I mixed that up with ordinary ivory black paint because that produces a drier and a denser paint. I put it into a jam jar with some turps and shook it all up and then I painted a black line. It was a big canvas, sixty-four inches high. Then I put a cobalt blue line above it and I covered the rest of the canvas in black which I hadn't expected to be doing.

Over a period of days, I put in some stand oil, which is linseed oil that is dried in the sun and is thick – it's like grease for cars, in my mixture and mixed it all up and I painted a black over black. Then I'd got a very matt black and the shiny black, although it had changed a lot from how I started. I then found some red, blue red, like an Alizaren red and I put it on and then I scraped black over the top of that because I didn't like it, but some of the red came through – paint has its own life. In a strange way although the painting is black it's about light. It's wonderful. I don't think it's right for the hospital but it's a wonderful painting and it's obviously the beginning of a whole new series. After that I painted and finished a smaller one, which is again mainly black. It is that line of infinity, which fascinates me.

▲ **Beach Painting Mount's Bay**
2000 oil on canvas 163x122
SC

▶ **Autumn Landscape**
1993 oil on canvas 60x70
MT

Dealers

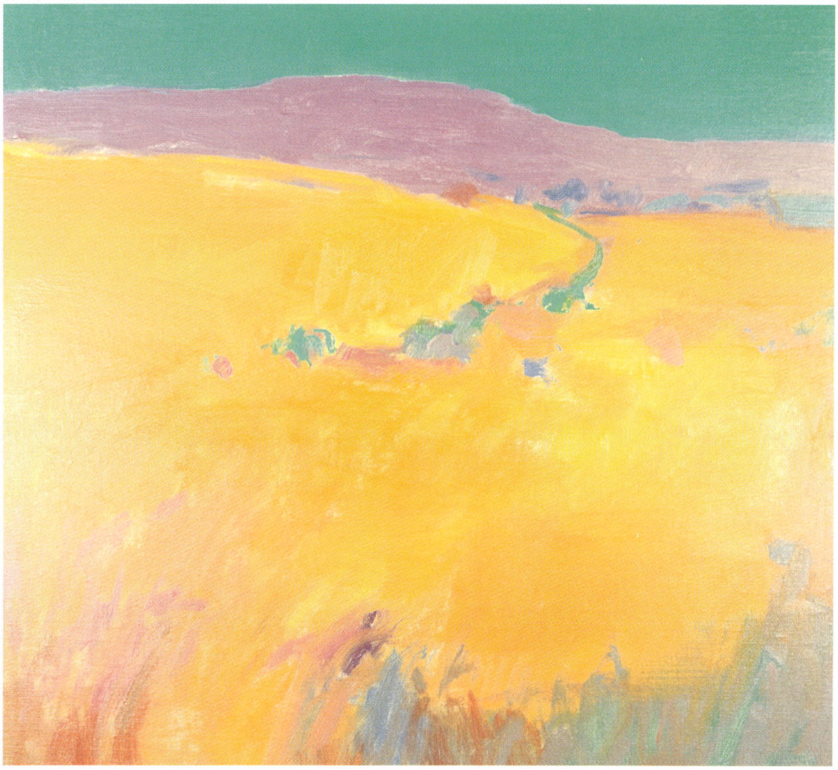

When the New York dealer took me on first, I rolled up the paintings and sent them to him. Ten days later he'd send some money. There are a number of dealers who do that. In the old days, of course, if you think about the Impressionists, it was always like that. Very often the dealer also sold paints and canvasses so the artists would go and say 'Will you put one of my pictures in your window?' The moment an artist's work began to sell the dealer would buy the paintings. The sale or return business is quite a recent thing – or at least a twentieth century thing. For example, Monet played dealers off against one another once he'd made his name. I think that in America they do it more that way – it gives it a bite. If you have bought something you want to sell it.

The American dealer paid me 25% of the wall price (the sum paid by a collector). This provided the cash for solo exhibitions, which can take up to two years to prepare . London galleries can take between 40% and 65% commission, depending upon the backup, such as expensive catalogues and advertisements. Public galleries take 33%, as do private galleries where no additional expenses are incurred, over and above their overheads.

There are pros and cons regarding direct sales but they do provide cash up front when working for a show. I found I was able to pace myself with the New York gallery providing a background income during the year to eighteen months of preparation for a solo exhibition.

Selling interior landscapes

When the interior landscapes were first shown in 1990 the gallery put everything behind them with a superb catalogue with a foreword by John le Carré and some splendid advertisements and articles in advance. One in particular was by Emma Burn in 'London Portrait' entitled 'Mauve over darling'. Americans and Japanese took to the work immediately at prices between £7500/8500 and the Brits followed on. Considering the artistic leap I had taken the sales were remarkably good. The guitarist Robert Fripp and Toyah Wilcox, both old friends, bought a number of paintings from the exhibition and later Robert used these as covers for his CDs. Gary Rhodes has many of my paintings in his large private collection as well as a group of paintings which he purchased for a new restaurant 'Rhodes in the Square' opened in 1998 in Dolphin Square, London. Since then he and his wife Jenny have become good friends of mine. They have bought some of the more recent work as presents for friends as well as additions to their collection.

▶ **Purple Interior**
2000 gouache
SC

▲ **Blue Interior with Figure**
2000 gouache 45x26
SC

▶ **Red Interior**
2000 gouache
SC

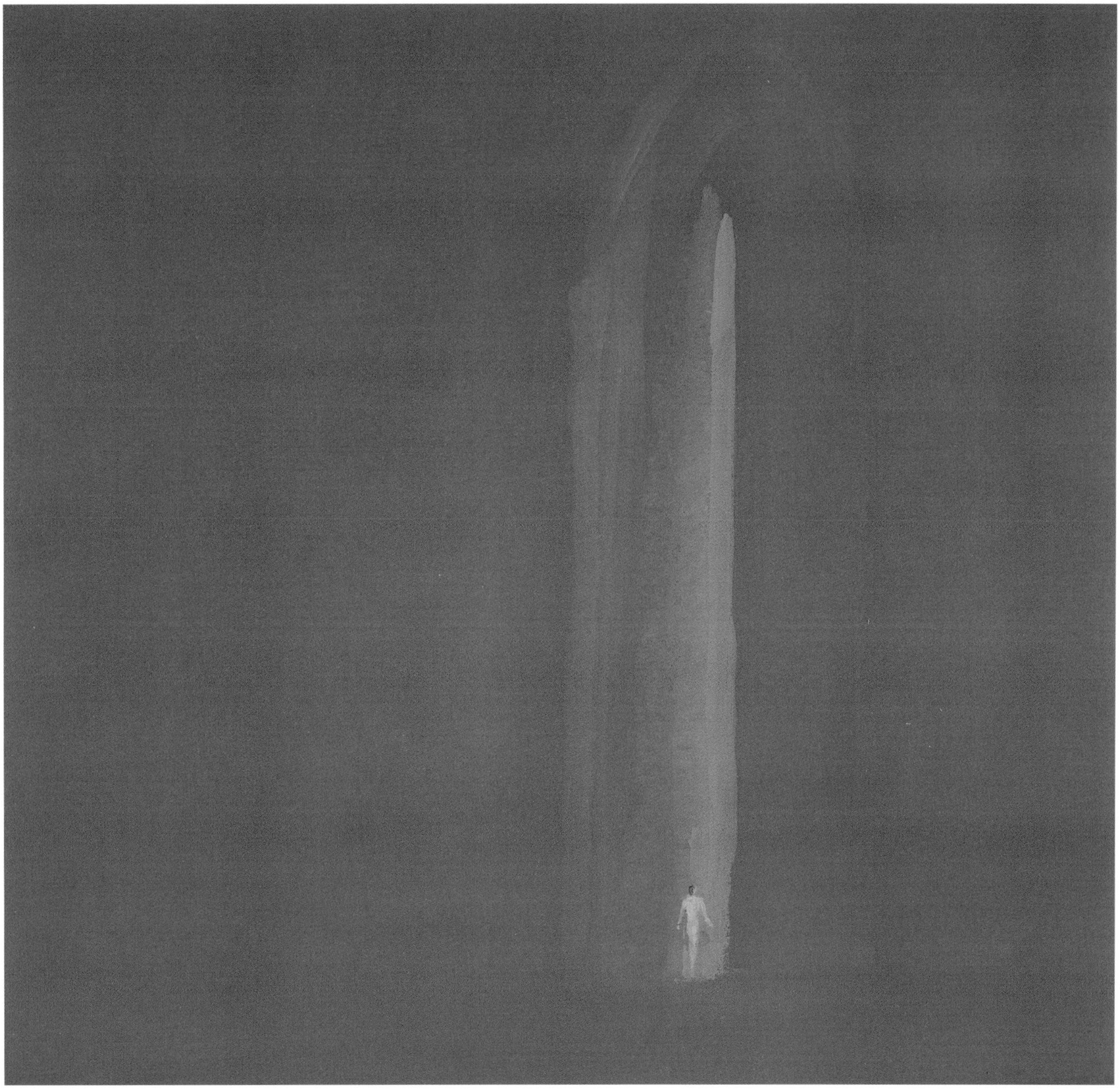

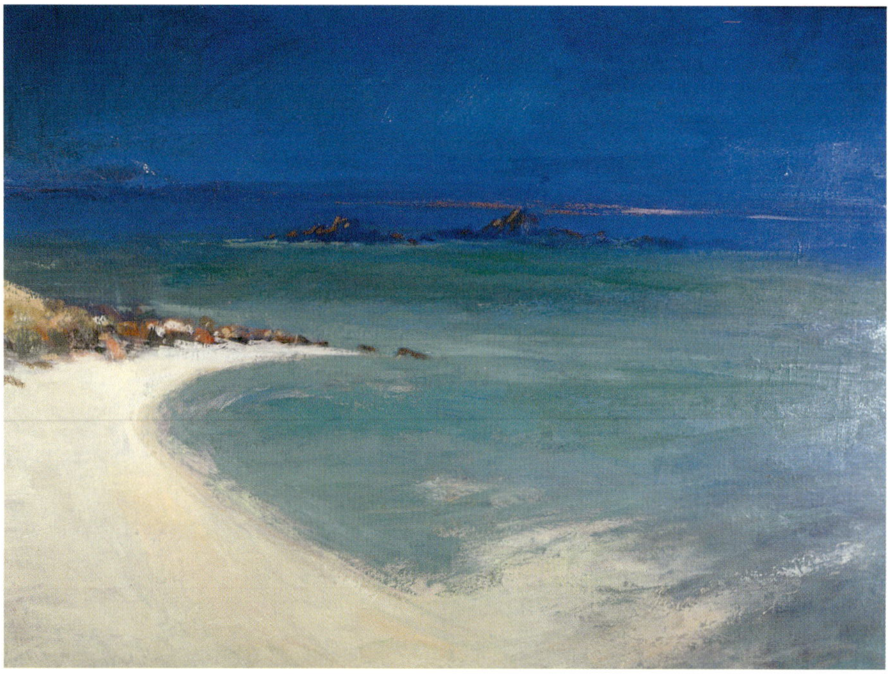

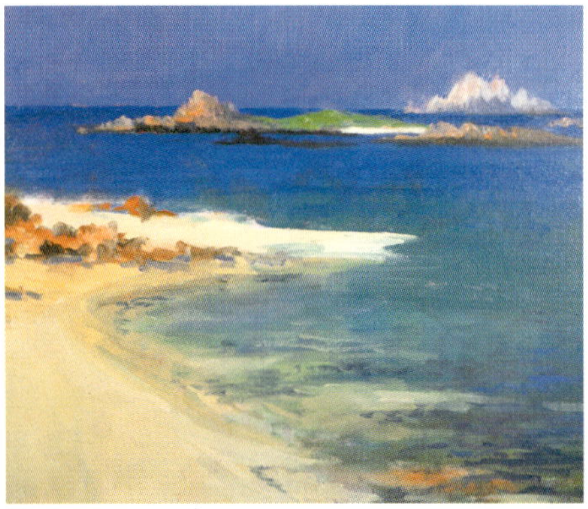

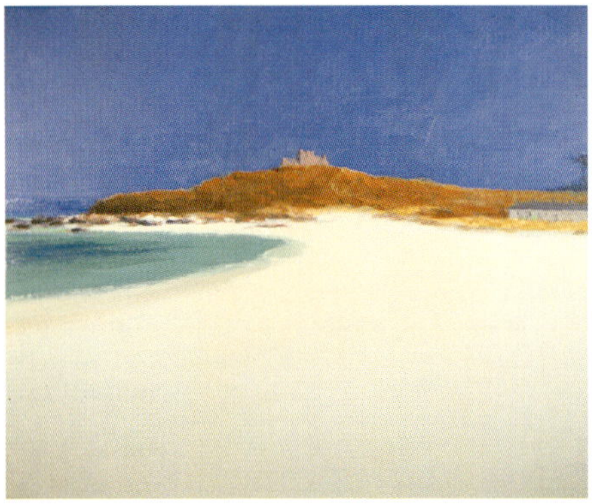

▲ **The Water's Edge, Tresco**
1992 oil on canvas 75x95
MT

◀ **Beach Study II, Tresco**
1992 oil on canvas 40x50
MT

◀ **The Blockhouse, Tresco**
1992 oil on canvas 55x70
MT

▶ **Quiet Bay**
1998 gouache 24x24
MT

▶ **John Miller and Boots Redgrave**
2001
MT

Selling the beaches

I began to paint the beaches following an invitation from Lucy and Robert Dorrien-Smith to stay in one of their beautiful cottages on Tresco and work for a show at the Gallery Tresco. The exhibition was successful and Boots Redgrave, with whom I have been showing for forty years, suggested I let her have some for her gallery in St Ives, the New Craftsman. She opened the gallery originally with Janet Leach in the mid-1960s to show pots by Bernard, Janet and other top contemporary potters. Soon the avant-garde St Ives painters were also exhibiting with them. It became an unpretentious but very successful gallery along the lines of the older Parisian galleries.

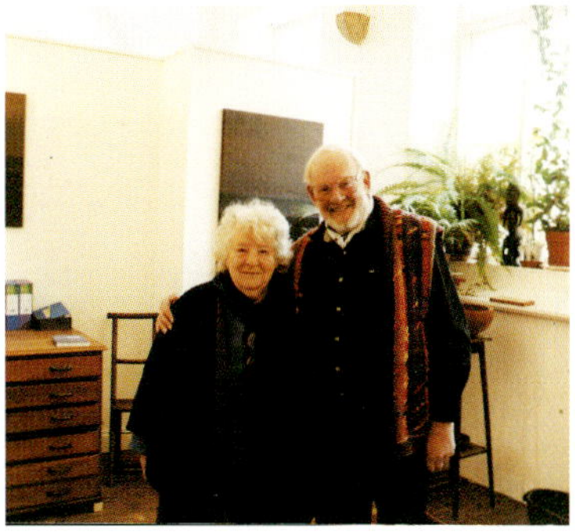

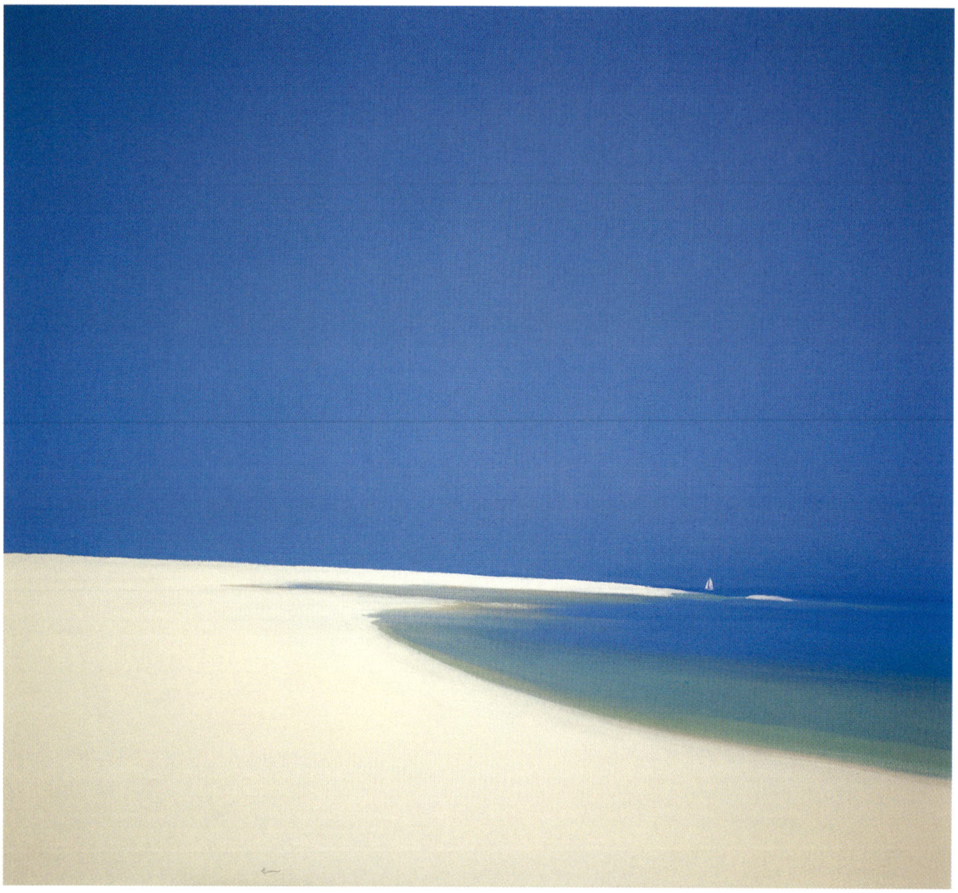

▲ **Sandspur with Passing Yacht**
1999 oil on canvas 85x90
MT

▶ **Summer Beach**
1999 gouache
SC

The dealer/artist relationship

Because the dealer and artist are a necessity to one another the relationship can be rocky at times. The dealer represents the artist and it's not simply a question of selling – it is about all the machinery behind the business of marketing. That's the age we live in. I think that marketing is a very special operation and it has to be embraced. The market has to be controlled too; you can't over-stuff the market because it gives the buyers indigestion.

Dealers take on other responsibilities, which the public don't realise, which is why I never resent the commission. People say 'Oh these enormous commissions' but, for example, a dealer will buy at the salerooms to ensure that paintings aren't floating into the market at knock-down prices, to use their terminology. They buy in and take them back into stock, so the dealers are putting money behind an artist's work all the time, as well as bearing the costs of the catalogues and running the galleries in very high rate and rent areas.

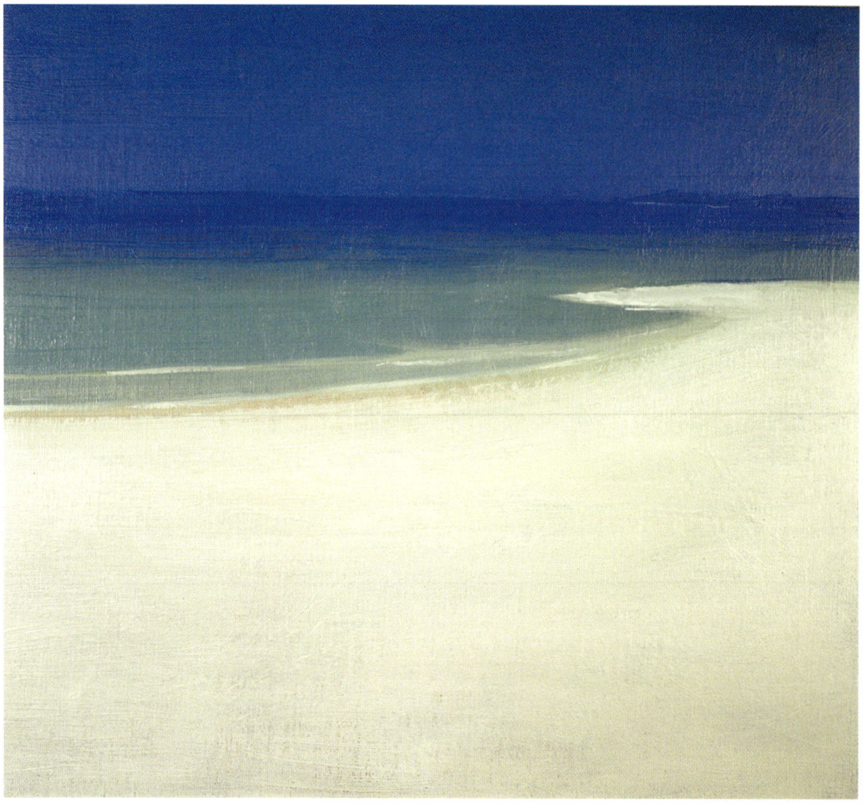

▲ **Beach Painting No 3**
1993 oil on canvas 40x45
MT

▶ **Lelant Sandbar**
1998 oil on canvas 65x60
Donated to Cornwall Macmillan Service
MT

The valuing of paintings

We all know that we won't buy anything unless we think it's worth it. If I want to buy a motor car, I'll go to the motor car dealer who's going to give me what I believe to be the best motor car for the deal. You don't go to a back street shop hoping to buy a spanking good car. We all have to be reassured that we're spending our money sensibly, whatever we do, and that's another part of the dealer's responsibility. The dealer has to be well established and to have proved himself to be reliable, knowledgeable and astute. People are more likely to go to him to buy a picture because they're reassured by his qualifications – life, business and art market qualifications.

Another very important factor is that artists make art and can't value it. It's almost impossible to value something you have made. An artist needs someone else to do that. If I had to think about the worth of a painting and how I was going to sell it and how much I was going to sell it for, it would totally intrude. It would make the actual making of the painting impossible. I have to be completely detached from that. Painting for me has to be about making something that communicates. Of course I respect the money, because after all painting is all I can do so I have to earn my living from it. If you think of a nineteenth century village, 'the butcher, the baker and the candle-stick maker' – each made his contribution and was rewarded for it. That's all it is with painting.

...and selling them

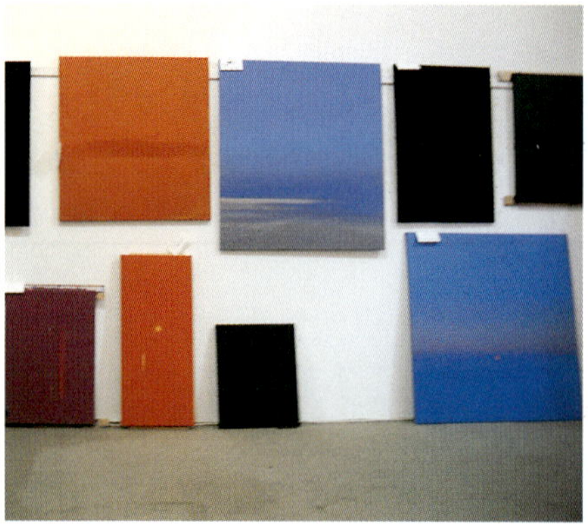

It's a curious fact that one dealer can sell an artist's work and another can't. In a way it's inexplicable although it must have something to do with a particular gallery's clientele and their taste. There was an instance of this recently before I joined the Portland Gallery when an American dealer tried to sell a beach painting destined for his gallery in the States to an English buyer without success – in the end I wrote to him and said 'Look, it's horses for courses. You know you're not able to sell these paintings. You have to acknowledge it. They just don't happen to fit into your flavour, the way you deal, or with your sort of clientele.' It's a mystery but it's true you can have two galleries side by side and one can sell a thing and the other can't.

If a dealer can't sell the work then there is no point trying to suit the dealer. Painting really is dragging your whole being up and using it and you can't perform it, you can't become a different person. In my own life, I've passed through many different styles but each of them has clearly been a representation of my own development as a human being and so they were honest in their day. I couldn't go back and paint the past and I couldn't paint anything that didn't come out of who I am at the moment.

▲ **St Mary's Studio**
AW

▶ **Trencrom**
1999 gouache
SC

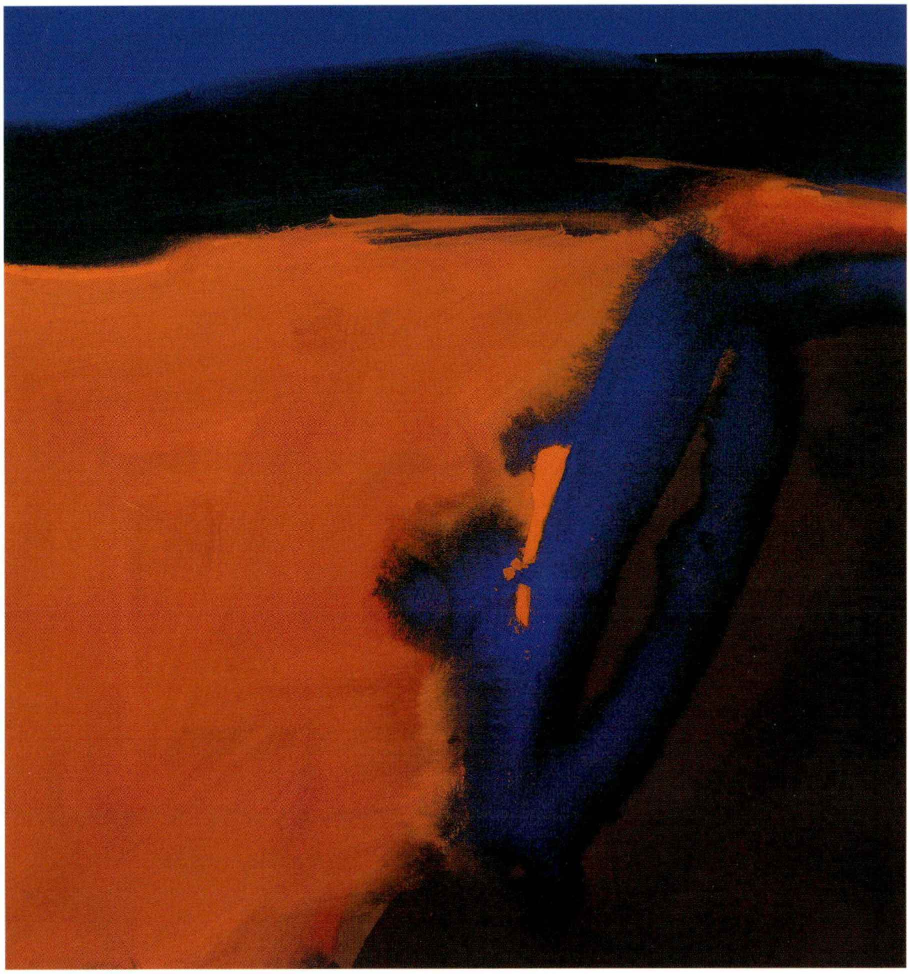

What to paint

As a draftsman, I could paint the green landscapes that I used to do or the trees, but they wouldn't succeed as paintings. At one time they were about the search for the Holy Grail through the trees and now I see the Holy Grail, for want of a better term, as a tiny sun rising or something quite different. You can only declare it the way you feel most able to at the time. I think that this makes things difficult for dealers because a lot of people, not just dealers, think that when you do a painting, you assemble it, having intellectually decided what it will be in terms of its construction and arrangement – it doesn't happen like that for me. Very often when I'm painting colour it will perhaps marry with an experience, and so another experience will start to overlay it and then the painting will start to go in a particular direction. Certainly that's how I paint. I'm an intuitive painter. Of course, the vision is always there, but it is how to describe that vision.

You go on painting something because you're still exploring it but if you reach the end of a theme you can't go on painting it under any circumstances, because it's boring. It's as simple as that. I think I am quite selfish in a way. I don't want to do something that bores me. I'm sure of that. I sometimes wonder whether all this 'highfalutin' talk is just to camouflage the fact that I simply want to please myself all the time!

The beach paintings have been hugely successful. I've been painting them since 1992. They have moved on enormously from the early ones and they've gone into something else so it isn't as if they are identical in any way. They've moved on to sunrises and other experiences of being on the beach. Now there are the black paintings, in the 'Looking at the Open Sea' exhibition 2000/2001 which extend the beach experience even further.

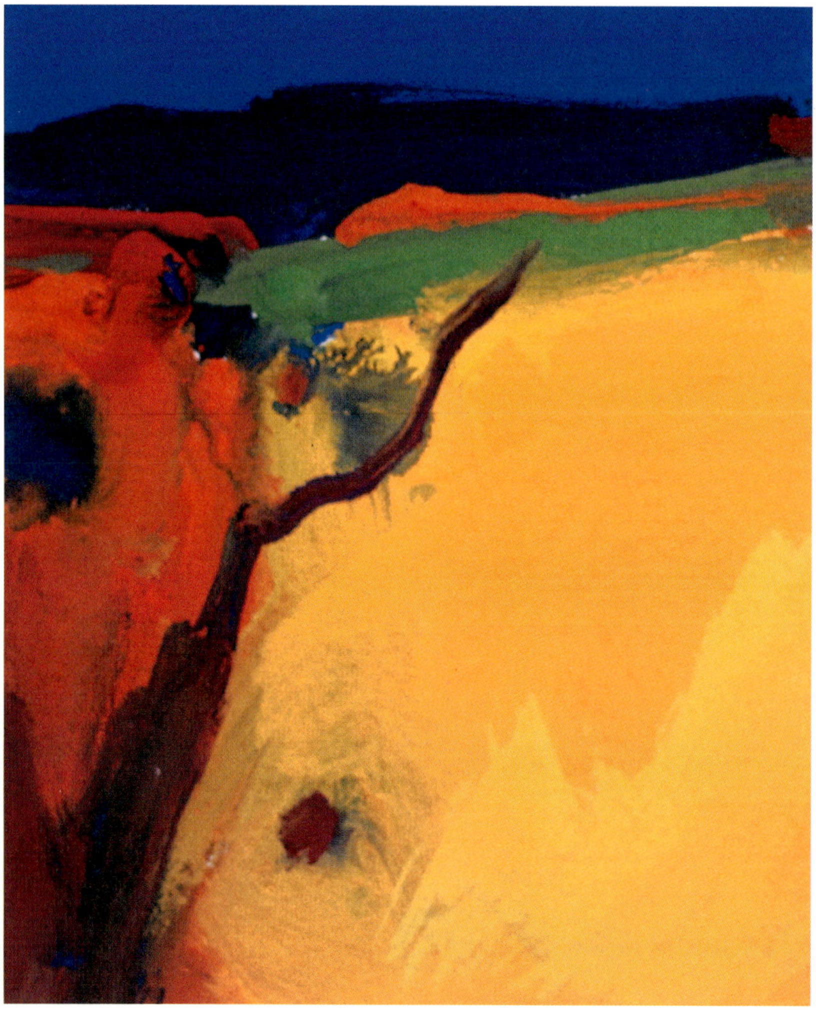

▲ **Lelant Downs**
1998 gouache 11x8
MT

A painter's integrity

If you're a painter, for better or worse, you explore your own experience of life and see to what extent you can share it with others. It is a lonely road. Van Gogh in his last letter says something like 'I have risked my life in my art and it has brought me close to dementia.' He never posted it and it was actually in his pocket when he shot himself, but that 'dementia' is how it has to be because one risks everything really. I'm sure of that. Without sounding pedantic, often there are choices and you know which choice you have to take. I turn down commissions that don't seem right to me, even though they would pay the bills. You have to maintain integrity. If you miss out on that, you let life down.

I have had some very difficult times when it was impossible to paint or to find the right way. Clearly there's something in me that has to serve. Maybe the part of me that wanted to be a monk. I did other extraordinary things as an alternative to being a monk but always I sought to find total commitment. I do find it in painting. Maybe I demand more of painting because of my personality. A number of painters teach so if nobody wants to buy their work it's not the end of the world because they're shown in prestigious galleries where paintings are appreciated and not necessarily purchased. At best they're bought for public collections. Sir Terry Frost is a very good example of this. Terry taught most of his life. His work was always highly regarded and acquired for public collections. His overall popularity came later in life – as with so many artists. I couldn't teach. Really and truly I've been learning all the time, I'm still learning. The little teaching I have done just exhausted me. Ways of earning your living, other than art, take up the energy that should go into painting.

People like Turner saw painting as a way of making a living. There was nothing wrong with that. We've become a bit precious about it now. Why shouldn't you use your talents to earn your living in the village like the boot maker does and to do it on the same level, not to see yourself as something different and special as a painter but say 'I'm the guy who does the paintings, so you can buy the paintings from me, you can buy the boots from this guy.' That's how I see myself.

I come across people who really do love the paintings and couldn't acquire them and that hurt me a lot. A few years ago I was surprised by all the prints of my beach paintings which flooded the market world-wide and which I had not given permission for. Now, I've changed my mind. These mass produced prints have made it possible for people to possess at least the image, not the painting. The painting is different from the image. I can take a painting of 6 x 4ft that I've worked on over some weeks and gone back to it time and again. I slosh paint all over it and think this is either going to work or it isn't. All that effort, and all that paint that's gone into it isn't to be found in a print. It's on the painting but it's not on the print and nobody can pick that up from the

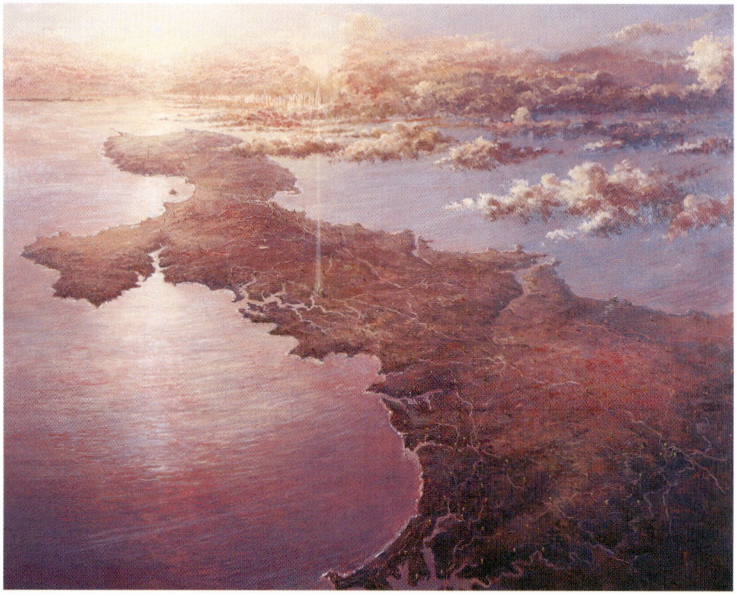

Cornubia
I was first asked to make a map of Cornwall showing every church. The idea was that of Dean Henry Lloyd who had obtained permission from the Chapter and the churchwardens. Once I began on the project my first drawings looked like a tourist's tea towel and I went into despair. I walked from the studio at Sancreed into the house and told Michael it was a job for a designer not a painter. As I prepared myself to phone the Dean I sketched a view of Cornwall from the air on a doodle pad making it into a landscape and not a diagram. 'That's how I could do it' I said to Michael. 'Then do it that way', he replied – so I did – and then telephoned the Dean. Although at first taken aback, he soon entered into the spirit of the painting. Over the following six months he visited frequently and made important suggestions so that the work grew in a harmonious way. After the unveiling a dear old canon gently described his disappointment having assumed his church would be lit up at the touch of a button!

▲ **Cornubia**
1980 oil on canvas 120x150

▶ **Simply River**
2000 London Underground poster

print. I suppose it has to be said that the colours never match and that the content is not as strong in a print as in the painting. It can't be and that's why I worry a bit about it only being an image, because painting for me is not just about an image it's about something that lies behind the image. I'm sure that's right and I'm sure that's where all the effort's gone into in my paintings. Matisse used to say, 'I want to make my paintings look as if they were done in three hours.' You hide the effort, nobody wants to see hard work. We're worried about seeing hard work. We want to receive something from a painting that's going to feed us. We can admire hard work and craft in other areas but we really want to be spiritually fed by a painting.

I am not against reproductions in principle because the images become universally available at economic prices. The London Underground poster of the Tate Modern 'Simply River' is a good example of reproduction with a purpose. It will be good to have the screen prints which are planned by Tom Hewlett of the Portland Gallery and Ann Viney of the The Art Group who produce posters, cards and prints of my work. Ann recently re-introduced Tom into my life. We had met when he signed a copy of his book on Cadell for me in 1988 and he showed a painting of mine in an exhibition he mounted in 1992 in aid of the St John's Ambulance. It never occurred to me that I would one day join his gallery, yet here we are planning a major show in June 2001 – which will coincide with the publication of this book – a week or two before my 70th birthday.

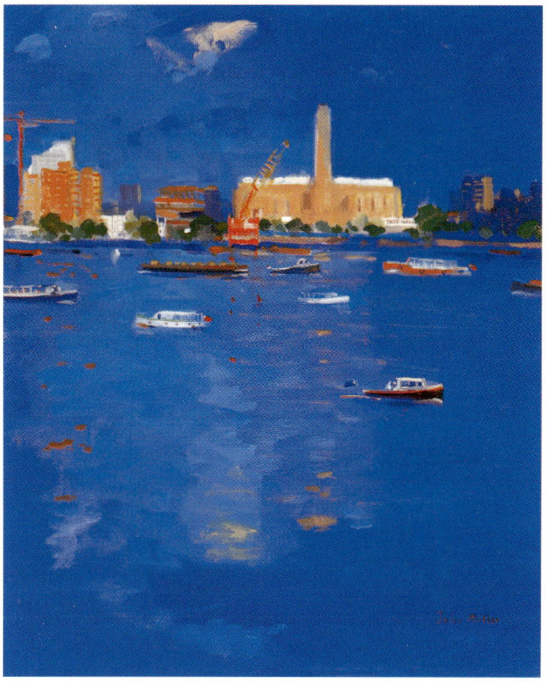

Simply River
When I was first commissioned by London Transport to create a poster for the London Underground showing the Tate Modern I really found it hard to believe. Michael Walton explained it would be the last in the present series which had started when the underground began. There have been around 2000 different poster designs in that time – many by distinguished artists. David Hockney made the Tate Gallery Centenary poster and Sir Howard Hodgkin a more recent one of Highgate ponds. When friends telephoned me saying they had seen the poster on the underground it gave me an enormous thrill.

Censoring work

Although the experience of life is reflected in my work I am always censoring it because I wouldn't want my own misery or my private problems to enter my art. It may belong in your own doodles, in your own working through. Somebody like Munch who painted 'The Scream' can make his misery speak to everybody about a universal experience. I think art has to be about that. Bacon too was painting universally, not about his own individual life. Goya's paintings of the war were Goya's comment on man's inhumanity to man at a time when, quite rightly, he'd seen that and he felt it had to be stated but, again, it wasn't his own misery. He was saying the world has to know this, not that the world has to know about me. I think that's the difference.

I drew my mother when she was dying and when Monet's first wife was dying he painted her. This may seem callous but as an artist objectively, you're there to do that in a way. You're there to make those observations, not comments. Hogarth was definitive in pointing up all the desperation of human beings, the follies and decadence of his age but you wouldn't want to hang a load of people falling around drunk on the wall, because Hogarth was an illustrator. You keep his work in a book and observe or as with paintings of the First World War, you hang them in a museum.

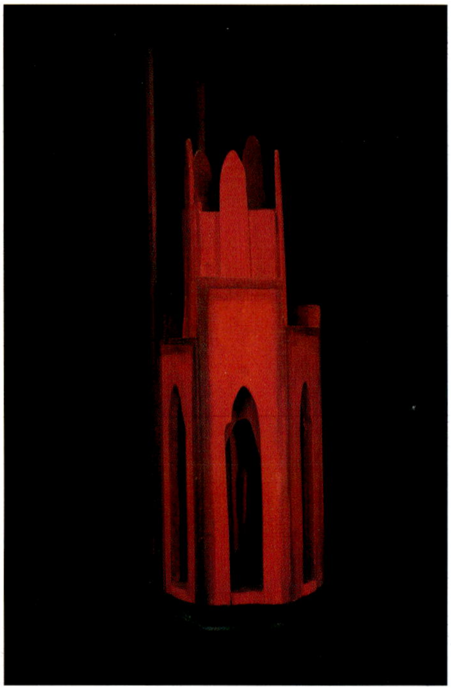

Standing Construction

There was a tremendous surge of energy at the time of the interior landscapes in 1990 which spilled over into the constructions. These began with all the surplus wood from reroofing Sancreed House – some ending up in a skip. When I was an ARP messenger boy I watched joiners, who had come from Bridgwater, take badly shattered and splintered wood from bomb sites and carefully cut out the good stuff with which they skilfully repaired broken doors and windows in houses like our own, which was ony partially demolished and therefore still habitable. I marvelled at their patience and skill. I have never forgotten how everything reclaimable was put to essential use. I still dislike waste and the arbitrary destruction of things which still have a usefulness. In many ways the interior landscapes were about enshrining something precious and the constructions became a natural extension. The figure in the landscapes became enclosed in a three-dimensional shrine. This called upon earlier carpentry skills although I was determined to avoid 'finish'. Both a visit to Egypt and my knowledge of gothic architecture contributed to this. Although they have something of Christian shrines about them I found in India years later primitive shrines that reminded me of that wonderfully creative period of work.

▲ **Standing Construction**
1990 wood 98x26
MT

▶ **Orange Interior**
2000 gouache 50x65
SC

Motives for making art

There are a number of different motives for making art. There's the very simple one of decoration – primitive peoples decorate their environment; they produce wonderfully decorative clothes and ornaments. We use art to declare political or religious beliefs and to impart those beliefs to people – art as propaganda. Conceptual art is to stun you, to awaken you, to make you think – Dali and the Surrealists would fit in here. Then there is topographical art: all those people who went off with Darwin and drew the topography of the places they visited. Similarly, there are the people who did accurate drawings of animals and plants or those who had the flair to go and draw the battles before they had cameras. Celebrating through painting I put at the top of the list because the others are utilising painting whereas once painting becomes celebration, it's purely that.

People have a very much stronger notion of what they want than the dealer thinks. A dealer once said to me 'I can sell anything.' That's not true of course. If people don't feel in touch with the work they won't buy it. There are some people who buy names and if they're told that this painter will be worth ten times more in fifty years' time, they'll buy it, they are really dealing themselves – they are buying the well established artists and more expensive paintings as investments. I'm really very small fry. I think it's over the twelve to fifteen thousand pounds mark that buyers begin to need to be told what to buy. There is a kind of financial barrier where people are beginning to buy for investment rather than for what it is that they're going to put on their wall for pure enjoyment.
I see publicity in the form of

interviews for articles or TV as part of the marketing of my work as important. I don't really want to do them. I would love to be without them, but can't be. I remember years ago saying to a friend 'It's just amazing how that particular painter is always doing the interviews, always doing this, always doing that.' He said 'Well, she does sell and at the moment you're not.' It's true. If you don't make the work available to people, you can't blame people for not buying. I'm a very practical person. I say that with a certain amount of sadness because as a painter I often think I should be up in the clouds a bit more. I am up there in the clouds but, like Turner, I'm also feet on the ground.

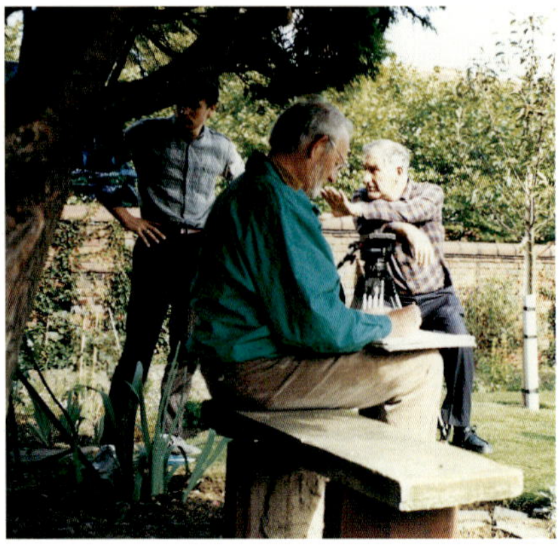

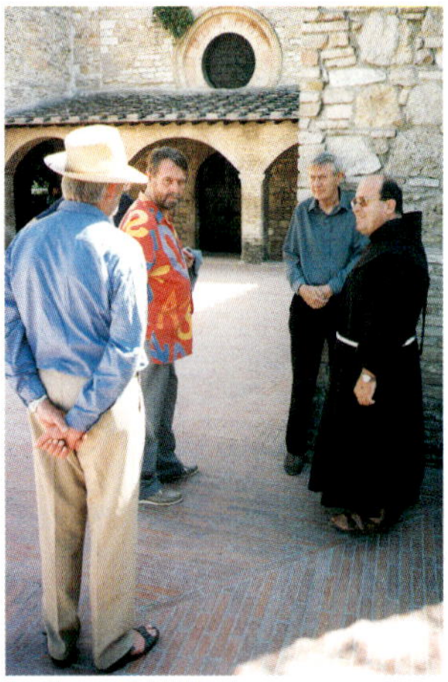

▲ **Filming for TV 'A Painter in Search of St Francis'**
1987
JB

▲ **Filming 'A Painter in Search of St Francis' at San Damiano**
1987
John Miller, John Bartlett, Brother Michael (out of habit) and a friar from the Assisi community
DH

▶ **St Francis and the Canticle of Brother Sun on Lelant Beach**
2000 oil on canvas 150x120
SC

Sketchbooks

I have always used sketchbooks. I still have drawings torn from the books I drew in the first years in Cornwall. In those days I selected those worth keeping and threw the rest away. I actually tore them out of the books. I stopped doing this when Dr. David Brown, then keeper at the London Tate Gallery, told me to keep everything. When I was a soldier in Malta I drew on sheets of paper and even pieces of cardboard. Everything was so short in 1950/51 following the war. There were no sketchbooks and pencils were still plain wood – utility.

Small sketchbooks are invaluable because they can be carried in a pocket and used for shorthand notes. Sheets of paper crumple up.

▲ **Cottage in Newlyn**
There are days in Cornish fishing villages when there is a strange stillness which gives a sense of timelessness. On those rare occasions when there is no-one about there is nothing to tell if it is a nineteenth century scene or a twenty-first – except for the occasional telegraph pole!

▶ **Farm at St Earth**
This is one of a number of sketches I made when staying for a weekend with Jean and Michael Cox at Tremellin when the light was warm grey with the sun breaking through a Cornish mist.

▶ **Cows**
At Sancreed I was surrounded by cows for most of the thirty-one years I dwelt there. They are such beautiful beasts with very gentle natures. From time to time I loved to go into the field and draw them for the simple pleasure of it. I did so again at Brunnion Barns. There the footpath went through the field of cows so I often walked there with our dog, Boss. Cows move so gracefully. This is drawing for the sheer joy of it like all the sketches on the beach.

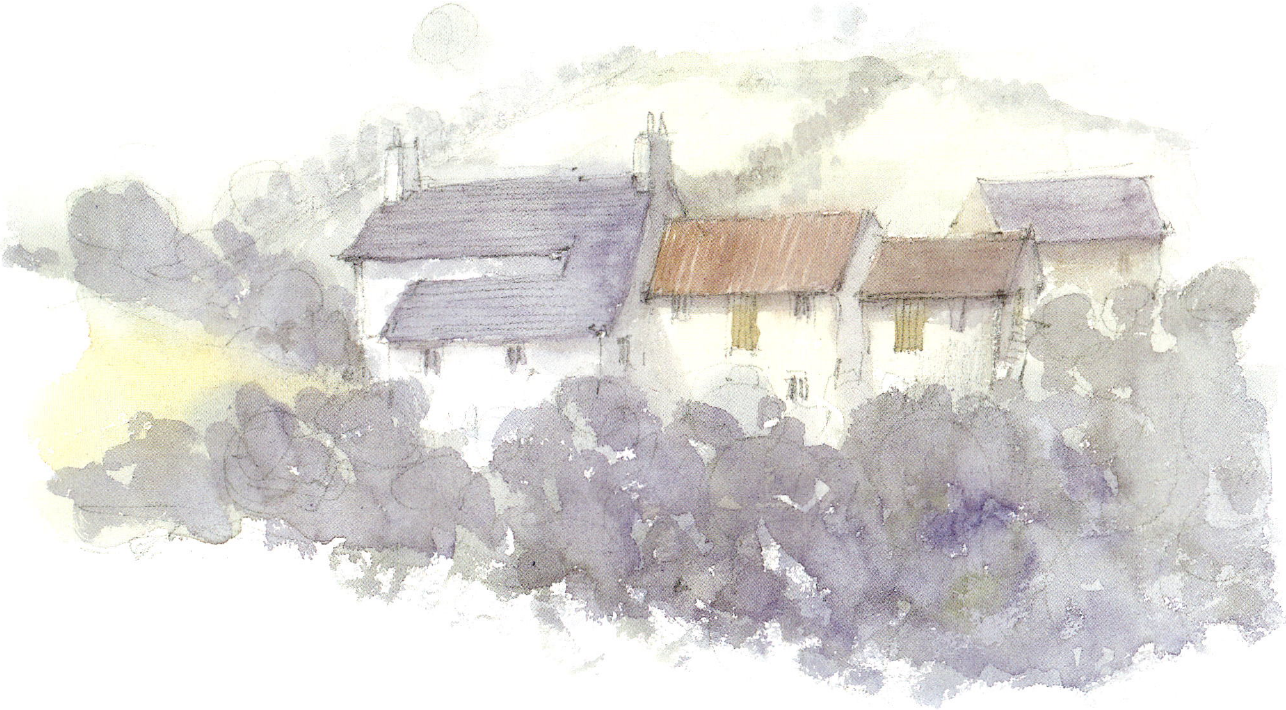

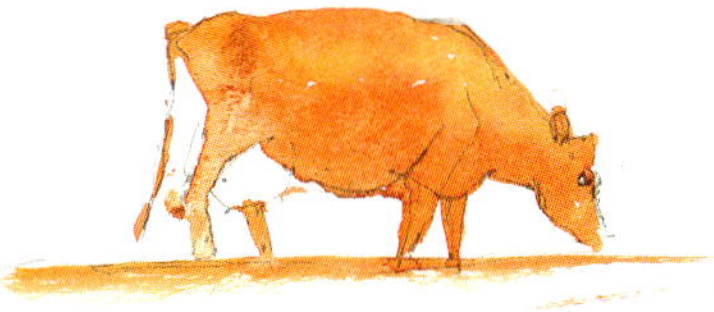

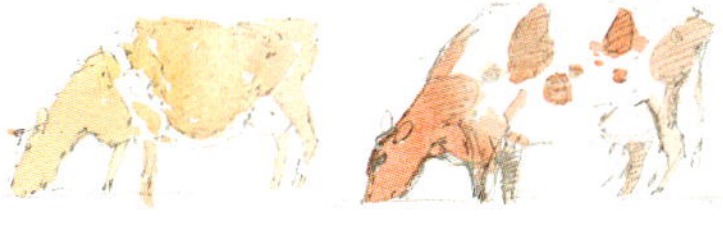

The moment I start to draw, I start to look, and then I begin to really see – and seeing is believing. For me it is far more valuable than thinking! Once I have drawn something I have come to know it and it has entered my memory. Because I have looked with such intensity, I have become conscious of the presence of what I have drawn.

I take large sketchbooks when I am setting off with the intention of exploring a place, or an atmosphere, or a time of day.

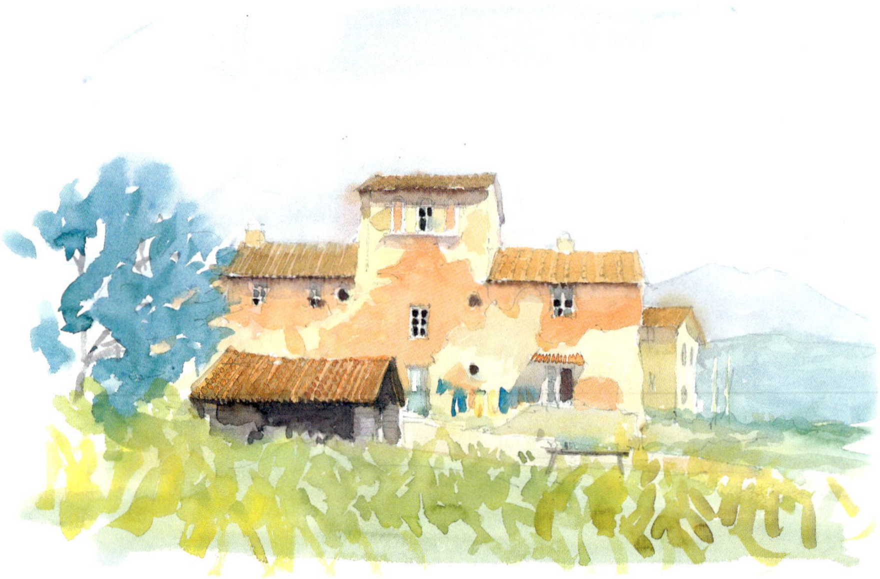

▲ **Tuscan farmhouse**
This is one of the studies I made when staying in Tuscany with Michael and Madeleine Canney. I studied Italian architecture for my architectural exams and visited Italy with a fellow student in the early 1950s before tourism. I fell in love with the land even then.

▶ **Assisi**
Whilst filming 'A Painter in search of St Francis' in Assisi I made numerous sketches in front of the camera as well as privately when we weren't filming. One of the advantages was that the crew protected me from curious onlookers.

▶ **Paraportiani on Mykonos**
When I make a study of a building I want to gather as much detail as possible. I can eliminate later but I cannot recall what I have not looked at. This is one of the studies of Paraportiani which I later painted in a much simpler way.

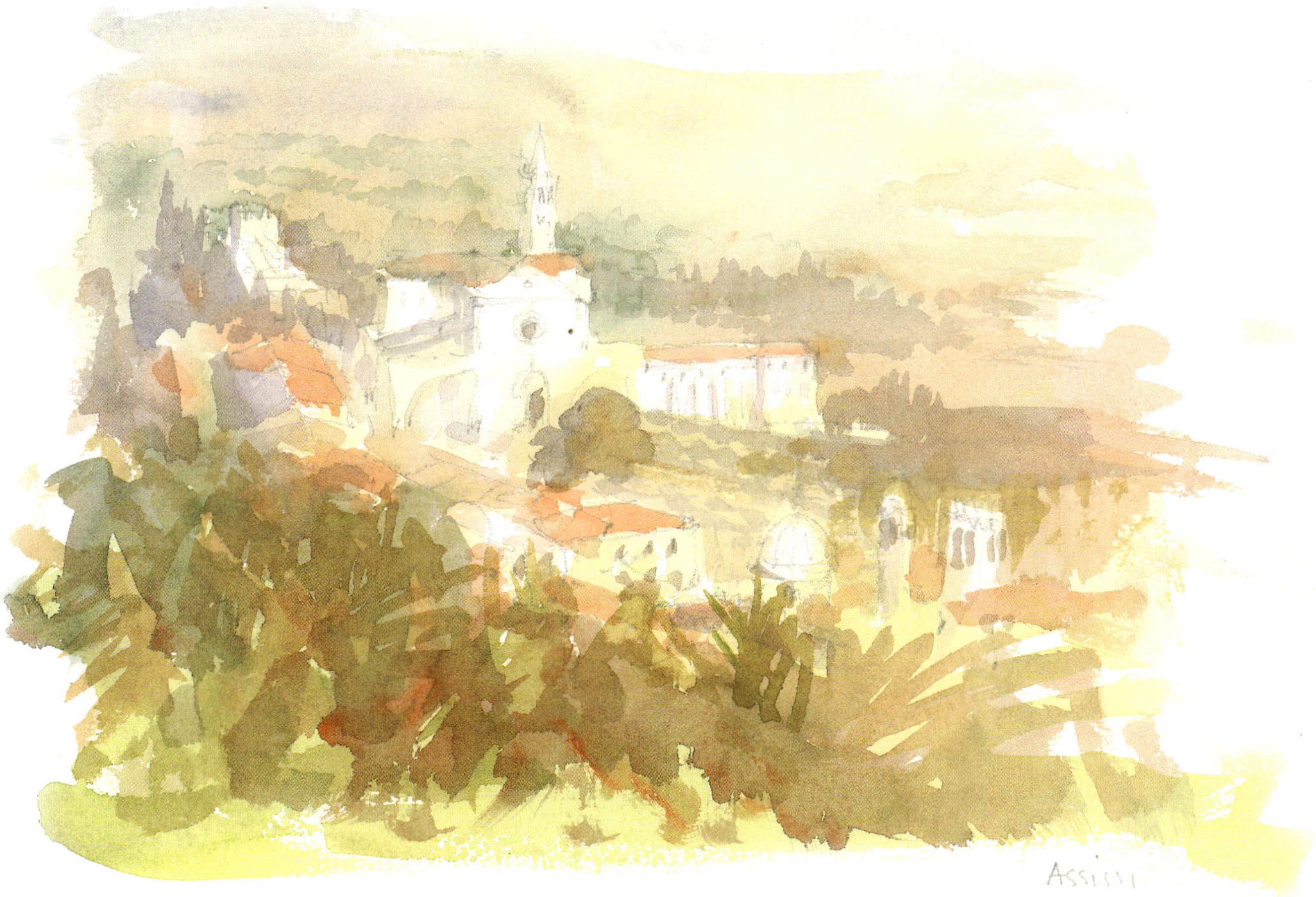
Assisi

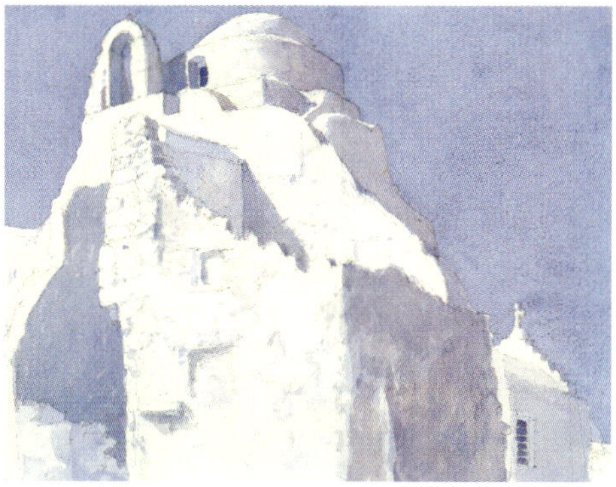

When I want to gather a lot of information in a day I make drawings and colour notes up the side – often with pastels. I then make fuller colour images back at base. Turner did this. He had a remarkable memory for colour. Often he used long pieces of paper no more than six inches high, which he rolled up at the end and unrolled at the other as he made his drawings throughout the day. There is an account of him colouring these at night in the tavern where he was staying with his marvellous travelling companions. Later these rolls of paper were cut up and sewn into book form.

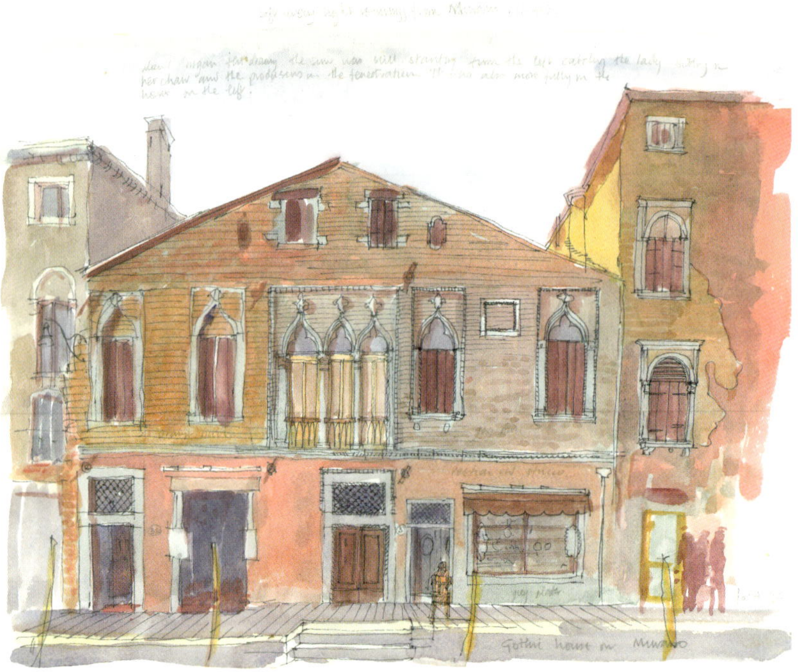

Venice
The enormous variety of facades in Venice has always fascinated me. They describe the history of Venice better than any book and show the way the architecture developed with the rise in wealth. Now many of the buildings are quite dilapidated showing the brickwork beneath the stucco and revealing the speed of construction – much like the Nash terraces in London. I love drawing these buildings. It can almost be like drawing a map for its own sake. Also looking and drawing helps me to soak up the atmosphere and character of a place.

▲ **Gothic house in Murano**

▶ **Buildings opposite St Eufemia waterbus stop**

▶ **Palaces on the canal**

▶ **The Fish market**

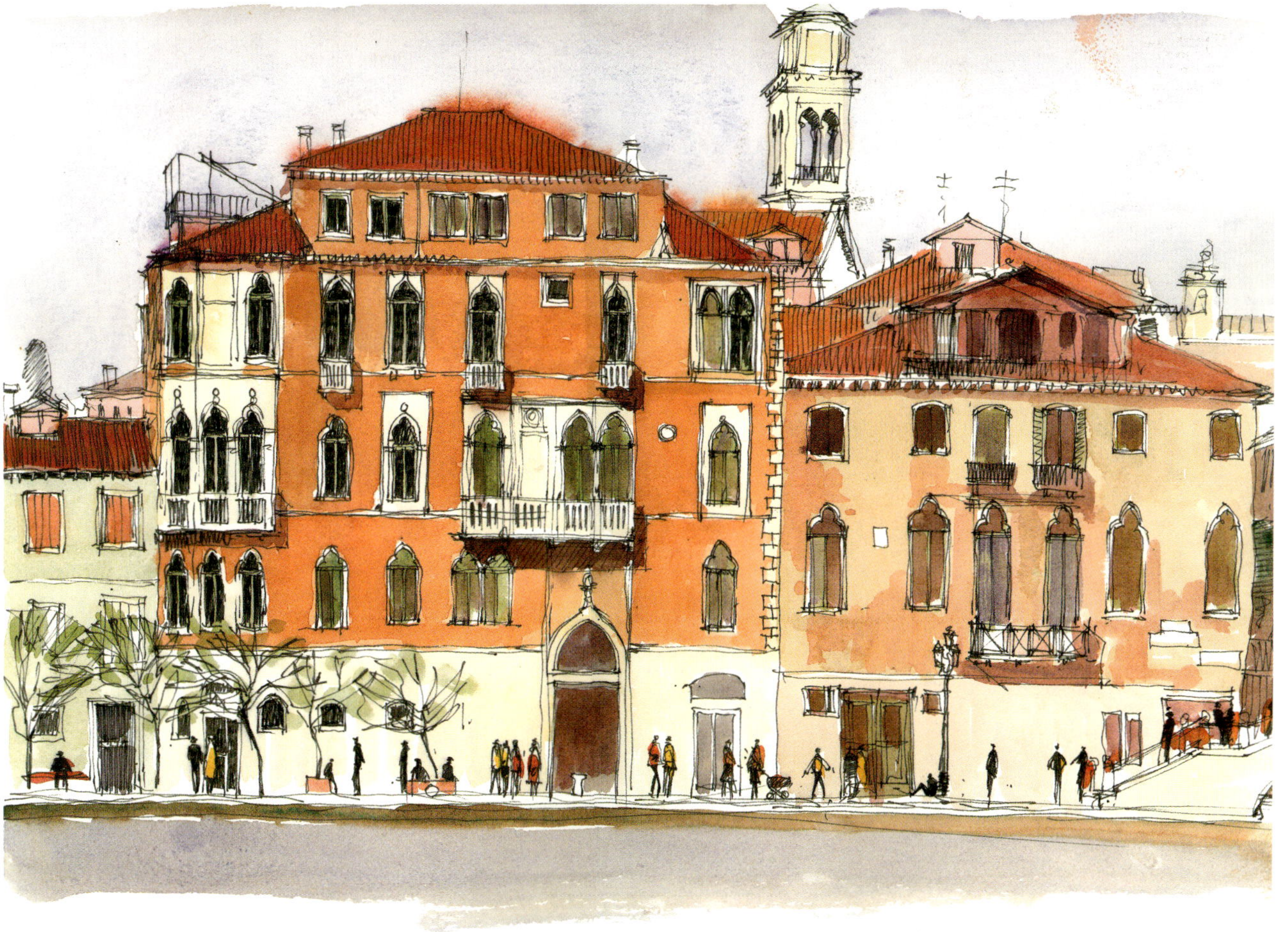

Buildings opposite S. Eufemia water bus stop 11.4.83

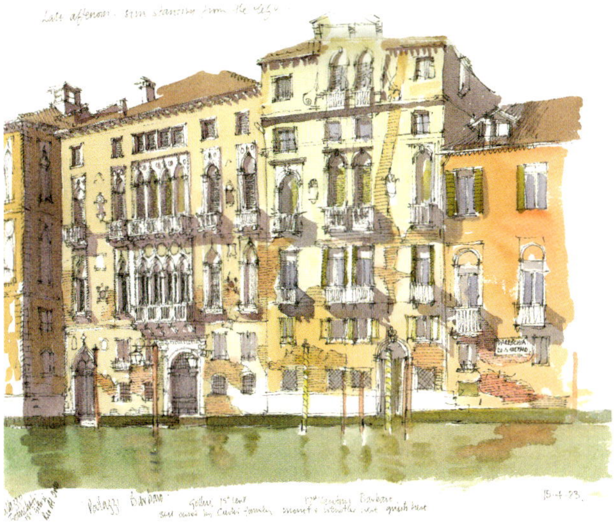

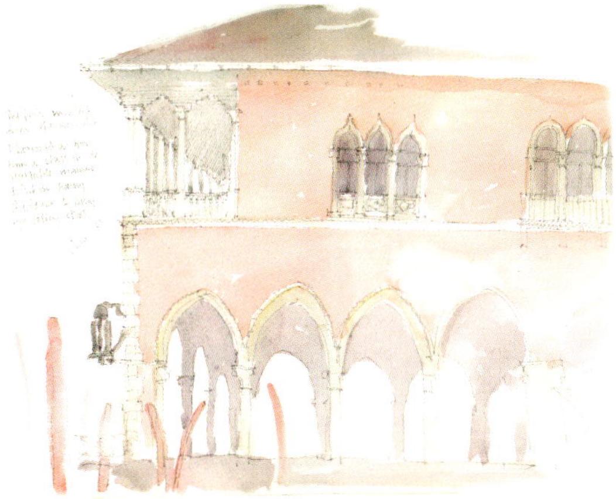

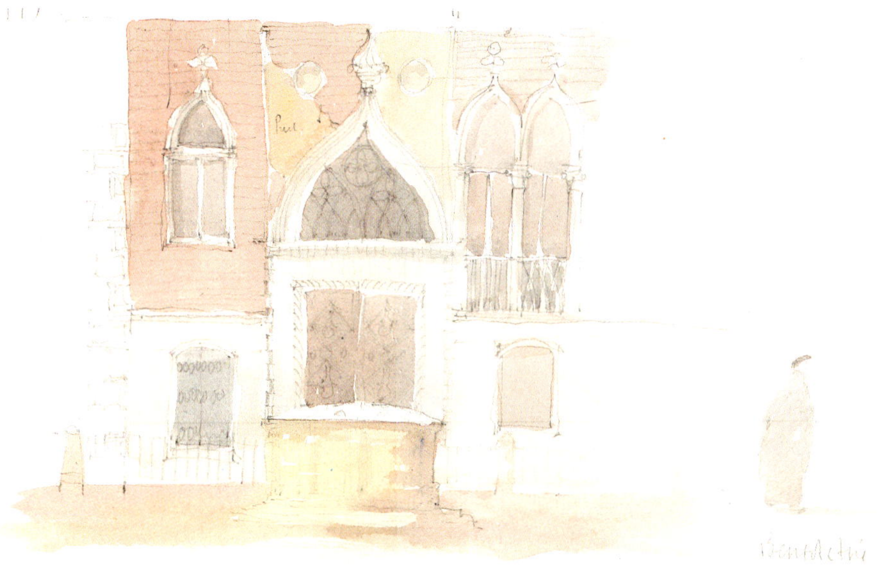

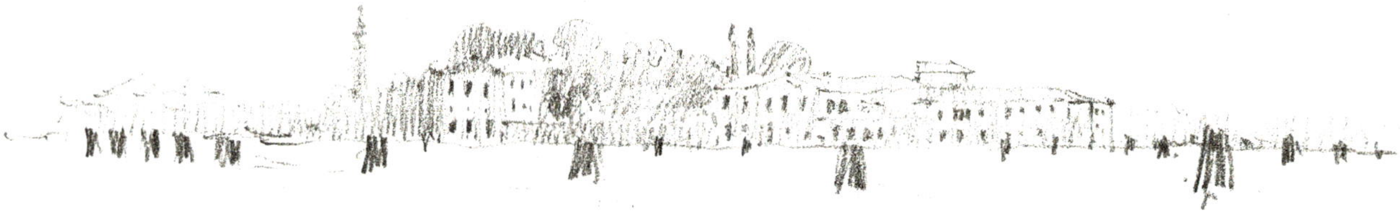

▲ **A well in the square adjoining San Stephano**
I would so like to make a study of all the wells in Venice. Every one of them is different and some have the most beautiful details. They also make a focal point around which people gather to pass the time of day.

▲ **San Servola from the Maritime Museum**

▶ **Venice – Pedestrian Bridge over a Canal**
1985 watercolour
MT

▶ **Santa Maria della Salute and the Grand Canal**
We had a superb drawing master at the school of architecture who made us really look. We were not allowed to do all that measuring by holding a pencil against the building we were drawing. We had to judge all the dimensions and proportions by eye. I can remember drawing a courtyard bay of Somerset House in this way. When I was there at Christmas 2000 I watched ice-skating!

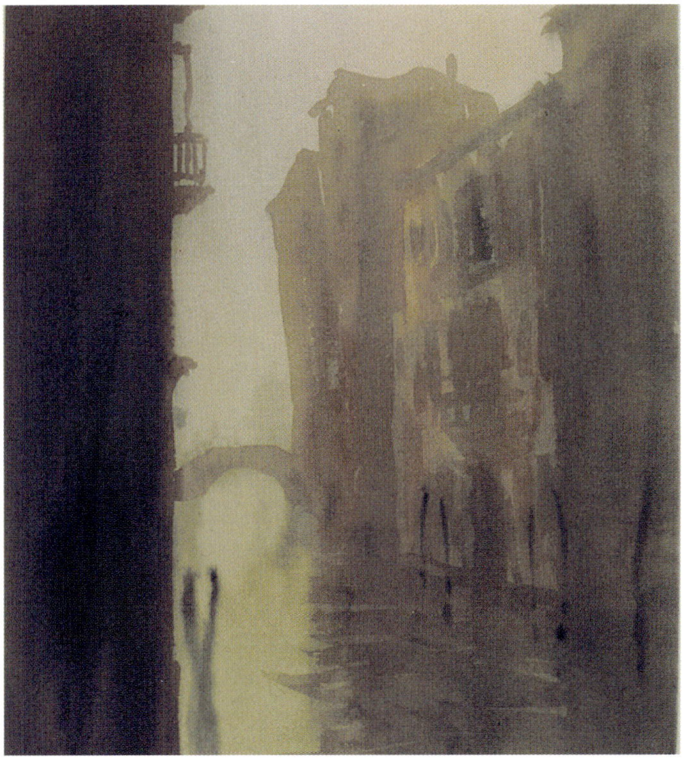

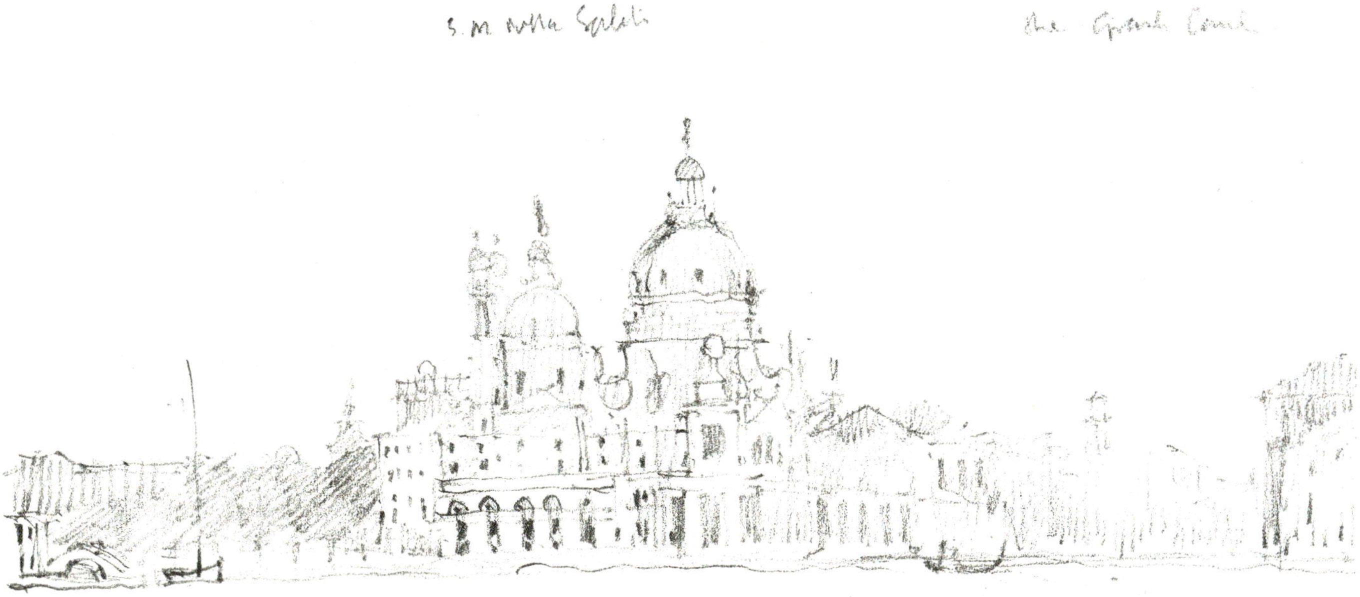
S. M. della Salute
the Grand Canal

Recently, I went on an expedition to Tresco and filled an A3 sketchbook with drawings and colour notes. I made colour images in the same book in the evenings whilst the wonder of the day was still fresh in my memory.

I never go back to remind myself of the detail I have forgotten. If I did I would over-emphasise what I had forgotten.

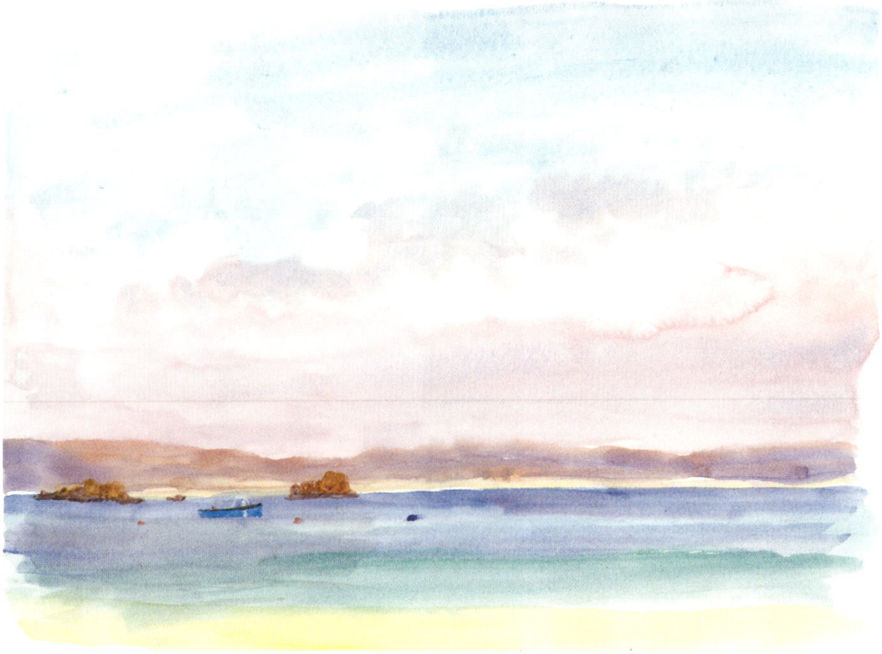

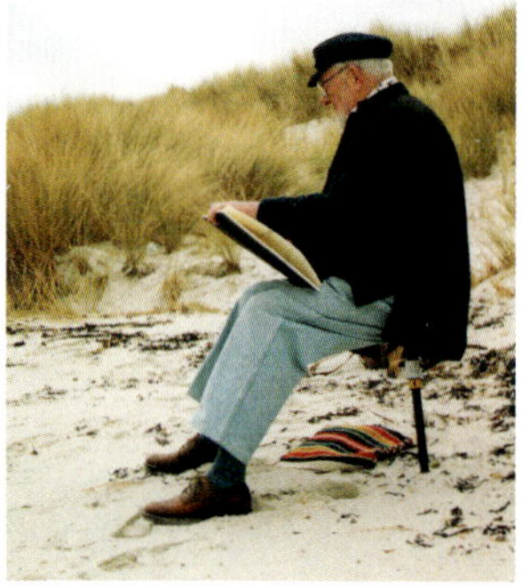

Tresco
Although I had visited Tresco on a number of occasions in the past it was not until Lucy and Robert Dorrien-Smith invited me to stay there in May 1992 that I walked the island with my sketchbook. I drew practically everything I could see and although most of the time the weather was perfect I even drew the view from my cottage in the rain.

▲ **High Tide**

▲ **Sketching on Tresco**
February 2001
MT

▶ **From Gimble Porth**

▶ **Rain – Tresco**

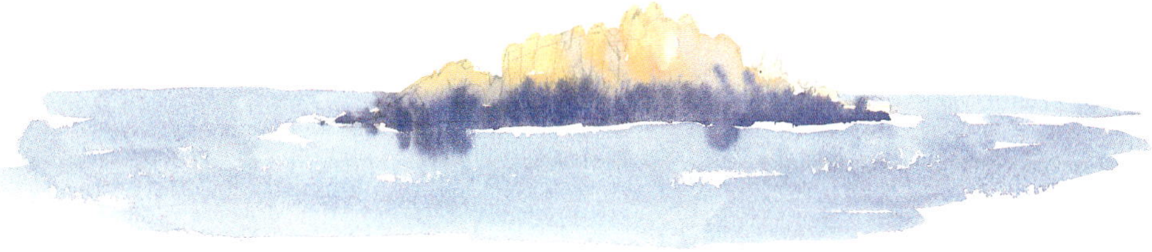

Very often the sketchbooks are put away and I never look at them again because I have imbibed it all in the process of drawing. I stopped painting 'plein air' many years ago because I always wanted to paint too much. I couldn't sort out priorities so I put everything in and choked the painting by observing and drawing on the spot. Working on the paintings from memory I only include what is essential. It is a way of focusing and refining.

I don't take photographs because it means the camera does the looking and not me. On the other hand, Michael often makes his own record of expeditions we go on together, which is always fascinating because they are beautiful portraits taken with his own eye.

▲ **Study of morning light**
Throughout my painting life I have made many, many studies of the colours of morning and evening light. So often the sky reflects the colours of the spectrum – when there is a line of sea this can reflect any one of the colours in the sky or remain its own colour.

▶ **Lelant – Study of the beach from the terrace 18.4.97**
Very often people don't believe the colours in my paintings until they see them from the terrace. Gouache is a good medium because of the richness and density of the colours.

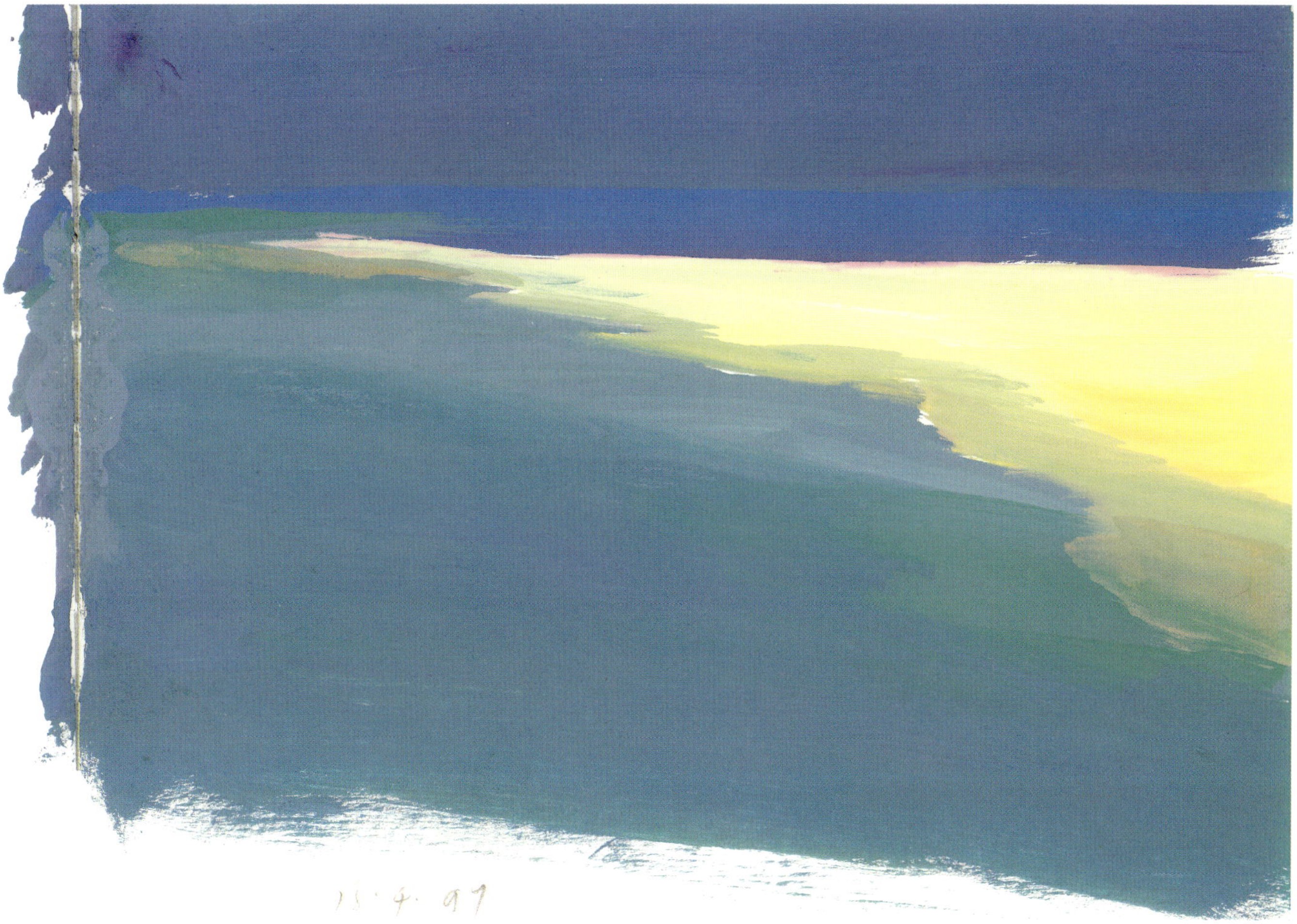

A painting day

I get up and I want to start painting around dawn. Sometimes I wake up to see the sun rising over the sea – that's wonderful because that in itself is an inspiration. On a perfect day, when I've got no distractions I go into the studio early and there are two possibilities. One, hopefully, there's a painting in progress because boy oh boy that's lovely. I can't wait to get back to it. If there isn't a painting in progress then it's different. Recently before I started to paint the triptych 'St Francis with Sister Moon and Brother Sun on Lelant Beach', I had a kind of vision of the direction it might go in and I actually put the canvasses, which Michael had made, together myself. I strapped them onto two runners and screwed them in and put on the tops and bottoms to attach them to the easel because I wanted, at that point, to be involved. I put it up on the easel. I thought to myself 'Now I've got to start it.' I got some colours out because I felt it had to be in a sort of orange to brown to yellow. I knew that much and then I went and fussed around Michael and made life difficult for him and asked him fatuous questions: 'How are you getting on with the framing?'

▶ **St Francis and Sister Moon on Lelant Beach 2**
2000 oil on canvas 101x96
SC

and that sort of thing. All delaying tactics! I spent quite a lot of that morning pacing around because I couldn't face starting it and then finally I did a separate small horizon painting instead and nothing on the triptych at all. The small painting was about the moon, because we'd had a full moon and when that moon rises very often it rises into a really big cloud and so I painted this cloud on a canvas and didn't put the moon on.

Although I'm looking for distraction in situations like this, I'm irritated by the distraction as well and so, I think well I'll just go and do some letters because I ought to do some letters and so I go and do the letters grumpily. At the same time I know that this is all a game - it's the dance in T S Eliot's 'Four Quartets'.

On the second day, I did get some paint on the triptych canvas and once I'd done that I was off. This was a particular painting that didn't go well. It didn't go easily. It didn't flow out of me and finally, it's very strange, I suppose there were four days when I was repainting it every day. I was wiping it out and repainting it until one morning in two or three hours it just suddenly went right. I knew that it was going to work first thing that morning and it was a big painting – it's 7 ft wide – it worked. I'd seen the moon; I'd seen a reflection of the moon, which was like a lozenge below it. I knew then that if I put that in that it would work – maybe I could do without the moon but in the end I had to put the moon in. It took me a week to finish the triptych and then I was in a good mood! That painting I subsequently destroyed. Some weeks later another version flowed from the brush like a dream.

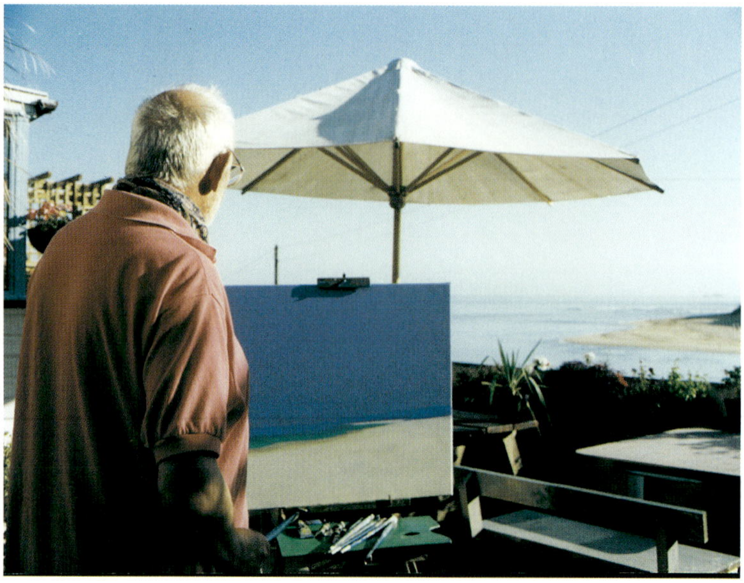

▲ **On the terrace at the beach studio**
MT

▶ **Evening Fishing**
2000 oil on canvas 65x60
SC

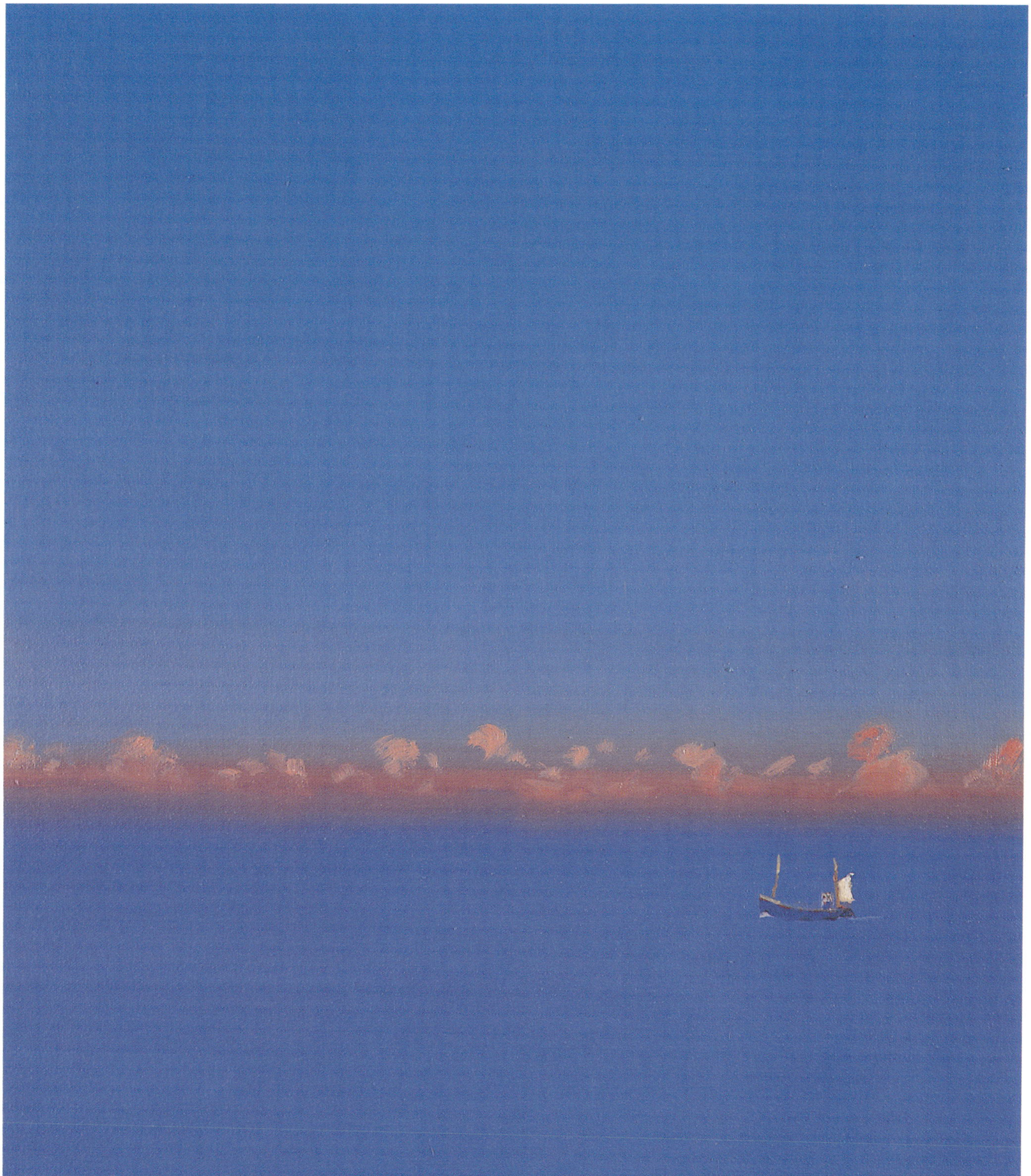

I often go on working in the afternoon – I try to discipline myself not to work on the main painting but to go back to one of the half a dozen paintings that are in progress. I go back to one that I know I can come to fresh in the afternoon. I get sleepy in the afternoons – I didn't used to. I really ought to be sensible and go for a walk. I have quite a battle with myself but I must drive on because I've got big exhibitions coming.

When I am on the beach it is easier. On the beach the routine is very different because I get up, go to the studio and I am being visually fed by everything around me. I am actually living in the painting and so I do my morning's work and I am not disturbed by anything down there. I go off for a mid-day walk along the cliffs, if it is high tide, or right along the sand. This breaks the intensity of work, which is important. Sometimes I can't believe how intensely I am concentrating. The work does need to be broken because it is obsessional. In the afternoon it is much easier to come back from the walk and go out and draw. I love drawing and I love just recording what I see. It's a wonderful thing because in a way, you're looking and everything passes through you and it comes out in the pencil.

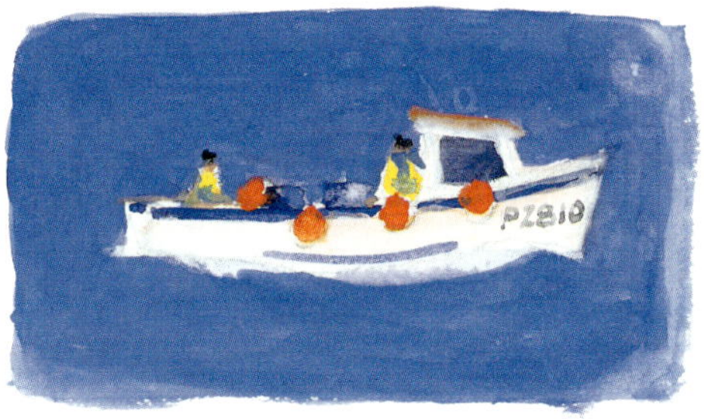

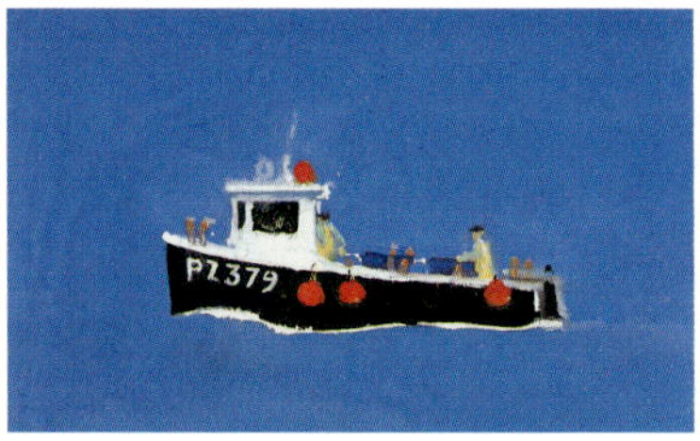

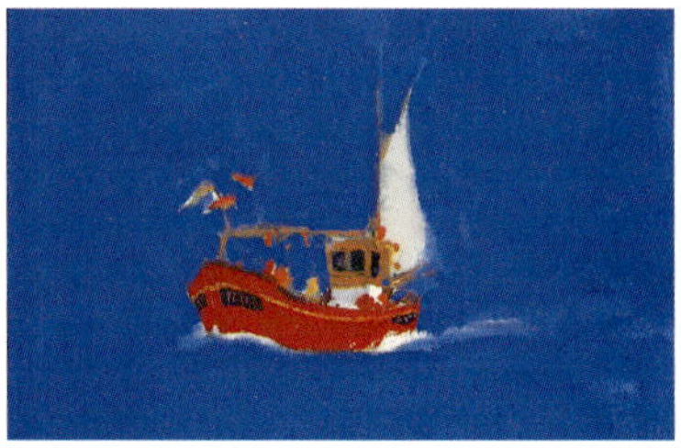

River Witch

Every day when I am at the beach studio I draw. I draw more or less everything I see. I watch the small fishing boats go out of Hayle harbour – some operated by a single man only – and I marvel at their courage and tenacity – they are the last of the hunters. They leave the estuary across a dangerous sand bar and follow their trade in a vast open sea in all weathers. They appear so vulnerable; Bishop Bill Ind reminded me of a Breton prayer:

O Lord the ocean is so large and my boat is so small.
Please take care of me.

One day I watched three men fishing from the shore with no success. A fisherman returning in his beautiful sailing boat enquired about their day as he passed. He immediately turned about and threw them three bass. It could have taken place on the sea of Galilee two thousand years ago.

▲ **Boat Sketch No 26**
2000 gouache 10x15
MT

▲ **Boat Sketch No 5**
2000 gouache 10x15
MT

▲ **River Witch**
2000 gouache 26x28
SC

▶ **John Miller & Michael Truscott in St Mary's Studio**
2000
SC

Of colour

Craigie Aitchison said, and I think he's absolutely right, that some days he can paint yellow and some days he can't. I think that he was saying for all of us that colour belongs, to some extent, to our mood of the day, not just to the painting. When I arrive one morning and look at the painting and think it's too brown, it may be that it's too brown for me that day. I don't know. Because I'm working intuitively I've got to remain open. If I start working it out in my head, for my kind of painting the intensity will be lost, so I do change the colours although I stay within the range. For example one painting was a rich deep brown and finally it was a yellow-orange with a big cloud. That cloud had wanted to be painted for a year. I saw a cloud almost like a boomerang and then I found a piece of wood at the wood turner, Anthony Bryant's place. I asked him if I could have it and I looked after it so that it was not thrown away by mistake. But one day I thought, 'Now it will make that cloud.' I was only four days painting it, but a year thinking about it. It has been titled 'Looking at the Open Sea'.

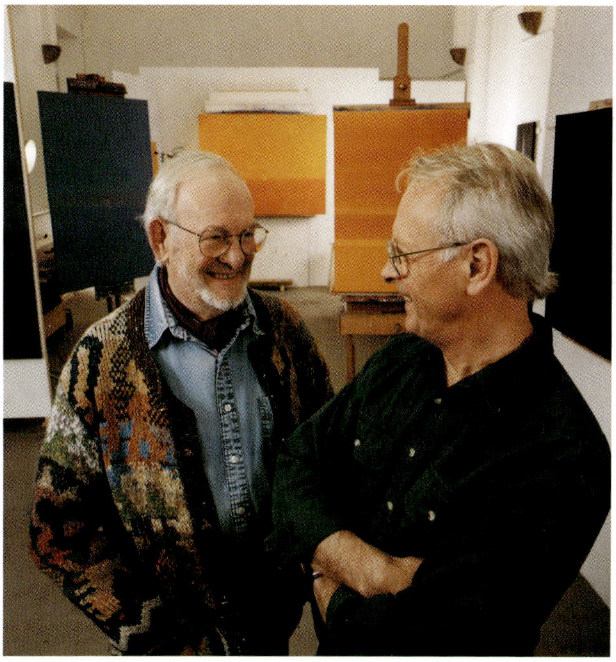

Of course I don't know if a painting is right. I often ask Michael what he thinks at that point. I value Michael's opinion because he's absolutely as straight as a die and he'll come in with some wonderful comments. The painting has to be left, turned face to the wall because I'm too involved in it and so now I have to leave it and look at it, as it were, with an innocent eye. Monet said the one thing that he could imagine being just stupendous was being re-born and opening his eyes again for the first time and seeing for the first time. In a way you have to see your own paintings for the first time. This is hard because, as soon as you look at it you think of all the battles that have gone on! I do have a peek at work, from time to time but ideally it really needs several months before I look at it properly again – I haven't always got that time. When work is going off for an exhibition I often have doubts, but it's too late then. Partly it's a battle with one's own ego because really it's letting go.

I'm mean with canvas because it was very difficult to come by when I was young. I hate to see it wasted but very often, at a certain stage, it's far better to get another canvas and just paint the picture in an afternoon. Then all the agony that has led up to it is left behind and the purity goes on the canvas. Very often that's what I do. I'm very conscious that Michael has given part of his life to making those canvasses and I don't want to just spoil them. It's his life he's put into it – his days, his hours and that counts for me. In the same way I look at old stone walls and see the men who built them, who hauled those stones and got them onto carts and donkeys. I think of all the effort that went into those walls, which we can so easily take for granted. I can't take them for granted because I am aware that somebody's life went into them. This awareness plays a part. Michael has made that canvas; he has stretched it. A lot of people can't stretch canvasses. They get rucks in them but he's got an enormous skill. You see him doing it and he's laughing but he's got the skill. I am beholden to that; I am responsible for making something of what he has started.

▶ **Looking at the Open Sea**
2000 oil on canvas 92x86
sc

Having a number of paintings in progress does not confuse me because I'm very selfish about the work. I'm going to work on the one I feel like working on. I don't ever feel that I have to work on one particular painting. If I don't feel able to, I don't and if it means leaving work in progress and even starting more, I'll do that. The work must be joyful; it mustn't be forced. It needs to be a joyful struggle. If it goes beyond a certain point it has to be thrown away because if you put too much of your own personal struggle on the canvas, it'll stay there and you're throwing that at somebody else. That's not what I want to do. I really want to be joyful.

I do believe that we can influence people much more deeply than we realise. Not just with words. We put our own spirit into something and if there's badness in that it will go on and on and if there's joy in it that'll go on and on.

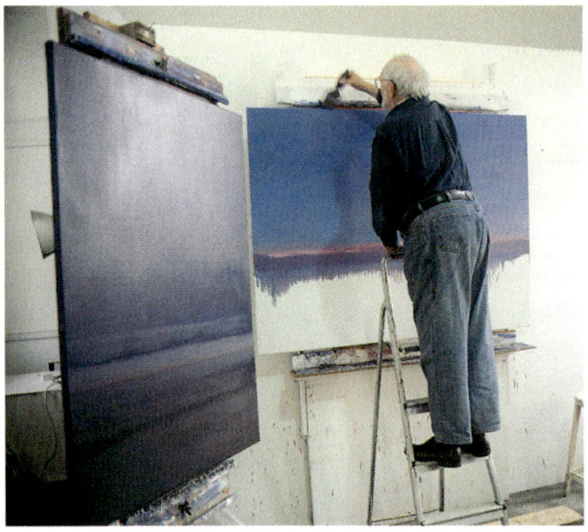

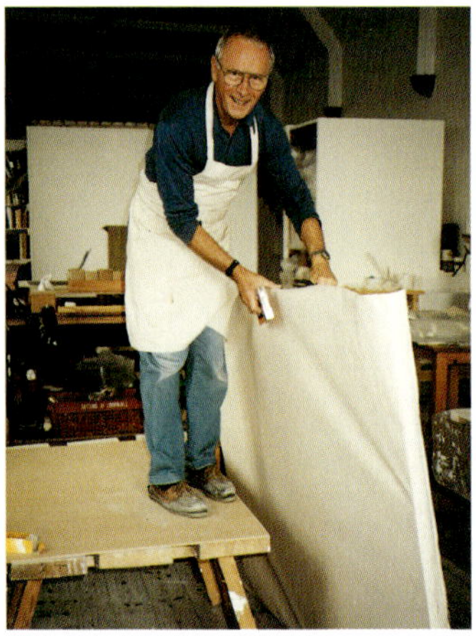

▲ **St Mary's Studio – working on the large sunrise painting for the 'Sunrise of Wonder' series**
MT

▲ **Michael preparing a canvas**

▶ **Distant Hills**
1998 gouache 22x20
MT

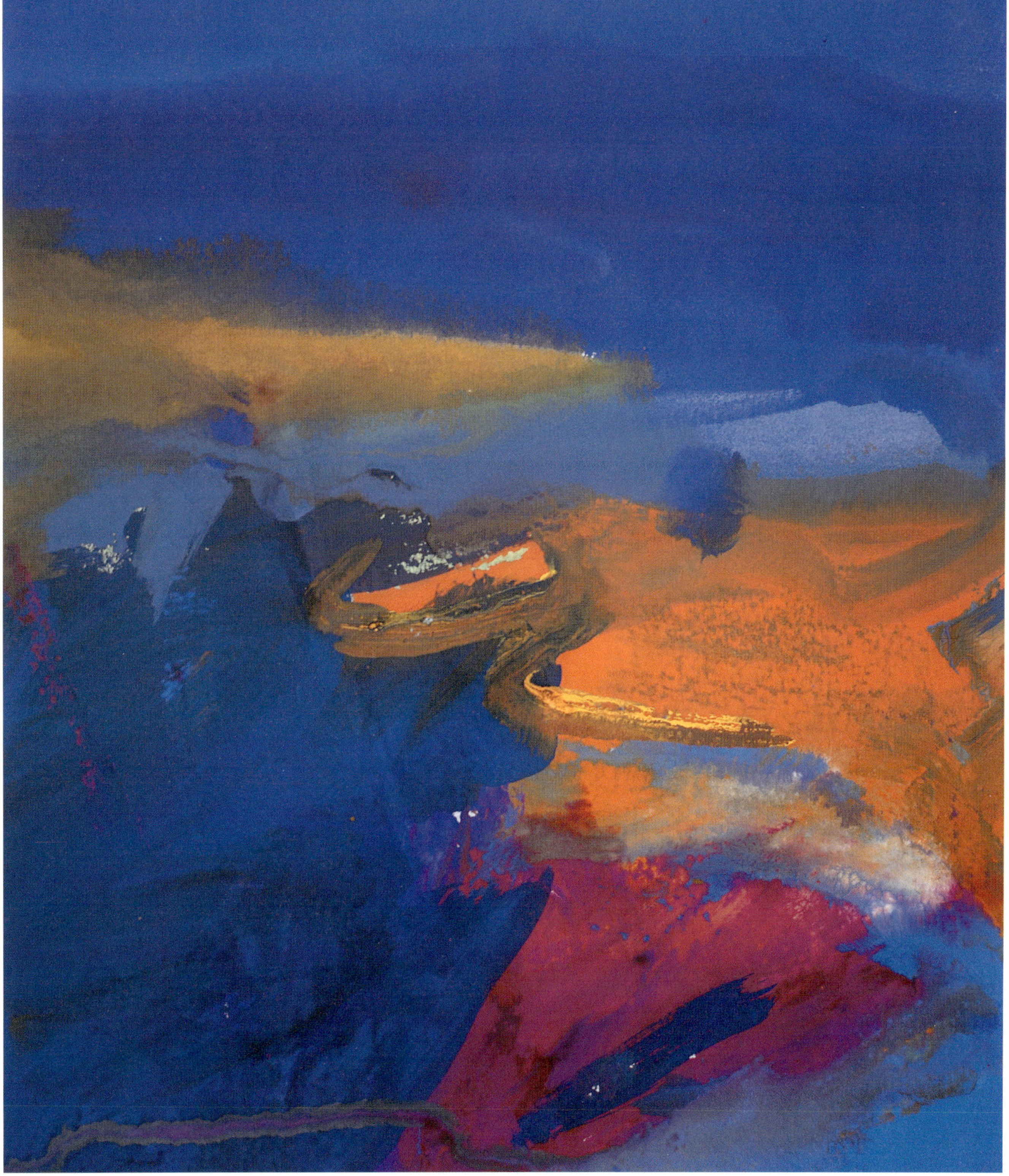

Of paint

Whcn I draw in the open air I often colour the drawings with water-colours. Naturally I sometimes make pure watercolour studies. More often I find gouache a suitable medium for this. Gouache is an opaque watercolour medium often given 'body' with the addition of Chinese white to the pigments. It enables me to paint on paper more directly in the way of oil paint. It is a beautifully fluid medium for making works on paper.

Mostly I use oil paints. I occasionally paint in acrylic but not very often. I like it because it dries quickly but apart from that I don't like it because it goes on in layers. I like using oil paint because it melds much more easily – it takes six months to dry properly. On the other hand oils don't dry quickly enough for me! All paints are pigment – let's take cobalt blue: the cobalt itself is ground down to a very fine powder and then mixed. If you want water colour, it's mixed with gum arabic; if you want an oil paint it's mixed with linseed oil, if you want acrylic it's mixed with white glue or vinyl. Basically, you have the pigment and then you suspend that in a medium. Oil paint is suspended in oil. You can buy it in tubes, which are all mixed up, or you can buy the pigment. I buy both and like to add to the tube pigment some of the actual pigment, the powder, because it makes it denser and drier. It's less spongy

▶ **Trencrom**
1998 January gouache 15x13
MT

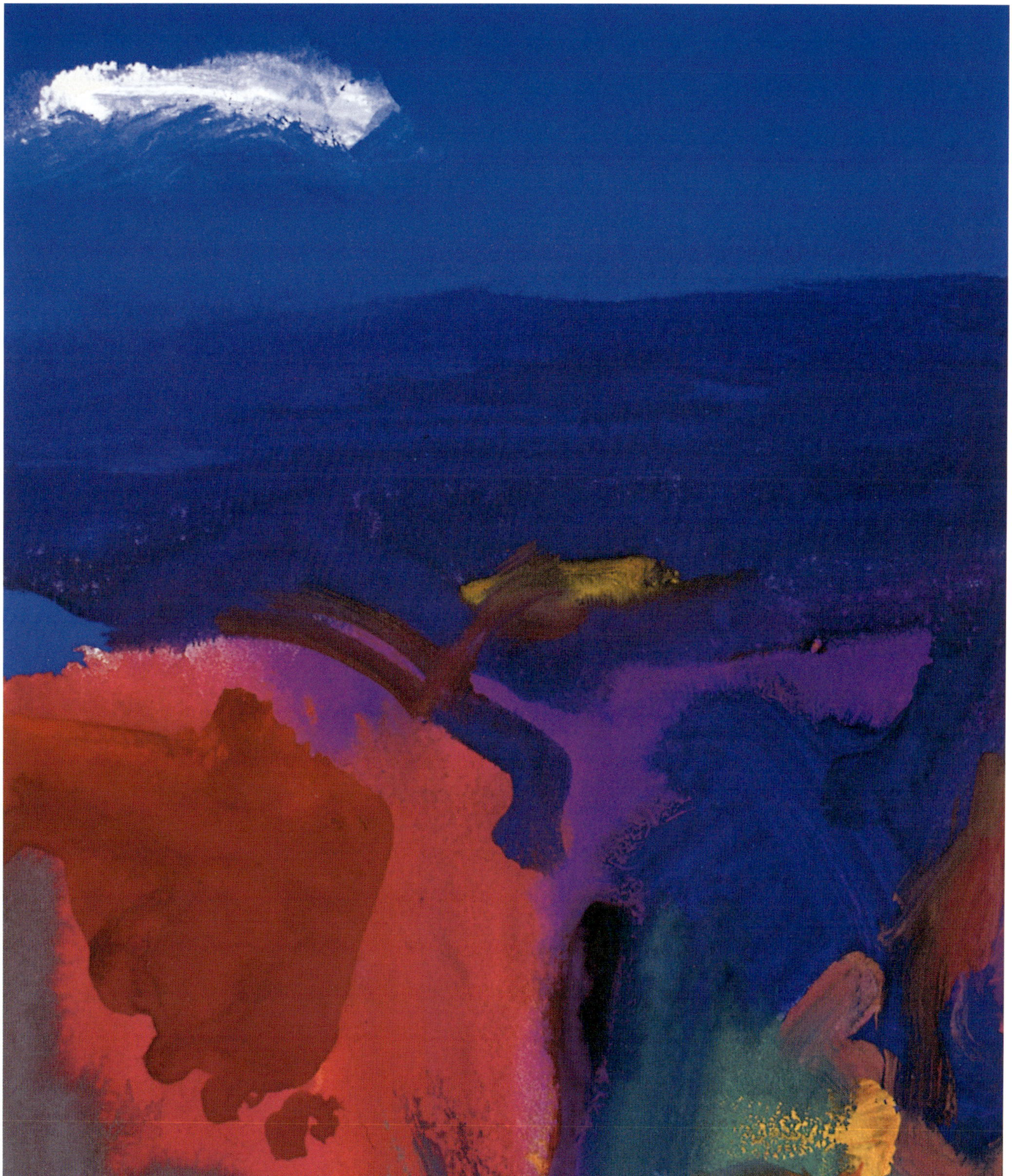

and drier to spread on the canvas. I also like the canvas to be a very absorbent one, not a sharp, shiny one and, in fact, for a long time, until recently, Michael has prepared canvasses with an American preparation, which makes them wonderfully absorbent. We've stopped doing that because he just hasn't got the time. We're buying canvas from Belgium that is very similar but it's not as good, obviously, as the thing you do yourself. All these things are very personal but very important.

When Sisley went to paint on the Isle of Wight he waited for his canvas to be delivered and couldn't paint on any other kind of canvas. Turner used to have a chap prepare his canvasses with layers and layers of gesso which Turner ground down and then put the next layer on. He used graphite to grind the layers down until they were like a plaster wall, because Turner liked to throw oil paint, almost like watercolour, onto the canvas and it would get absorbed in and then he could add thicker paint. He could put washes of paint on and on. You eventually discover which materials suit you. It suits me to have an absorbent canvas because I like to be able to go on painting into the paint using thin paint. It also suits me to have a dry paint because, in a way like Turner, I like to be able to put paint on that I know will stay there and perhaps be able to wash round it. Also if you have dense paint and thin paint then the painting has a bit of life.

▶ **Autumn Landscape**
1999 gouache 18x15
MT

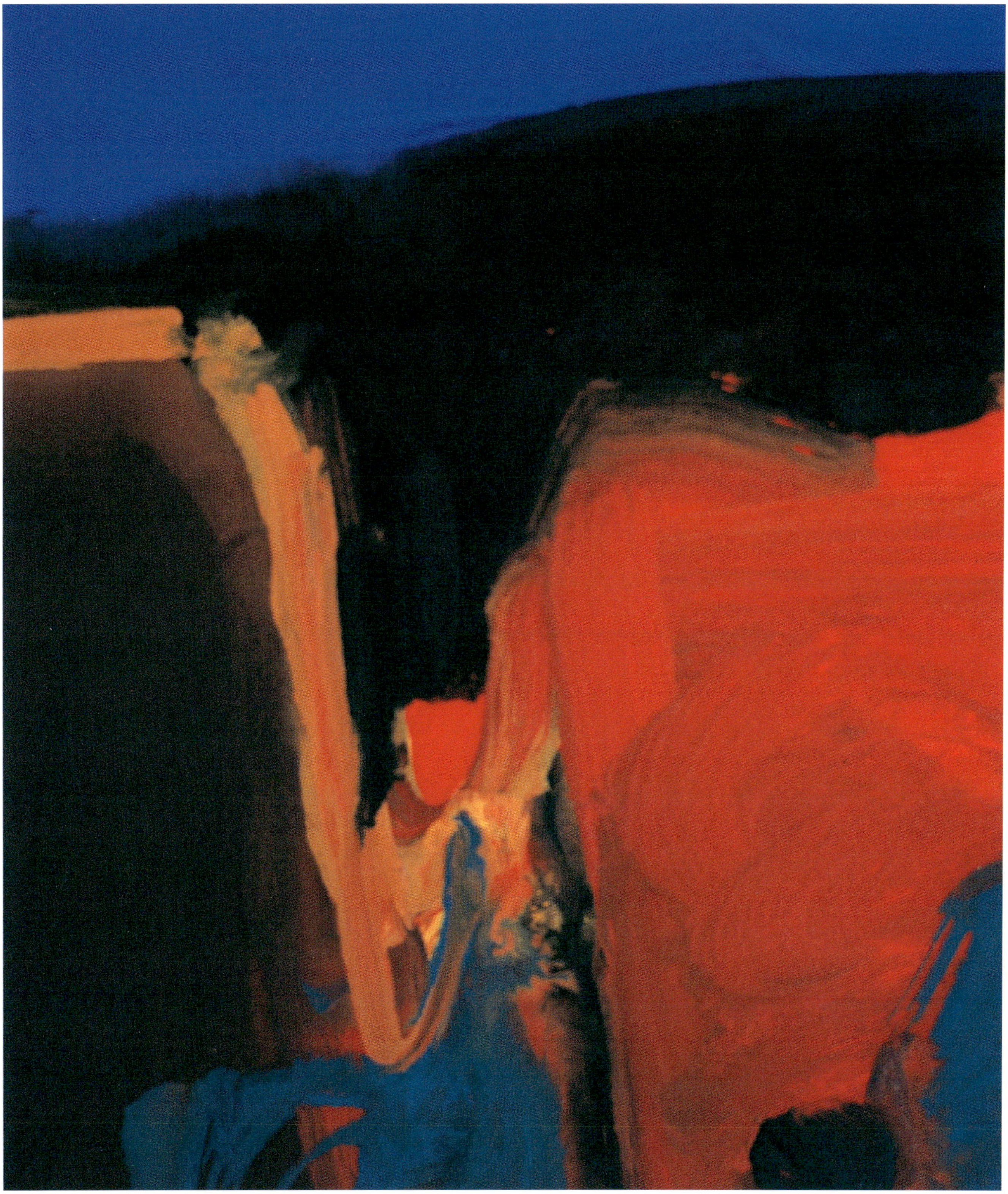

Because I feel so at home with watercolours and gouache, I spend a lot of time trying to make the oil paint behave like water-based paints. There is an intoxicating sensuality in the way gouache behaves at the junction of two colours. I sometimes paint on raw canvas with oil colours in an attempt to achieve this – as did Van Gogh.

I mix pure powdered pigments into the paint from the tubes with linseed oil that's been dried in the sun, called stand oil, turpentine and cobalt dryers which are used by printers as a drying agent. You just put the tiniest, little drop in a quantity of a mixture of turps and a tiny amount of the stand oil. You need very little, so much so that if the following day you leave it uncovered and the turps evaporates, the stand oil will become too dense and it'll make the thing too oily and shiny. There's an old adage which says 'thick over thin, fat over lean' and that's the best bit of advice that anybody can take about painting because you must start with thin paint and it must be lean paint, it mustn't have much oil in it and as it goes on it can become denser and oilier if you want it to. It's rather like painting a house. You paint a house first with a primer, which is very chalky and absorbent. You then put on an undercoat, which

▶ **Autumn Penwith Moorland**
1992 oil on canvas 90x120
MT

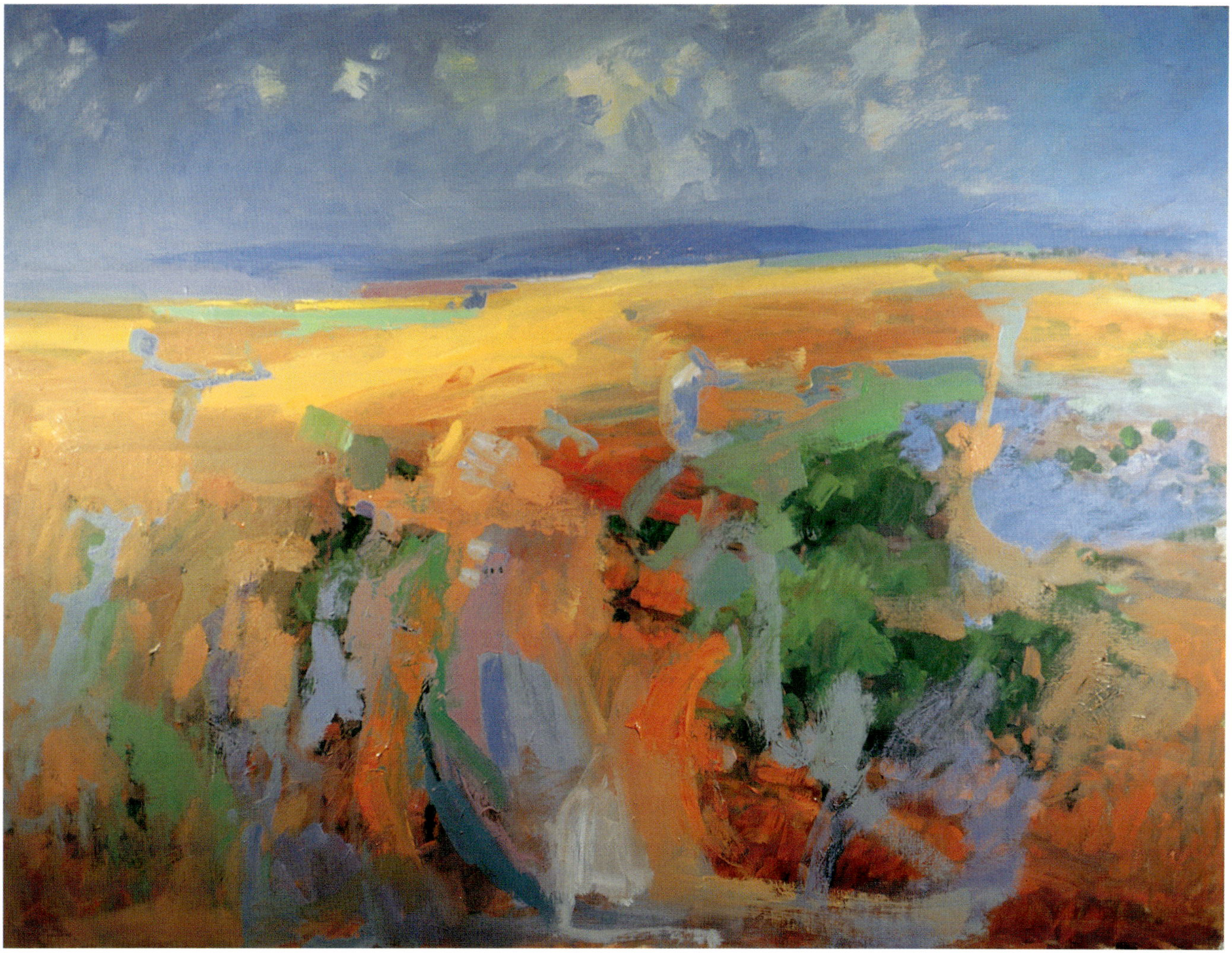

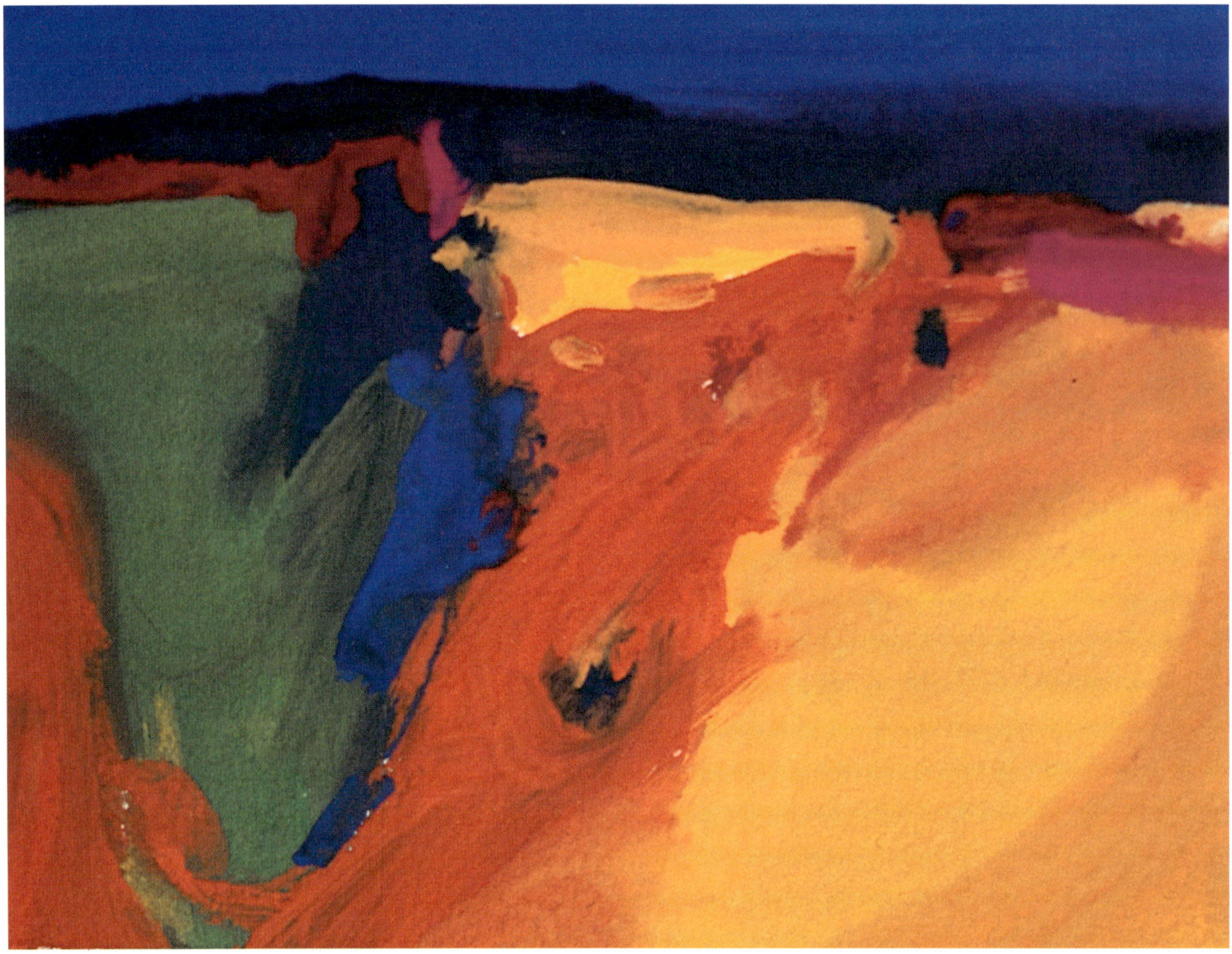

▲ **Moors**
gouache 1998 18x15
MT

▶ **Lelant Downs**
1998 gouache 10x15
MT

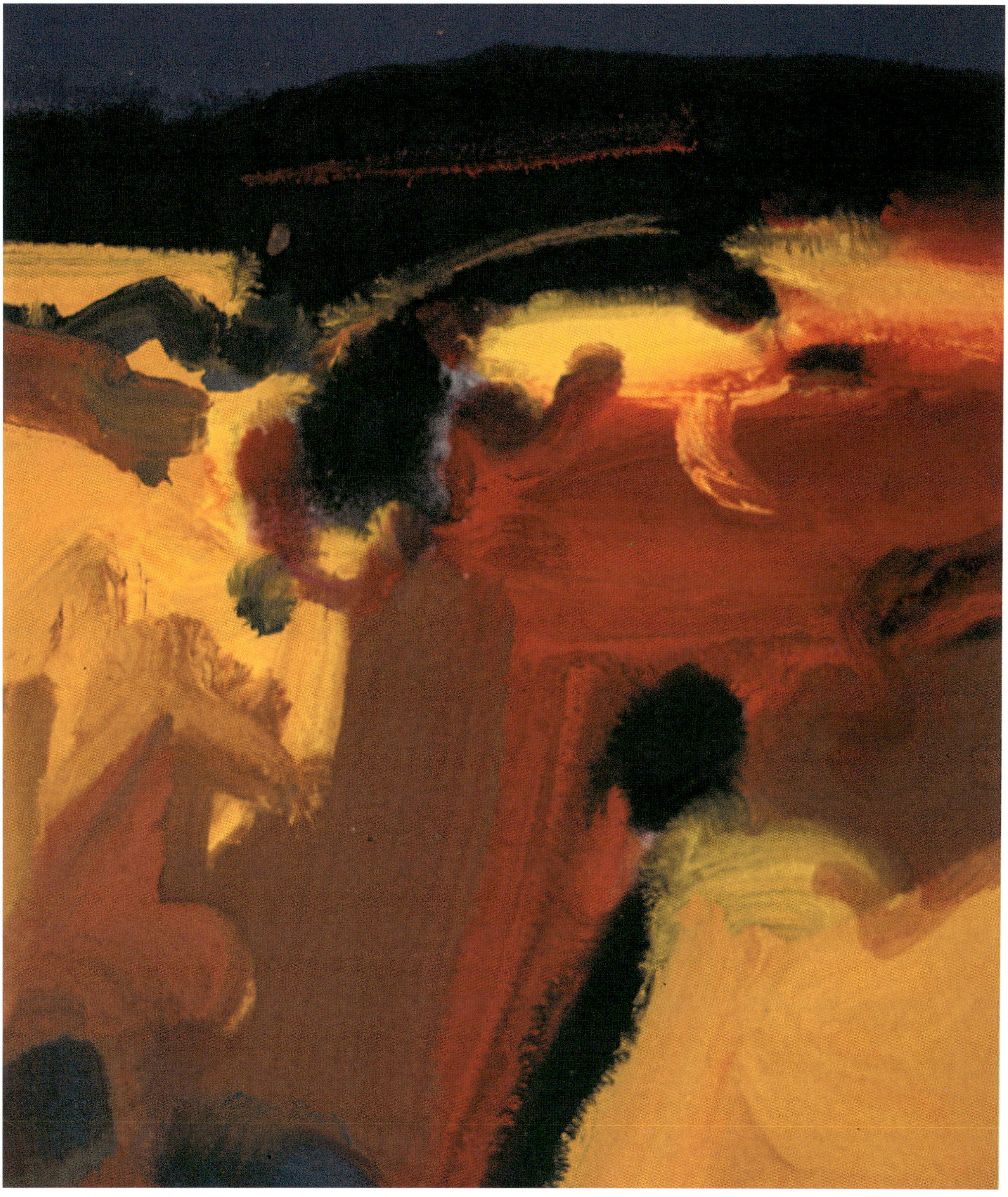

the primer absorbs and it's very flat and then you put your shiny coat on. But once you put your shiny coat on you can't put any more on because it won't let you. It's like trying to paint on glass. It's just the same. They're the same paints. One of the comments made about Van Gogh is that however much he threw the paint on he did know how far he could take it before it became dangerous, because paint cracks. If you put a thin layer over a thick layer then the thick layer will take longer to dry than the thin layer and therefore will crack. You've got to know a bit about the technique to make sure the painting is going to last. But having said that, I try to forget about technique and develop the work naturally. People say 'Oh how did you get that effect?' I really don't know how I get effects. If that's all you're aiming at, you're into craft rather than painting.

There are all kinds of brushes from beautiful little sable brushes, which I find important when I'm painting my tiny little figures, through to hog brushes which have quite stout hair and which the Impressionists liked. They're very good for putting blotches of paint on. I use very few of those because they actually take the paint off my canvasses. I paint with very fluid paint and if I use a hog brush it very often removes the paint. I like very fine hair. The Italians make some marvellous great fat brushes, which are very thin. They're like the brushes you paint the house with but instead of being thick they're thin and wonderful for putting on my very fluid paint. I don't use a lot of hog because they're really for impasto, which is thick paint and I don't work in thick paint. I also like to keep the paint wet. Because I was taught by these two old girls to do watercolours when I was about six,

▶ **Purple Meadow**
1999 gouache 15x13
MT

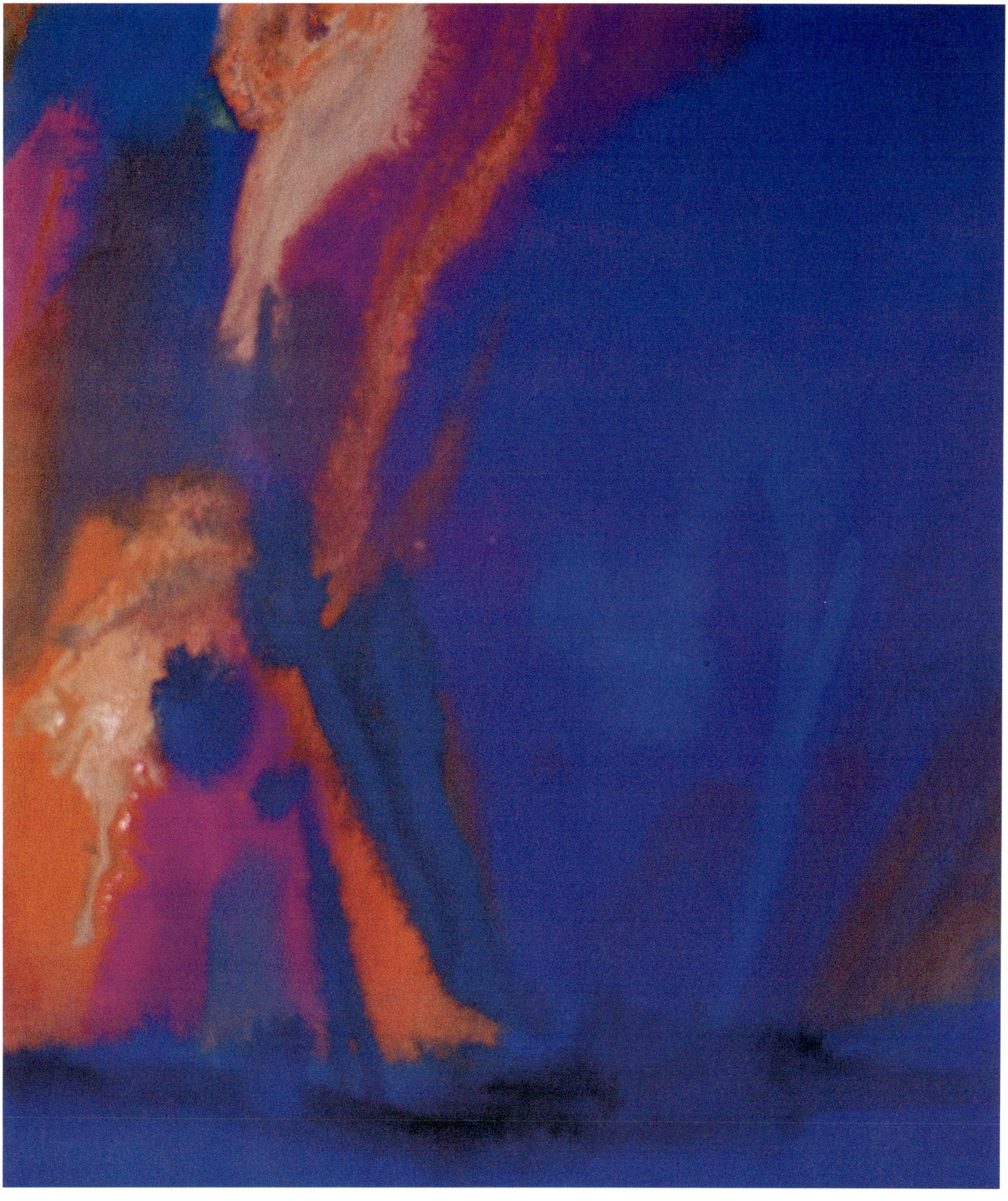

I've stayed with those techniques. I use a house plant spray with turpentine in it and I spray the painting and keep it wet. This helps to keep any brushwork out of it and it keeps it fluid. It makes it a wonderful sort of fluid arrangement on the canvas.

The mixing of colours is very personal. Everybody has their own colours that they feel comfortable with. I feel comfortable with red blues rather than green blues and also oranges, which happen to be in the spectrum the opposite side to blue. Like Turner I don't use a lot of greens; I don't feel very comfortable with greens although I like them when I see them in the landscape. The closest Turner got to green was almost brown. Green is a very difficult colour for some people. I love these rich dark greens that are near the blues you get in macrocarpa plants. Although I love painting in what appears to be a primary colour, a lot of it's much greyer than it appears. It still has that impact of colour but if you were to look at it on a white sheet you'd find it's very much greyer and yet on the canvas against other colours it looks blue. In the end the mixing of colour is intuitive; it's a feeling for the mix rather than a scientific technique. I've read Goethe and Kandinsky on colour, but it's all too formalised for me. I have to just paint the colour that I feel.

▶ **Autumn Moors**
1998 gouache 22x20
MT

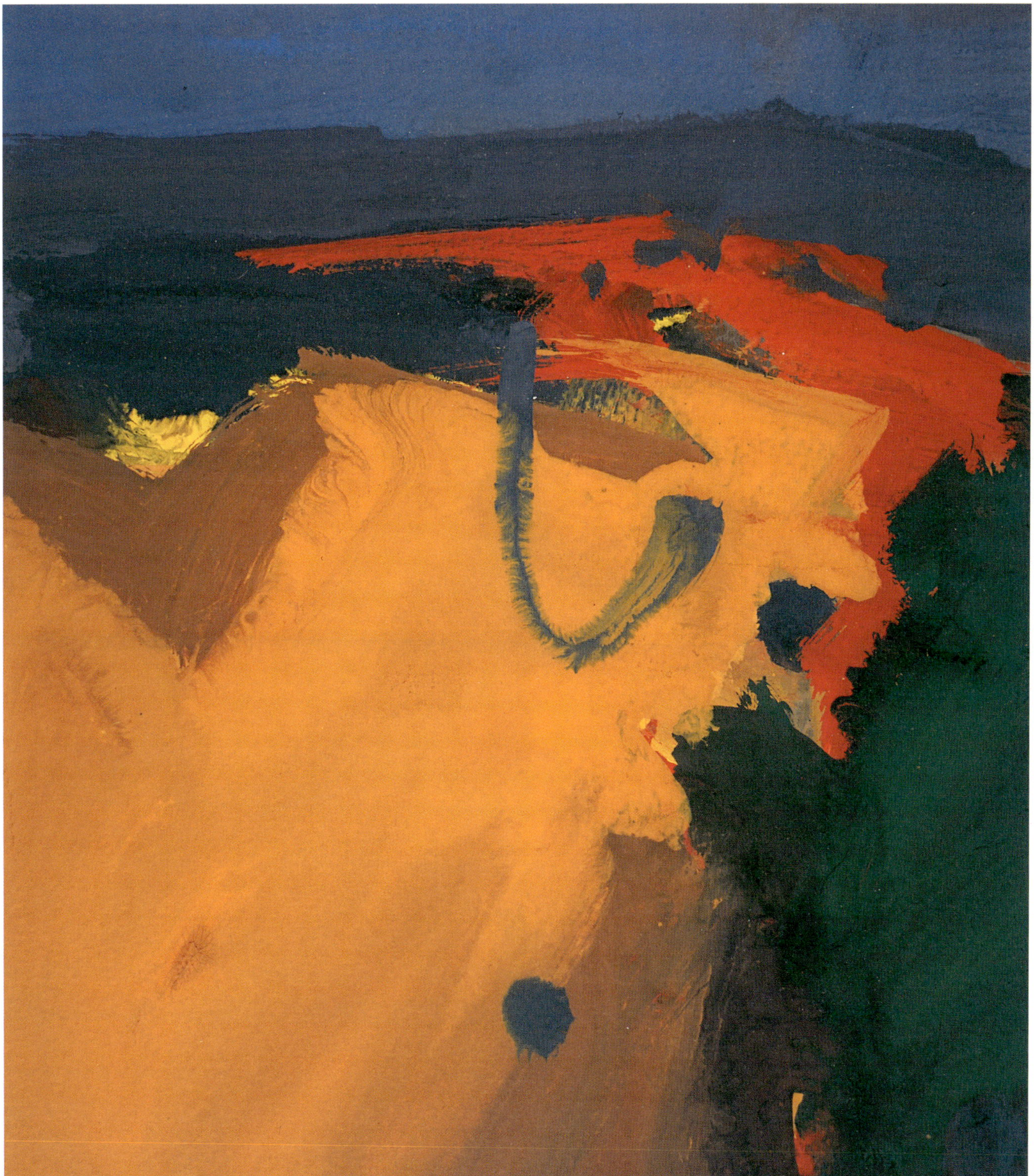

Before I start a blank canvas the mixing of the paint is part of the preparation ritual as is the lack of distraction. The calming of one's self also is important. Finally I've had to find a replacement for rolling my own cigarettes, because that was very much part of the ritual, to sit back and roll a cigarette which was Gauloise pipe tobacco and then place it into a holder. This enabled me to sit in front of the painting during that preparation time.

The technique for some people is to keep the paint slightly unmixed so that when it goes on you get flecks of different colours in it, but that doesn't interest me. I mix the paint thoroughly with a palette knife and sometimes I put it in old dishes or even in a jam jar if I want it quite thin. I shake it all up and then I pour it into the dish and it's beautifully fluid – it's closer to watercolour than oil paint – which I suppose is how I began.

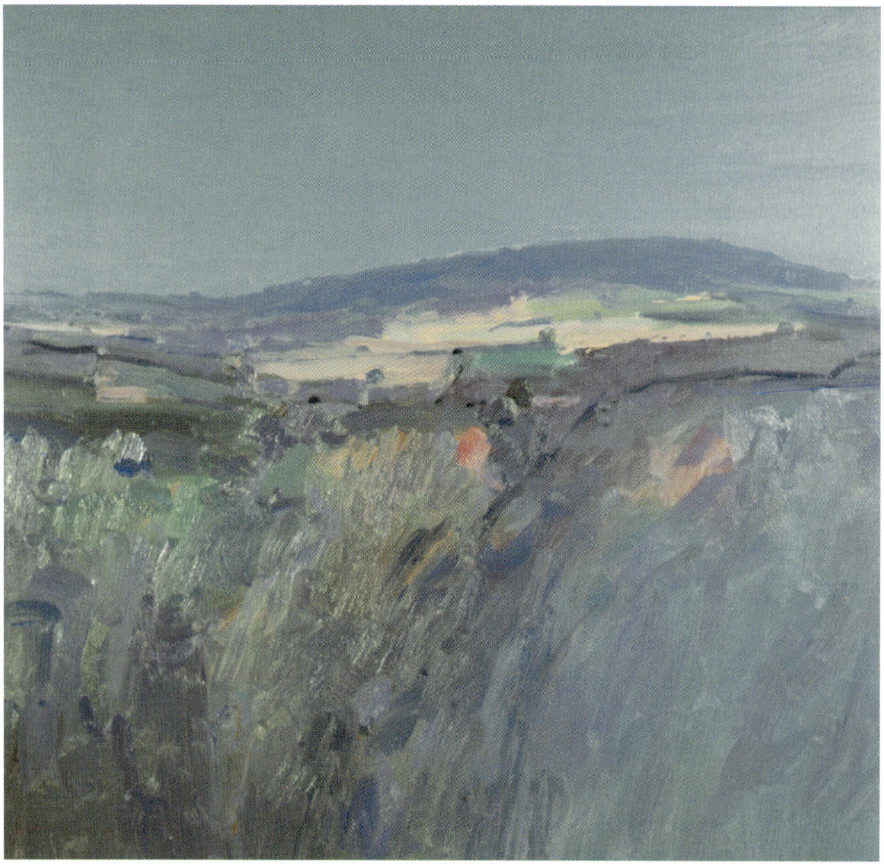

▲ **Autumn Landscape, Cornwall**
1992 oil on canvas 60x70
MT

▶ **Spring Fields**
1999 gouache 18X15
MT

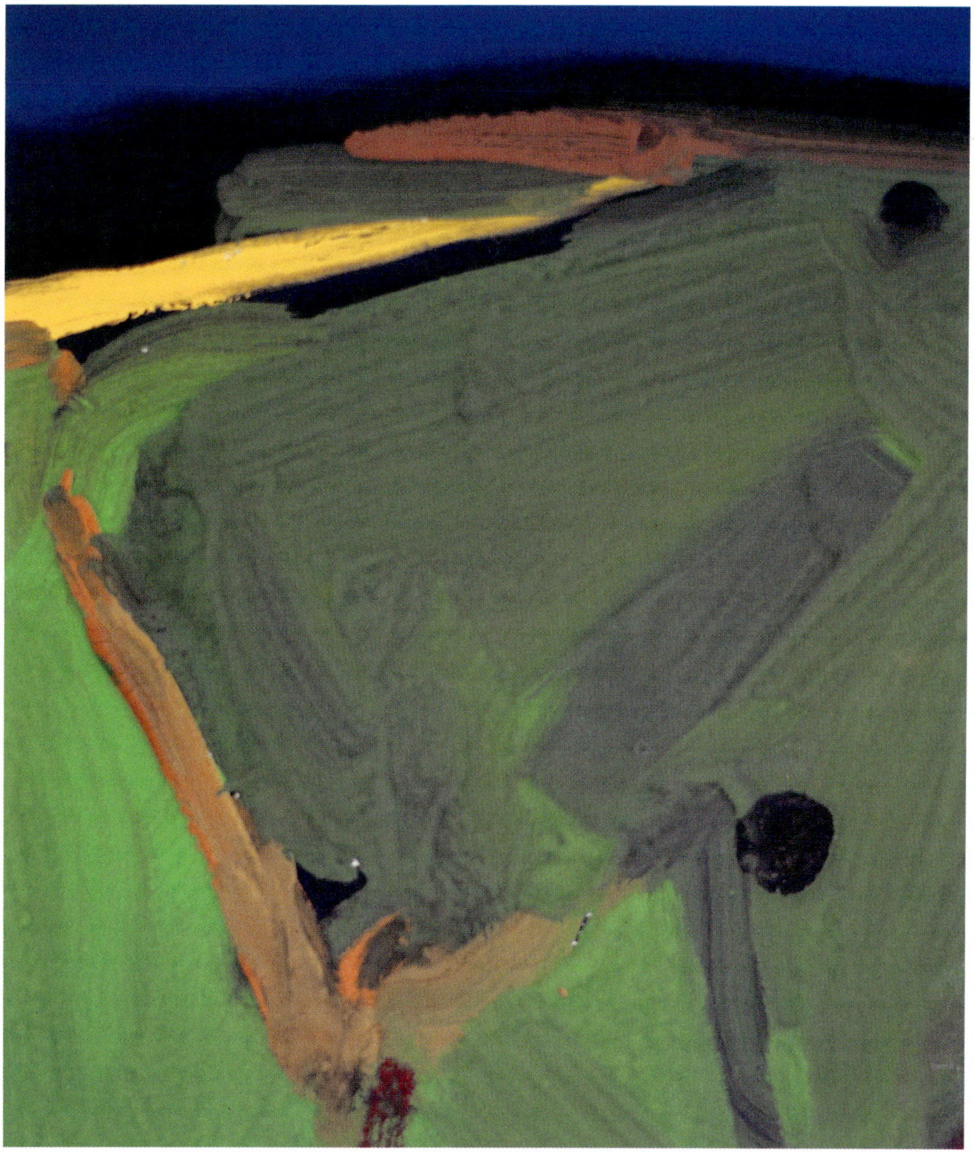

Beach paintings

Very often I cover the whole canvas with paint, like a wash. It depends what I'm painting but if I'm painting a beach, for example, then I very often cover the top with a blue, which I've enjoyed making; I've enjoyed mixing the blue and trying it on bits of paper and seeing it against other paintings. I like to see the blue against another colour so I go to another painting that's got other colours in it and see what it looks like. Bonnard used to pin his paintings – he didn't put them on stretchers, they were just the canvas – up on the walls everywhere, and then if he found a colour for a painting he was working on and thought this is a wonderful colour, he'd go around the whole lot and see if he couldn't find somewhere for it!

I find brushing the colour onto the canvas a very exciting moment. Very often it is blue, of course – the blue of the sky – and I paint this to somewhere near the horizon and the wash it thin at that point with turpentine. I will then bring up a colour which I have probably taken an equally long time to mix, which is close to the sand.I am now left with an unpainted area in the middle. That's where I've got to paint infinity. I start to work the edge and the shape of the sand that goes on forever and then it gets wiped out and then it drives me mad and then – and I never know why and perhaps I don't want to know why, because the adventure wouldn't be there – it begins to speak about moving into infinity and then, I start to find a colour that's going to link these two. Maybe I will leave it because the next stage is much more difficult to describe. The relationship between the two colours is so critical that I might paint the blue all over again. I couldn't count the

▶ **Midsummer Bay No 23**
2000 oil on canvas 60x85
sc

times I've come back to the sand and painted it over and over again. Then one day it's finished and somebody says 'Oh it's so calm' and it's been such a battle and I think I can't believe that it's calm but there you are. People say that.

I don't know what I'm striving for in that infinity and the relationship between the joining of the two colours. It's something beyond. For years I used to look at St Michael's Mount and see it as a magic place and then one day Lord and Lady St Levan asked me to go there with a view to painting a series of ten paintings. The warmth of their patronage and the frequent visits to St Michael's Mount at that time, and since, have meant I have become familiar with it – although it still remains magical. Nevertheless it is no longer beyond my reach. The joining of those two colours is about somewhere beyond my reach. Whether it's a beach, or a passage in the interior landscapes, or that thin line of light under a cloud and beyond the sea, or ashore, or a landscape. If I reached it, I would probably stop painting.

I'm always striving to go beyond the last painting. I've done a lot of beach paintings, but I've not been bored by them. I go down to the beach house and there's a new shape there and it stops me in my tracks and I simply have to paint it. It just fires me again. I go down there and see an amazing little orange line on the edge of the horizon and I want to paint that. I've never become bored with the beaches. It's amazing because in effect, they're very similar but in detail and in experience, they're entirely different. Every time I paint it's a whole new challenge.

▶ **The Morning Beach**
2000 oil on canvas 150x120
SC

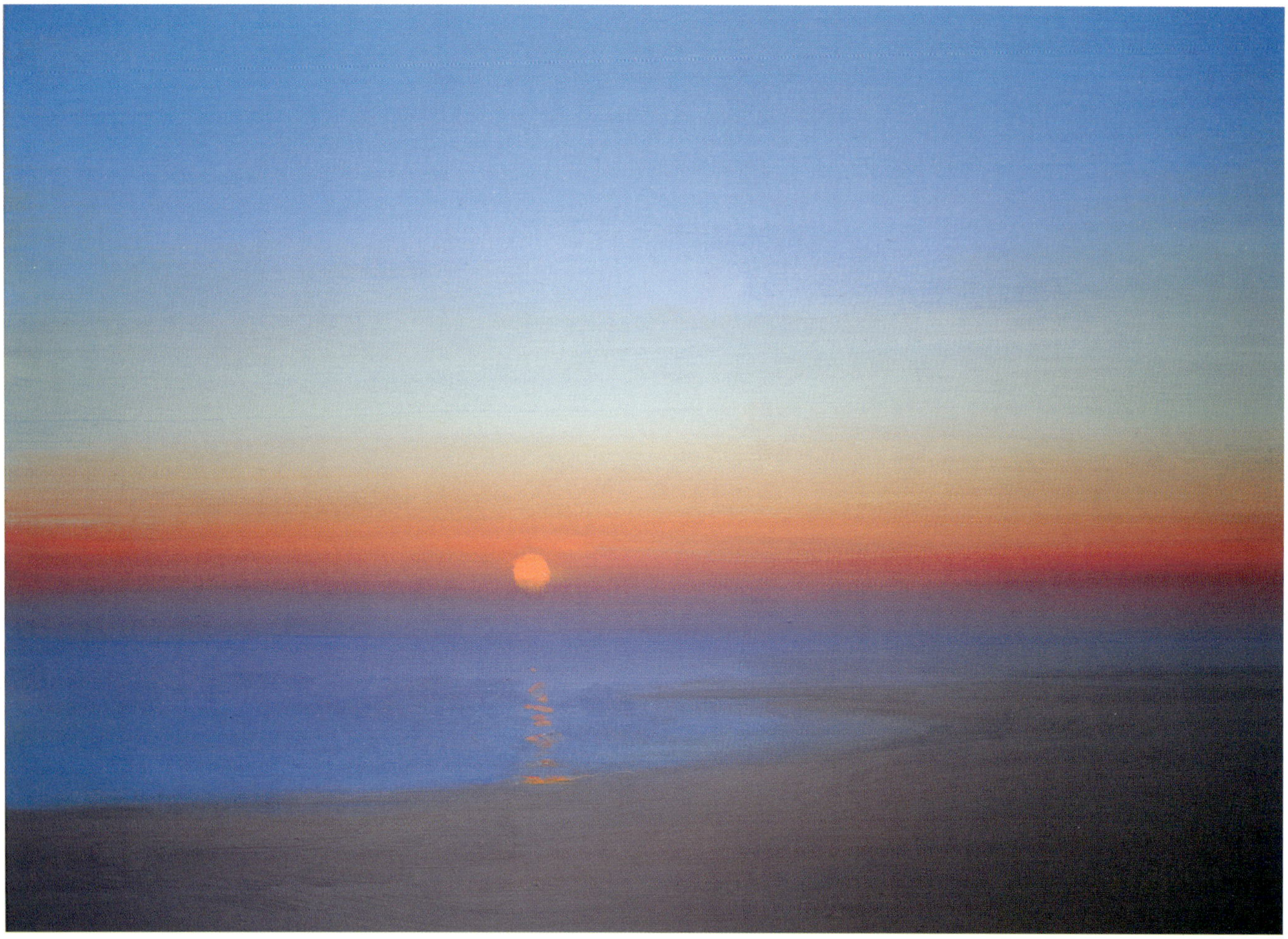

▲ **May Sunrise**
1999 oil on canvas 92x86
MT

▶ **Cornish Crabber on the Tide**
2000 oil on canvas 92x86
SC

It is difficult to describe what my work is about. It is not about reproducing objects with paint, nor is it about ideas. It is more about how certain images, however simple, can evoke an emotional response in me. That experience is often so powerful and profound that I feel bound to convey and share it. The lifelong search has been for ways of doing this. Sometimes I wonder if, because the experiences are so abstract, it would be more practical to celebrate them with words. But how does one describe the sun rising through mist with words? I suppose that is partly why I left art school after a term. A lot of time was spent there making alternative compositional drawings of the project until it was killed stone dead for me. Even now I want to scream when I hear people making remarks like, 'I am not sure if it is quite resolved in the bottom left corner' or 'The colours are too cool in places'. I want to be more like children who simply go for it and produce wonderful evocations of their experience until we persuade them to become analytical and self-destructive. I have a book full of children's drawings, poems and declarations which their school presented to me following a day's visit to the studio on the beach. I value this above so much conventional art because it is full of immediate and honest responses to experience.

Because art is essentially a personal and individual response to experience it cannot be categorised. Of course we need to know the craft and use of materials before we can fully celebrate, but when the craft becomes our single aim the spirit of art dies. John Ruskin, the 19th century artist, critic and social reformer wrote, 'When love and skill work together expect a masterpiece'. Love comes first. As with art so with life. When living is simply a craft we live like robots. Love enables us to throw out the craft – how can love commit evil? That is why I can only paint out of love. When I have set out to paint something purely commercial, because I needed the money, the paintings always turned out to be a failure. On the other hand when I make a painting for someone as a special gift it always comes out right. All this does mean putting the whole of one's life into the work, and this can at times be hard on one's friends. I recall one occasion when I was due to go to a friend's firework display and noticed the early evening light contained all the colours of the spectrum. I felt bound to make a record of this. I knew it might never be quite the same and that my own response might never be quite so intense. It meant cancelling the visit to my friend's firework display which grieved me because I hold courtesy high on the list of essential virtues.

Because my paintings are not specific, in the way of a still life for example, it's impossible to measure the work in relation to time. There is a moment when the painting of an apple as a still life comes right. An account of Cezanne painting a portrait of his dealer tells how after one hundred and seventeen sittings the dealer said, 'I really can't spare any more time,' at which Cezanne exclaimed, 'oh, don't say that. I have at last got the colour of your coat right'. More often than not my paintings don't come right until the work seems to take over in the final stages and the completion takes place in silent timelessness. It seems to be about letting go – as though art can no more be possessed than God. When learning to ride a bicycle, it was only after I stopped trying too hard and let go, that I found myself riding on the wind.

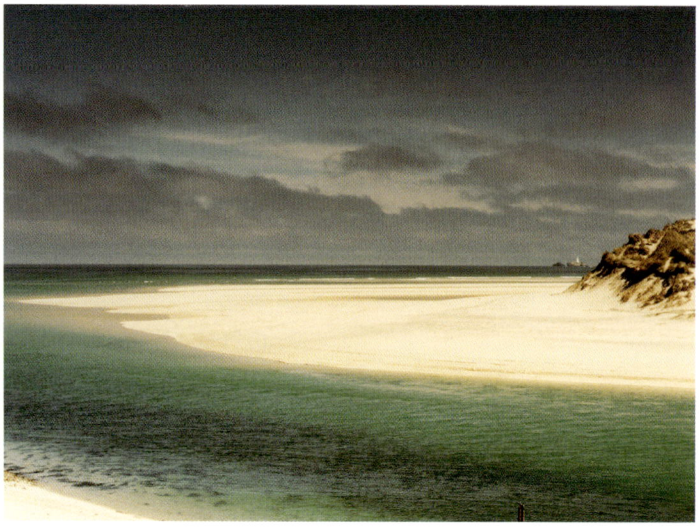

▲ **View across the beach at Lelant**
MT

▶ **June Beach**
2000 oil on canvas 75x70
SC

An outsider?

I first became associated with the art community when Michael Canney and Peter Lanyon invited me to apply for membership of the Newlyn Society of Artists in 1961. I became chairman during the latter part of the 1960s and into the 1970s and redesigned the gallery to bring it up to date with new public health regulations. At the same time part of the curator's flat was incorporated into the exhibition space on the ground floor. Michael Truscott and I put an enormous amount of energy into the Society during those years, undertaking the administration when the gallery was without a paid curator.

When the emphasis changed and the Newlyn Society became a small part of a larger organisation we found ourselves out in the cold. Nevertheless this did lead me to show in private galleries in London, Bristol, New York and Vancouver and brought my work before a wider public.

I came to know a lot of members of the Society in those early days and have good and close friends in the art community. Artists seldom talk to one another about their own work – with some exceptions! They talk about galleries and percentages and VAT and about who is showing where and how the sales are going with this gallery or that. They also talk about critics and artocrats – the ones to avoid are those referred to by the late Professor AL Rowse as 'third raters' – the ones who learnt it all by rote like a stamp collector but believe themselves to be the bee's knees. Eventually they run out of steam and go abroad or join some equally uncommitted profession.

Other Inspirations

When we were in Edinburgh recently, we looked at some marvellous 14th century art and Impressionist paintings there, which had been collected by Lord Lindsey – a special exhibition, and you could put your nose on it. Wonderful. One of the things I saw in that was the richness of dark colours, which made me want to come back and have another look at black. I was also putting my nose on a couple of Monets and the richness of shadows. There was a haystack and there was the same pointillism in both of them – they had such richness in the shadows and yet they weren't black, because the Impressionists didn't use black except for Manet: he could use black, like velvet. The others wouldn't use black, they would mix ultramarine and burnt sienna or burnt umber which nearly makes black – they make wonderful sorts of moody blacks.

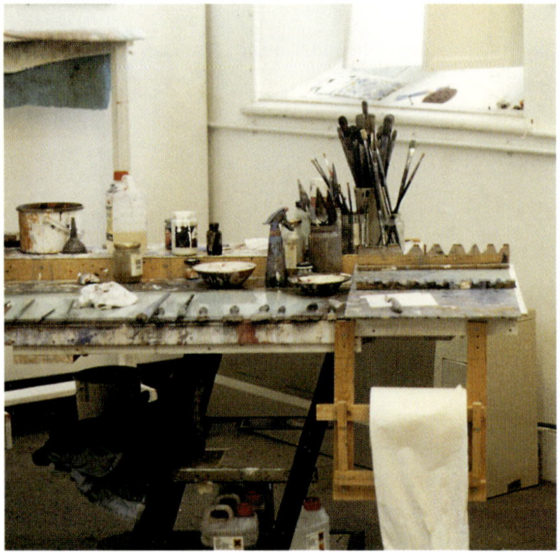

▲ **St Mary's Studio**
MT

▶ **Beach Figure with Orange Sun**
2000 oil on canvas 92x86
SC

One of my endless joys is the discovery of new colours. Every time I start a painting I find new colours. This happens whilst I am mixing colours, before beginning to paint. New colours also emerge during the process of painting. These can be very exciting because they are accidental.

Stanley Spencer mixed every colour exactly as he wanted it and put it on like painting by numbers. If you see unfinished work by him, you can see that he's drawn the whole thing very accurately and then he's painted. I couldn't work like that to save my life. I have to have my colours on the palate side by side and try them on bits of white paper against each other and so on.

I remember going to meet Deirdre, Gotch's granddaughter, and seeing his studio. He would work out a painting in greens. He used green and he would do wonderful tonal paintings in green and then he'd move over and he'd start painting it on another canvas so that he worked his tones out as somebody might take a black and white photograph and say 'Well that's my tonal values' and then he'd work his colours out in the next one but he'd be looking back at the tones – very much employing the techniques and methods of the old masters. I bought a canvas from her where he'd prepared the canvas with various recipes of colours and he'd written them in a marvellous script on the side.

▲ **Shore Dance**
2000 oil on canvas 70x75
SC

▶ **Morning Star**
2000 oil on canvas 92x86
SC

When I look at the landscape or the sky or the sea, I see colour in light. It is really all reflected light. That's what I have tried to paint. One day I had a unique experience when visiting the Tate Gallery to look at Turners in their original Duveen rooms – before they were moved into their new wing. The electric lights failed and I saw the paintings in the natural light Turner had painted them in. They had become iridescent and this inspired me to continue with my own personal search.

When you paint in watercolour the white of the paper shines through the paint and is a source of light but once you're painting in solid pigments, the light is reflecting off them and it doesn't become a source of light. The wonderful thing about watercolour is it becomes an abstraction from the beginning because you're not trying to record things as you see them. You're making an image that is the same sensation hopefully, as is the reflection of the actual surface of the paint. Watercolour is a very different and fascinating medium in its own right. A really good watercolour is very rare. Some of Turner's watercolours are beyond description. When I manage to make a good watercolour I have taken a leap and moved out of time and space.

▶ **Sunrise over St Michael's Mount**
2000 oil on canvas 100x80
sc

I am always amazed when a painting sells and imagine it to be the last. Because I earn my living in this way there have to be sales. I believe a painting only finally comes to life when it is viewed. It's a bit like the Trinity – there is the artist, the painting and the viewer and each is an important part of the whole. I am passionate about sharing all that has nourished me and therefore may nourish others so, sometimes in spite of myself, that is the way it has to be.

Breathless, we flung
us on the windy hill,
laughed in the sun
and kissed the lovely grass

Rupert Brooke
'The Hill' Dec 1910

Reflections

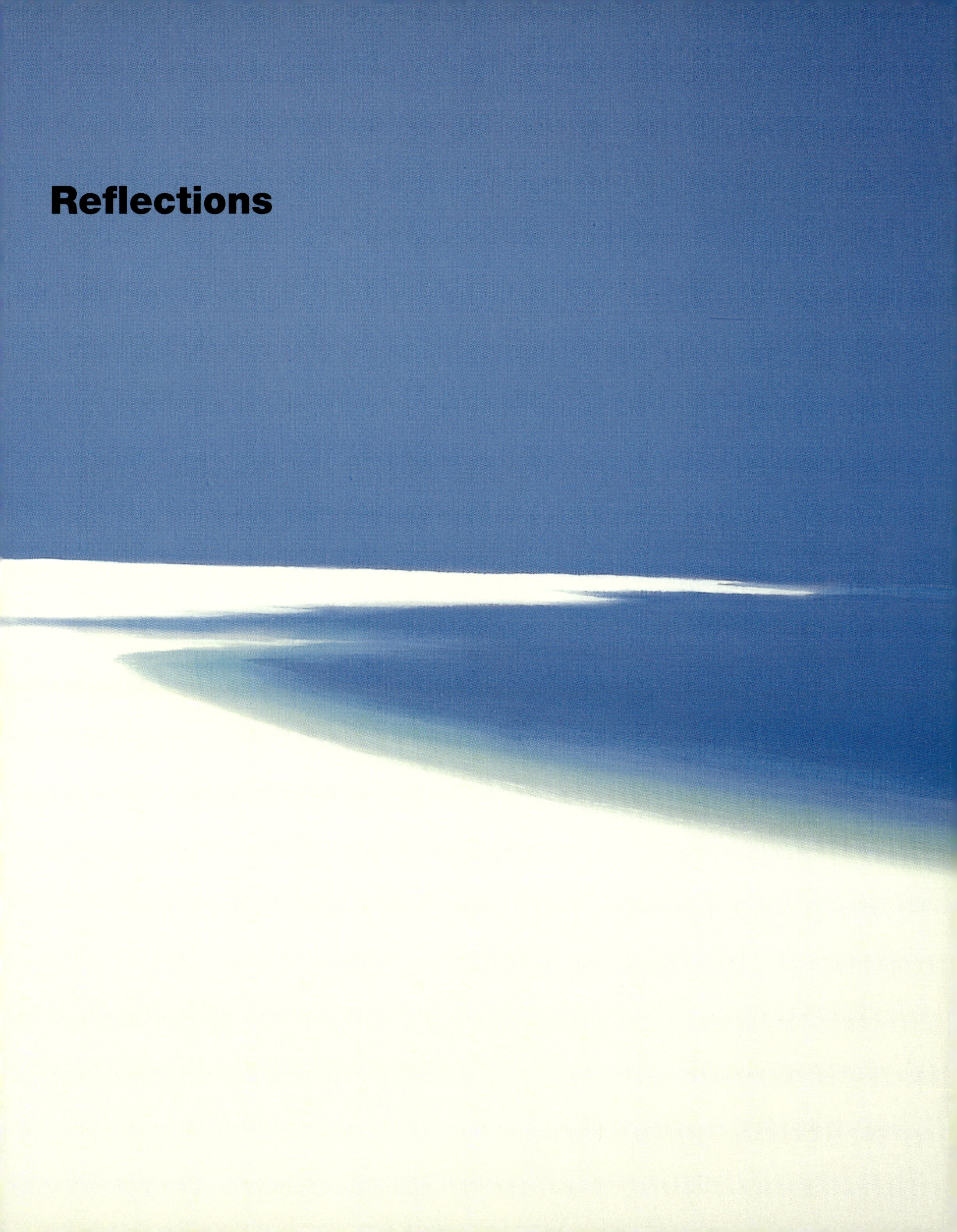

128 Cliffs and Rocks Fishing Boats in Old Newlyn Harbour 1960

When I first came to West Penwith I was impressed by the massive granite cliffs towering above the ocean. Their weight and construction gives them an architectural quality and the strength to withstand the force of the sea. I wanted to convey this and found I could best describe it using a palette knife. I so lacked the technical knowledge required for this that I came at it almost like a caveman. Perhaps there was a naivete that I have long since lost. The fishing vessels in the old harbour at Newlyn presented a different impression altogether. First I made the outlines in black and then filled in the colours. Both these pictures are more about illustration than painting. My cliff paintings were first shown at the Newlyn Gallery and then by Commander England.

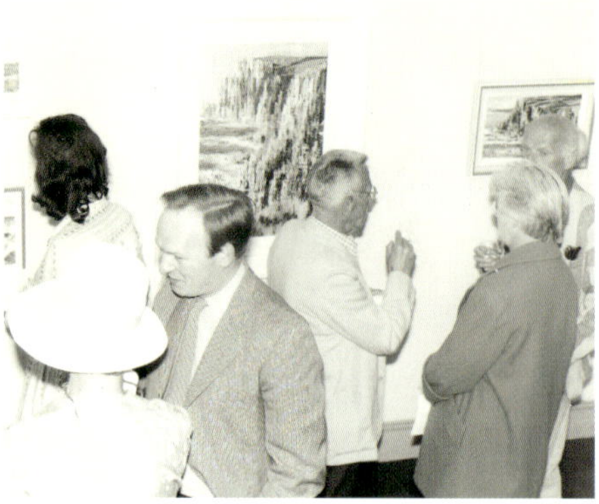

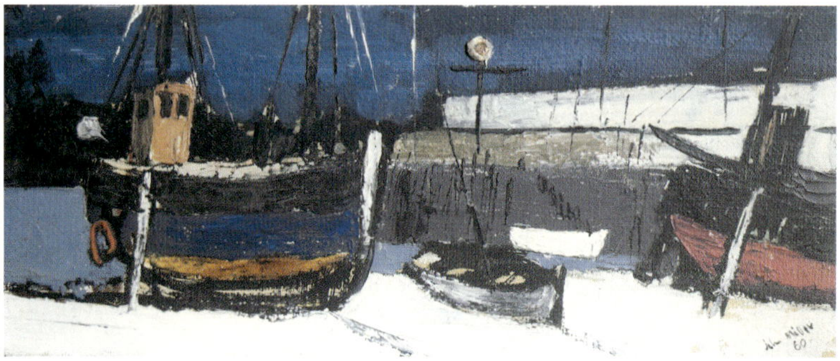

▲ **Exhibition at Newlyn showing an early painting of cliffs, rocks and sea**
about 1960 oil on board

▲ **Fishing Boats in Old Newlyn Harbour**
1960 oil on board 19x46
MT

▶ **St Just Landscape**
1964 priced at £16 oil on canvas 40x91
MT

St Just Landscape 1964
priced at £16.00

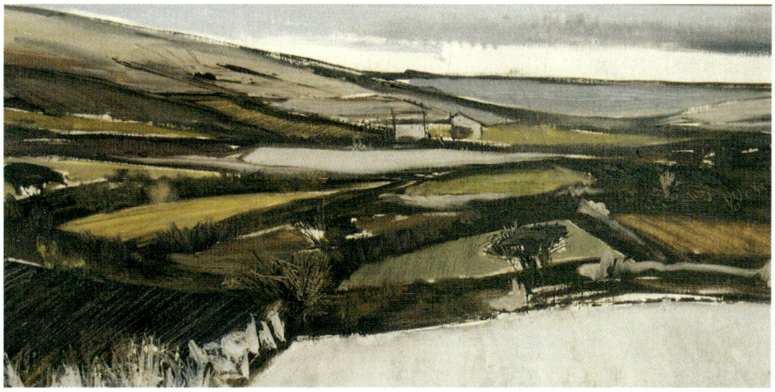

We lived at Joppa Cottage near St Just between 1961 and 1964 when we moved to Sancreed. By this time I was beginning to look at art and going to exhibitions in London as well as taking part in exhibitions at Newlyn. I was becoming familiar with how other people used paints. This painting was influenced by Ivon Hitchens' work although it doesn't look like it, because he painted inside a forest. The influence is in the use of paint and the brushwork. I found a way of describing the open moors, which is what I was really beginning to look at.

There was an exhibition at the Tate 'Painting and Sculpture of a Decade 1954-64'. It included people like Willem de Kooning, Mark Rothko, Clyfford Still and Franz Kline. I loved the work of Kline, because he used a black line and lumps of colour. All those Americans were beginning to influence me. It's interesting that although I was familiar with Peter Lanyon's work because I knew him through the Newlyn Art Gallery, I wasn't familiar with the other St Ives painters and so was not influenced by them. I'd met Karl Weschke and become a close friend – we have been ever since but I see Karl as a one-man band really. He's not part of that group. Much later I became familiar with Patrick Heron for example and met Roger Hilton, Bryan Wynter and Terry Frost. In those days I was more influenced by the people I was finding in London. There were English painters in that exhibition too, such as Craigie Aitchison, Ivon Hitchens and Robert Medley,the then avant-garde painters. It was a turning point, I think, for British painting because it brought together the best of British and American contemporary art.

Icarus
Lazarus 1966

I think that by this time I was beginning to paint ideas rather than simply what I saw. Also, I was still enormously interested in St Francis and in the notion of having another chance in life, as when he embraced the leper. Maybe my father's death in 1966 brought some of these ideas and thoughts into my mind. The paintings were really about that. They were about Lazarus, who had a second chance and Icarus who had a chance to rise above himself but went too far. If we're given opportunities we must use them, not abuse them.

They're figure paintings, which is unusual for me, although I often have small figures within my work. I draw friends, if they'll pose for me. I probably draw figures as much as I draw anything else, but not recently. The last time was when Rory, a dancer and friend posed once a week for me over a period of a year, which provided a lot of wonderful stuff for the current paintings. I think that the presence of a figure in the landscape became very important for me at that time. I was also beginning to really push paint around and use more descriptive colours – blue, violet, pink and white.

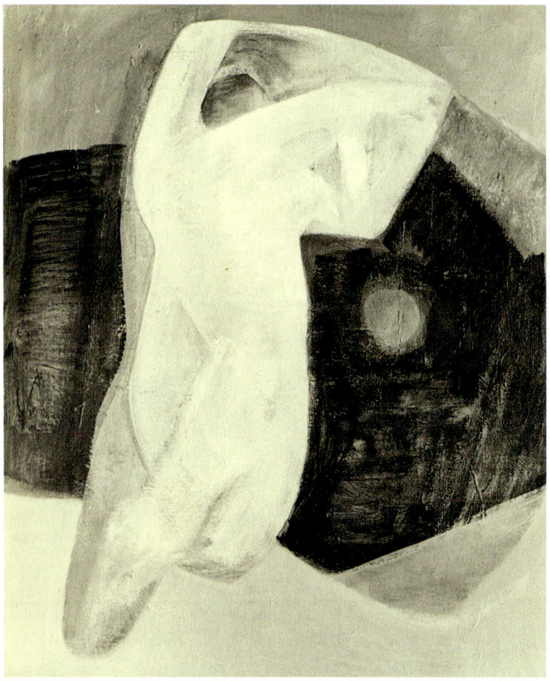

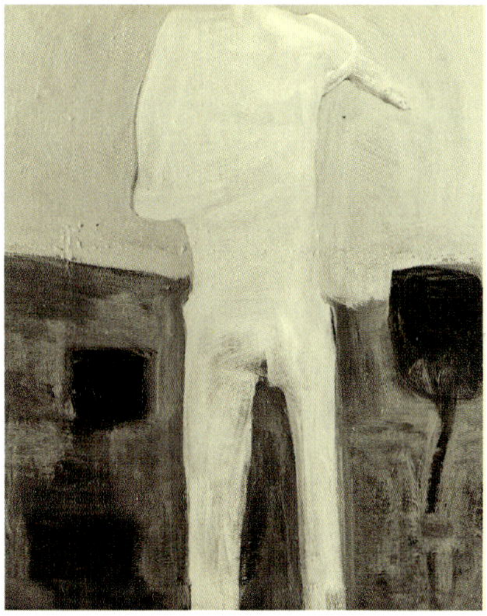

▲ **Icarus**
1966 oil on board 90x76

▲ **Lazarus**
1966 oil on board 60x45

I was still working at architecture so I was only able to give myself a short bash at painting and then knuckle down to the architecture again. The work wasn't flowing and growing in the way it has since the 1970s when I was able to paint all the time. That lack of interruption is very significant because I think one tends to rush into things if you've only got a certain amount of time. I think that it's important for the work to grow almost unconsciously. I find myself following it rather than pushing it. When it begins to grow then I have to take hold of it and push it, which is quite different from force-feeding.

132

Trees
Sancreed Church
1975/1976

By this time I was really celebrating Sancreed. I was living at Sancreed and I was painting Sancreed and everything around Sancreed. I was just in love with it: that's why I painted it. Sancreed was very enclosed – it was a typical old vicarage with very mature, big dark beech, elm and a lot of sycamore trees round it and a wonderful garden. It was like being in the rain forest. The trees came right over the drive. What I was painting became enclosed. I was interested by detail at that time. I painted the details of the hedgerows and the church beyond the hedgerows – thistles and all kinds of lovely wild plants. Then the time came when I wanted to look beyond and I found the trees were in the way. But the winter trees enabled me to see beyond and I began to describe space in much the same way as Gordon Craig did in his stage sets where he used flats which you moved between. He was working in the 1920s and 1930s. I was enormously impressed by the way he made architectural use of space. The trees provided the same thing for me. I was really painting the spaces between them.

I used very muted colours and greys because the colour was secondary to the physical interruption of space. Strong colours would have destroyed the space beyond. When, much later, I found ways of describing space with colour the composition had to be simplified.

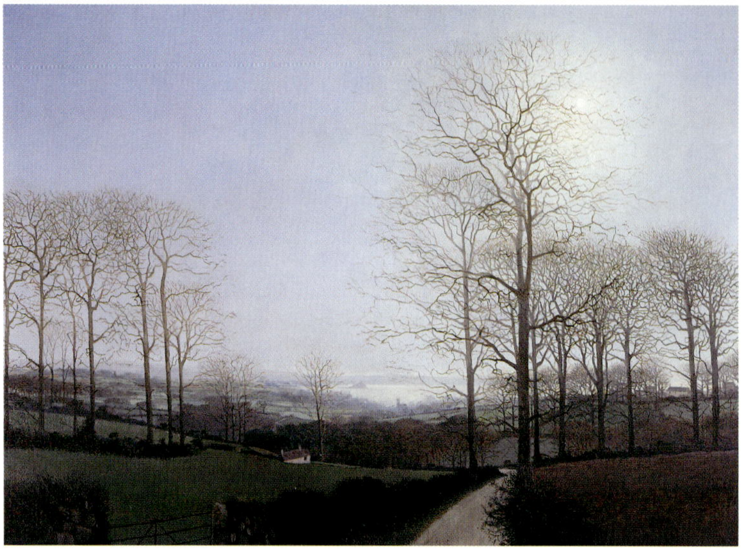

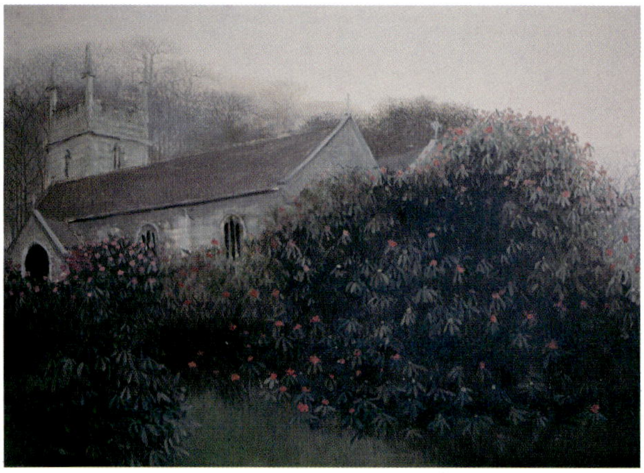

▲ **Trees**
1975/1976 oil on canvas 102x135
SC

▲ **Sancreed Church**
1975/1976 oil on canvas 70 X 55
MT

▶ **Sancreed Beacon**
1992 oil on canvas 70x92
MT

▶ **Farm at Sancreed**
1985 oil on canvas 35x45
MT

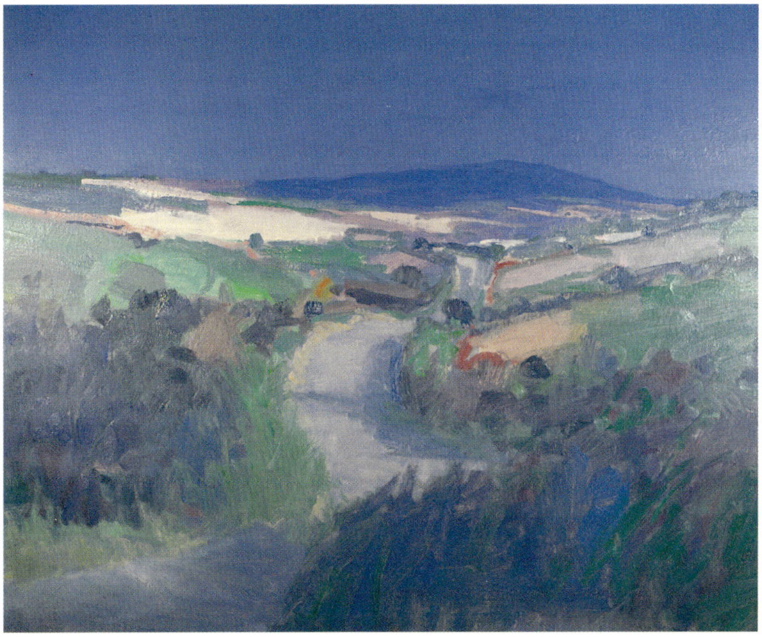

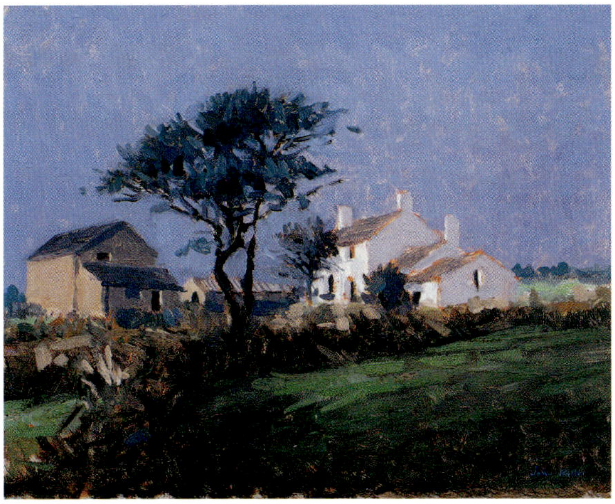

Romantic landscapes - Sancreed Beacon The Farm at Sancreed

When the winter faded into spring and then into summer and the greys gave way to a blaze of colour and light I was confronted by a completely new set of impressions which have engaged me, on and off, to this day. There is an almost uncanny stillness to Cornwall on a windless day. Everything appears to shimmer and there is a sizzle in the air which is unforgettable. I first drew upon the French Impressionists whose subjects in the South of France were not dissimilar. I devoured a book by Bernard Dunstan called 'The Techniques of the French Impressionists' and learned an enormous amount.

For the first time I went into the landscape with my oil paints and fixed a sizeable canvas on my easel. I started early in the morning so that by lunchtime when Michael found me with a flask and sandwiches there was something to show him. I was painting 'en plein air' like the Newlyn School artists and the Impressionists before them. At first the work remained disciplined in the manner of Pissaro and Sisley. Gradually the colour crept in in the manner of the later Monets. That period of intense search and discovery was crucial. I was starting on the threshold. All that I learnt then undoubtedly subscribed to the later semi-abstract landscapes of the late 1980s.

134 Venice - Summer Salute Moonlight Over Venice

I went to Venice in 1975 with Robin and Marika Hanbury-Tenison who took us for a three-day break. We went in October. It was wonderfully misty and moody – we walked everywhere. Marika, being a cookery writer, always found the most obscure places where local people ate, so we had a scrumptious three days. I did lots of drawings. I painted from those with a colour wash but they were very architectural. They were colourless because Venice was colourless – interesting greys. When we returned later for a longer period in 1979, I saw the sparkle of real winter sun. I saw the numinous quality of the domes in that hazy light which seemed to be what I had looked for through the trees. There's a link, there's something starting there, something beginning to say to me 'You can paint more than you see.' It was the first time I found that to be possible.

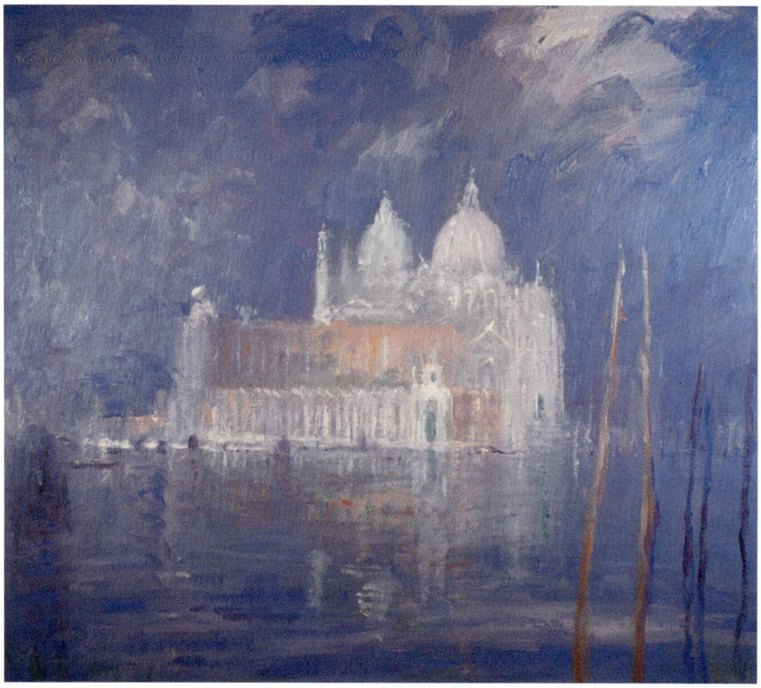

▲ **Summer Salute**
1992 oil on canvas 61x71
MT

▶ **Moonlight over Venice**
1992 oil on canvas 51x61
MT

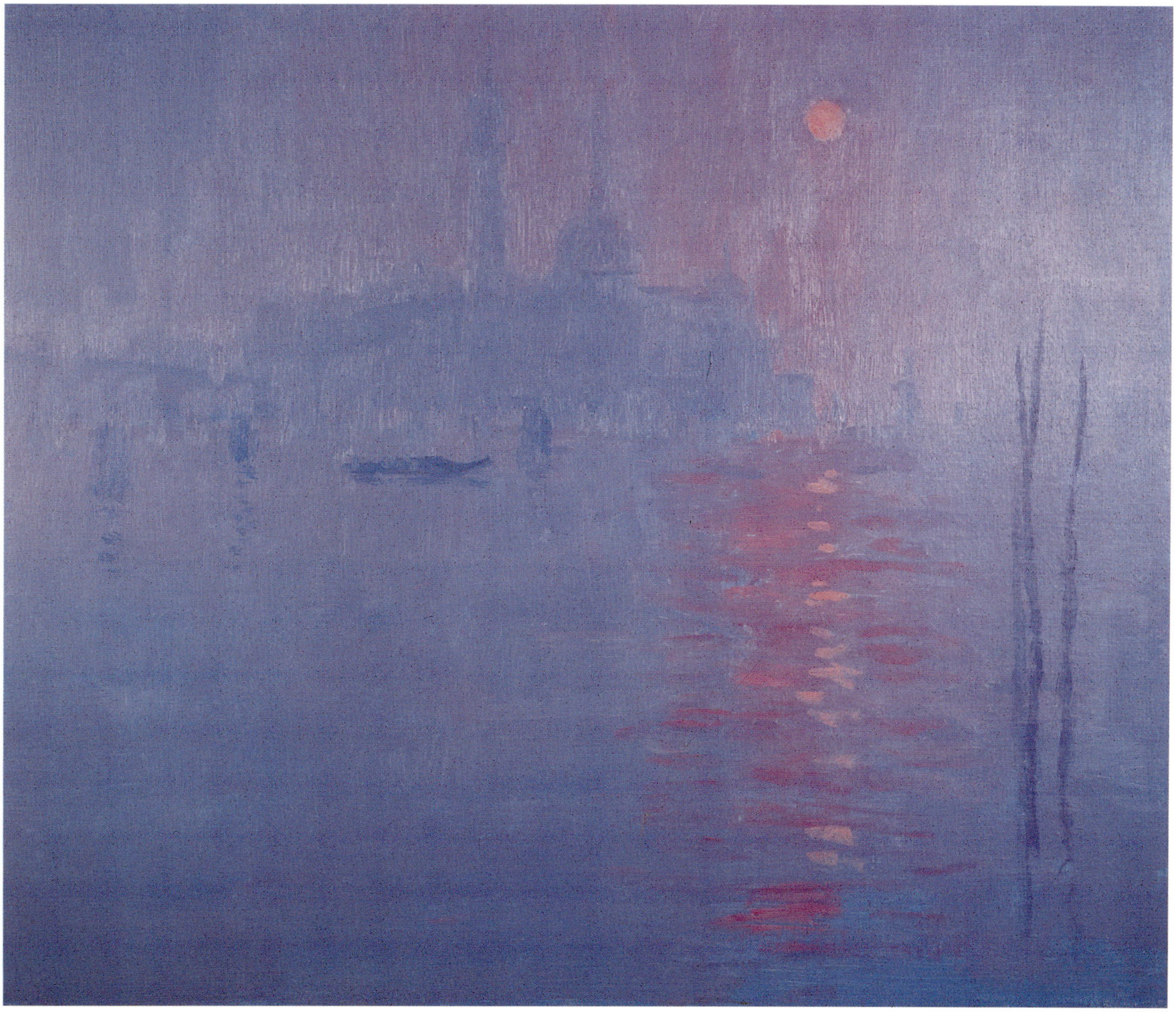

136 **Greece** 1986

Paraportiani Church of the Fisher Folk, Mykonos

On a lot of Greek islands the fishermen have their own church. Paraportiani is very ancient. It's on two floors and they keep putting more whitewash on until it looks like icing sugar with no hard edges to it. I was particularly impressed by the densely blue sky like rich velvet which I felt I could touch. The shadows on the white buildings were lighter than the sky, whereas in this country most of the shadows are darker than the sky. I loved the ancient quality of that building. I did lots of other drawings because I set myself that sort of task knowing that I would go home and it would be too late if I hadn't drawn something. Really it was that building that hit me and I drew and drew and drew that church and I loved it. There were houses around. When I was drawing it one day an old man came along. I hadn't put in a very high television aerial. He pointed to indicate he thought I ought to put it in, which I did to please him. It did and he went away happy. One of my watercolours of that church is in the Victoria and Albert Museum.

▶ **Paraportiani Church of the Fisherfolk, Mykonos**
1986 oil on canvas 66x60
MT

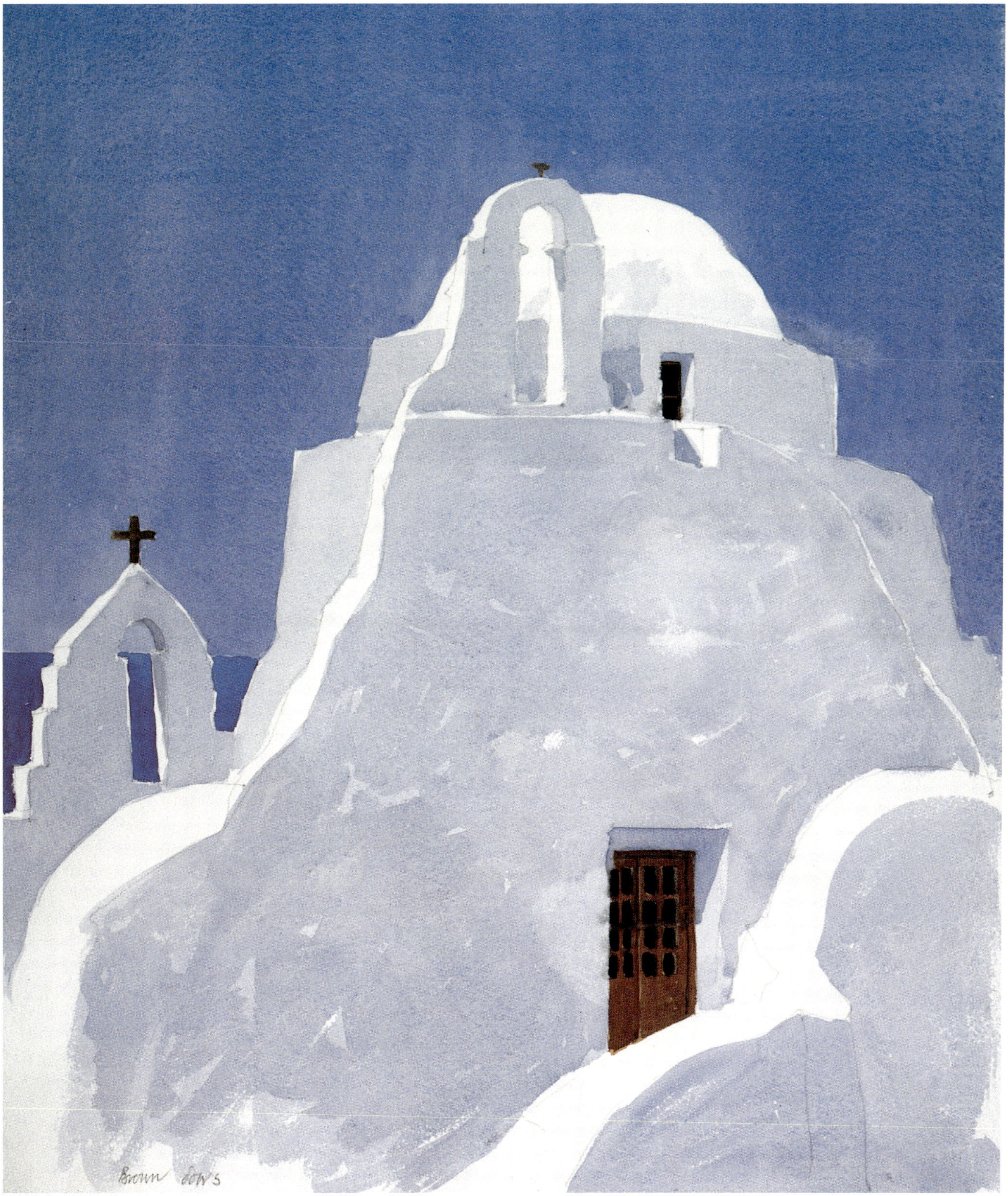

Expressionist landscapes
1987 onwards
Cornish Meadows
Penwith Landscape
Spring Beacon

Corfu, Crete and Mykonos awakened me to intense colour. That's when I saw what Matisse had found in Morocco and in southern France. It was the first time I understood what Gaugin and the Pont Aven people who influenced Matisse, were talking about – concern yourself with the fact that you're putting something on a two-dimensional surface and don't play games with that surface. Accept it's two-dimensions and use the colour and the shape to speak of space. Then I began to see the Cornish landscape again in two dimensions and in colour and I found ways of describing this without delineating. That was an enormous breakthrough for me, a wonderfully exciting period – the work was really beginning to move.

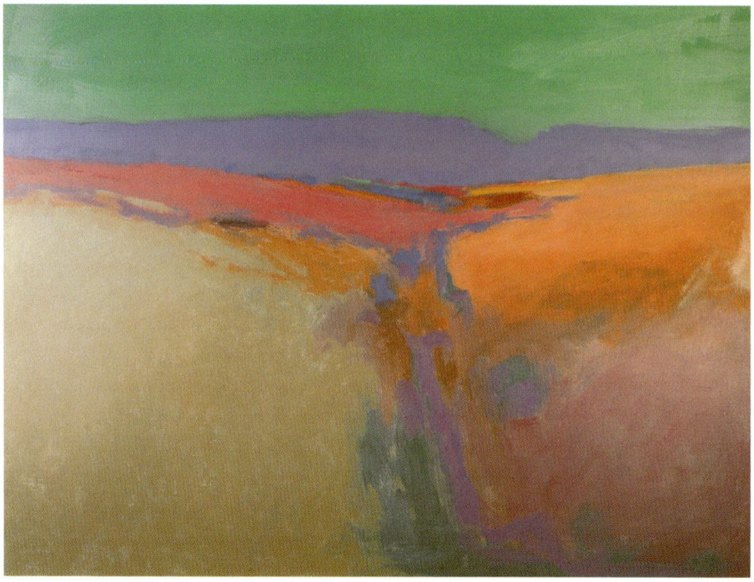

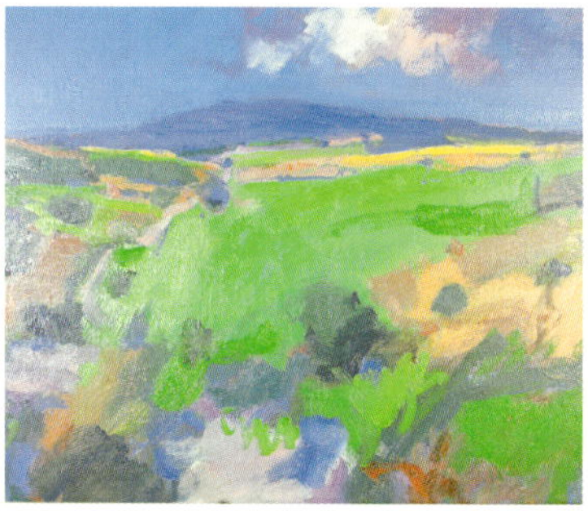

▲ **Cornish Meadows**
1993 gouache 24x20
MT

▲ **Penwith Landscape**
1990 oil on canvas 71x96
MT

▶ **Spring Beacon**
1993 oil on canvas 50x61
MT

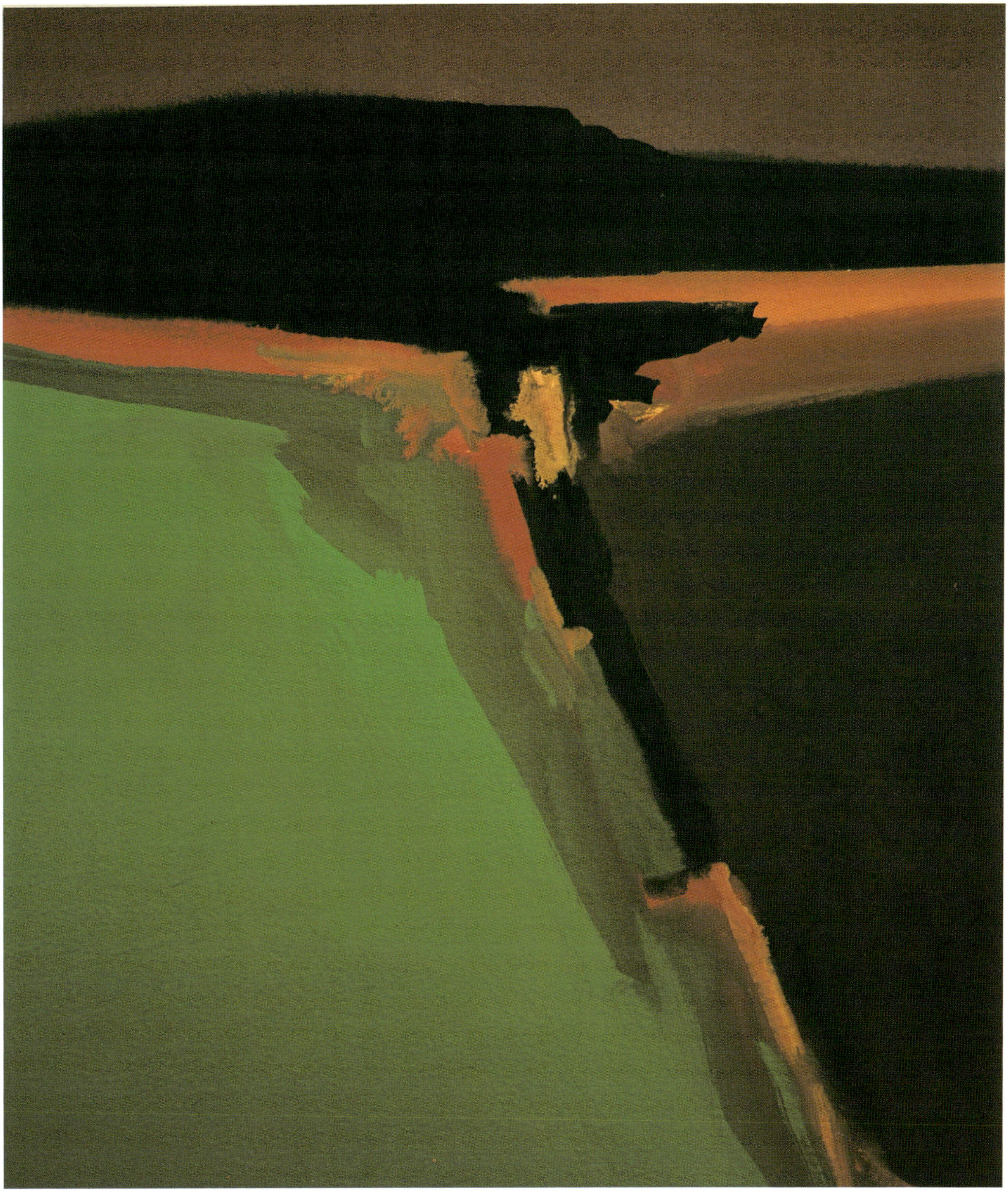

140 **Interior landscapes** 1989/1990
Orange Interior
Purple Interior

These landscapes had an intensity I found appropriate to Mother's illness. She couldn't move her body except her eyes. You could give her a kiss on her cheek, which she knew about and she could follow you around the room with her eyes, but she couldn't move at all. She was like that week after week. I knew that she was totally aware of us. She knew we were there; she heard what we said but she couldn't respond at all. For some reason that I can't understand I wanted to paint the landscape in an even more intense and rich way because I felt that would come through to her. The landscapes got more and more intense and when she died I found I could describe her departure in colour. Having been in a comatose state, she suddenly came to herself, smiled at each one of us and died. It was so beautiful that I wanted to describe it. I had been painting her prior to

▲ **Orange Interior**
2000 oil on canvas 51x46
sc

▶ **Purple Interior**
2000 gouache 54x66
sc

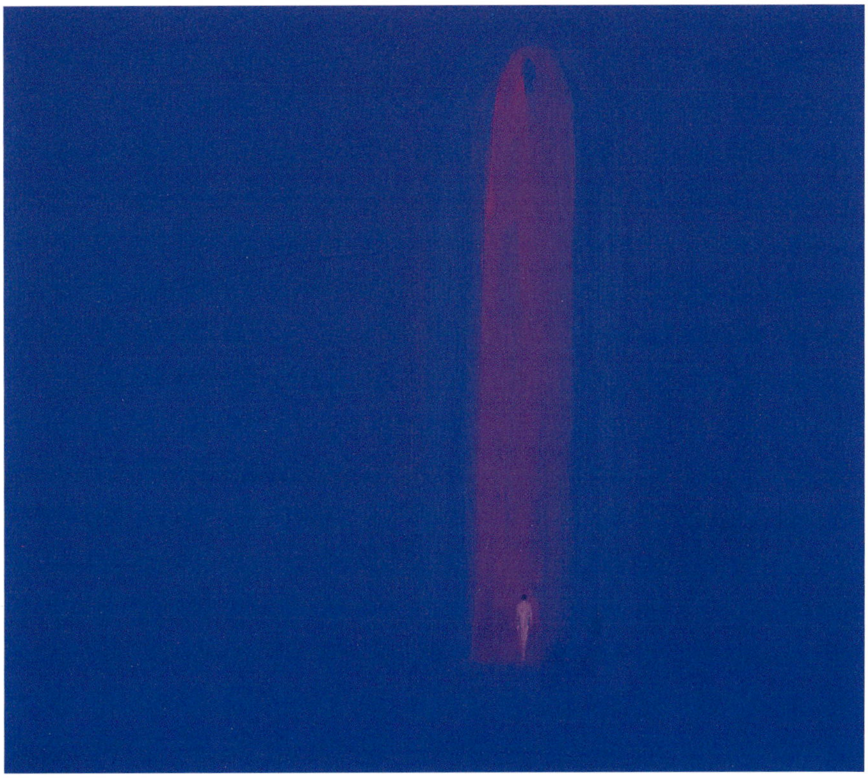

her death. The paintings were big colour fields with Mother located within them. I did make quite a number of paintings of that process of dying, but these were joyful paintings of a wonderful death. That's where the interior landscapes started. They've moved on enormously since then. Now I find myself painting them for entirely different reasons. The figure is Everyman and the shaft of light has become a symbol of something else. Either one's able to enter into it or one turns away from it or one dances because it's good, or one cowers. All kinds of things are going on in them so it's now a little different, talking about other things. They have become about life now – the dreams and the aspirations – the hopes and the failures – the tenderness and severity – above all the extraordinary possibilities open to us when we tune into life and take it on – the pure joy.

142 **Beaches**
Tresco 1992
Lelant 1999

The early interior landscapes had become an exploration of something going on in space described with great sheets of colour. Where on earth could I go next? At the time I thought 'This is it. I'll never paint anything else.' Fortunately Robert and Lucy Dorrien-Smith invited me to go to Tresco and Jane and David Cornwell took us to the Bahamas. In both those experiences I saw pure white beaches and a meld of blues and greens. That was wonderful because it was an exterior landscape in the manner of the interior landscapes. I leapt into that and found it was just right; it was carrying me through to wherever I was going. The part of the painting which fascinates me is the line that separates the blue from the white; the shape of that is everything. I was very worried about it getting corny. That's why I got the house on the beach to observe it more closely all the time. I have to observe before I can paint. I enjoy painting when I go down there and if I haven't been there for a while the whole beach will have shifted – the shape is quite different. That's wonderful because it steams me up. For me everything grows out of observed experience, although in the end it may be about interior experience. I'm not an abstract painter. Definitely not. I am painting my interior response to an exterior vision.

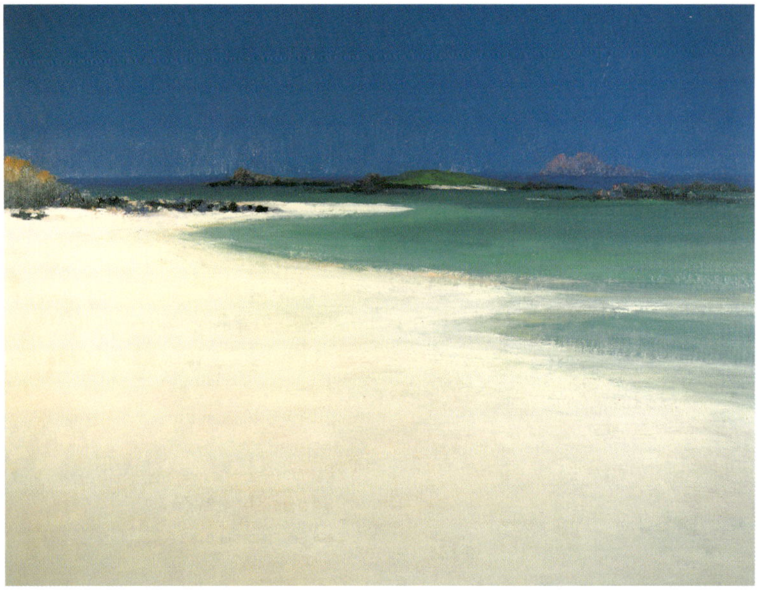

▲ **Beach on Tresco**
1992 oil on canvas 61x81
MT

▶ **Lelant Summer**
1999 oil on canvas 76x71
MT

Horizons
Morocco 1990
The Sheltering Sky 1990
Mount's Bay IV 2000
Mount's Bay September 2000

I began to see the horizons. I remembered the desert which I'd been to as a soldier – the edge of the desert is fascinating. I tried to paint the horizon when David Cornwell took me to Jerusalem because I saw a sandstorm. When you see the black line, you know the sandstorm's over. We saw it coming, swirling towards us like rain in a tremendous wind but once you're in it, or perhaps on the edge and when it's leaving you behind, that's when you see amazing colours beyond that black line. I saw this again on the edge of the sea and I attempted to paint it. I think it's only now that I'm succeeding. If you look hard, if there's any delineation between the sea and the sky at all then there's a line somewhere and often lines above and wonderful sausagey clouds above that which hang over the horizon, leaving a little gap that you can just see beyond.

▲ **The Sheltering Sky**
1992 oil on canvas 91x96
MT

▲ **Mount's Bay IV**
2000 oil on canvas 92x86
SC

▲ **Mount's Bay September**
2000 oil on canvas 100x75
SC

▶ **Morocco**
1992 oil on canvas 75x90
MT

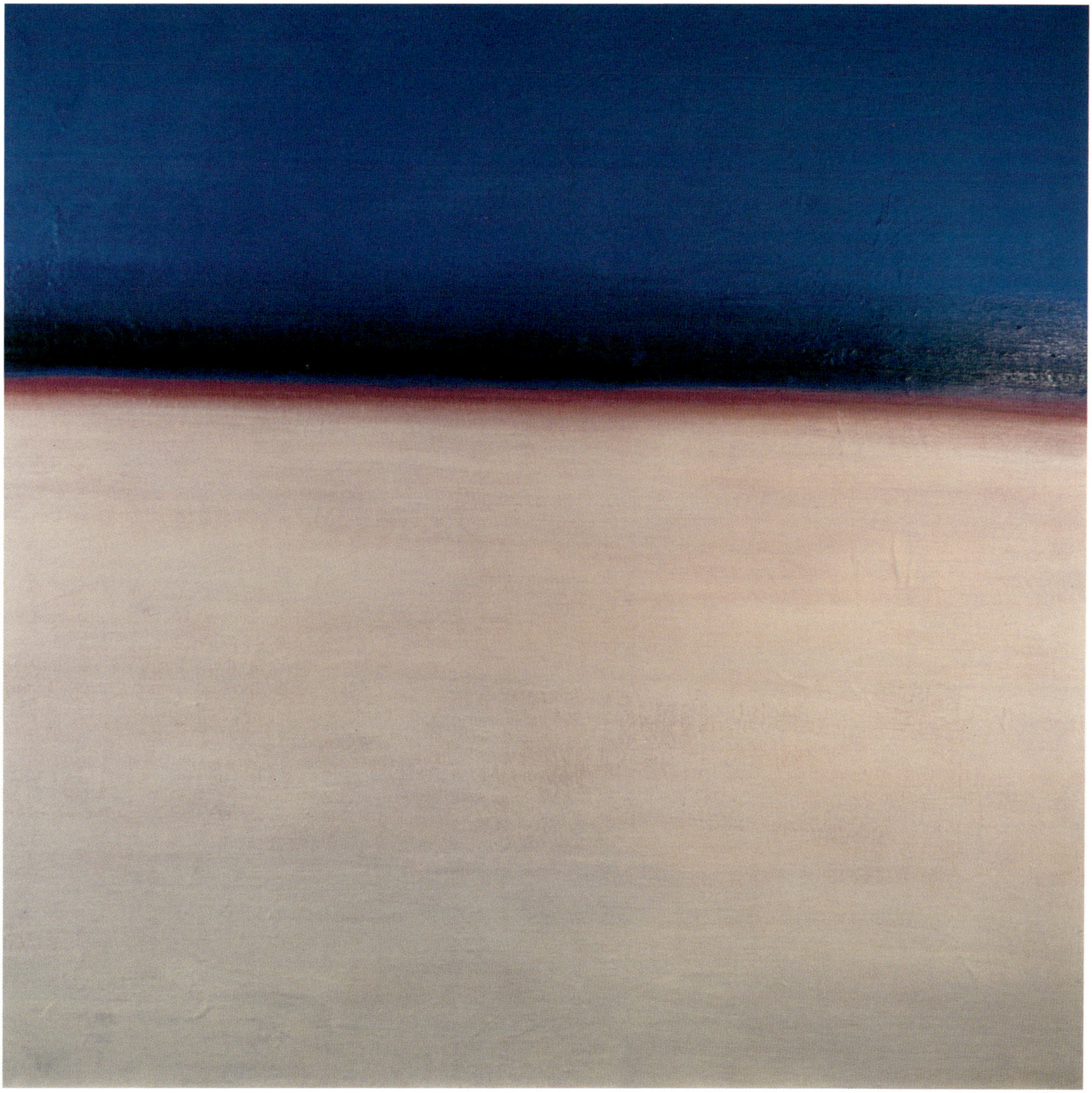

Sunrise Moonrise

At the height of the summer, if you walk onto the beach at Porthkidney, the sun rises over towards Godrevy. On wonderful early morning walks there, seeing that sun rising, coming up through haze, it became another symbol of renewal and energy so I found myself painting the sunrise. Then I became aware of the moon hanging over the sea. All this was a new experience for me because I had been living in the middle of the land and only just moved to the edge of the sea. I'd painted suns, rising through the trees and moons at Sancreed but these new paintings became far more symbolic of life because of the openness of the sea and the shore. The sun rises and sets in its time in the way of the waxing and waning of the moon. I find that amazing because although we know that the moon affects the tides nevertheless that timeless order leaves me filled with wonder. I always think this when I see a new moon. My grandmother used to say 'Don't look at it through glass and turn over your money.' There are all sorts of pagan ideas to do with the moon. The sun is a very deep symbol of life and when my father was dying I was quite sure that if we could keep him going until the sun rose he would live. Moving to the beach became a wonderful opportunity to go on painting and observing the passage of the sun and moon.

▲ **Moon Rising over the Bay**
2000 oil on canvas 107x97
SC

▶ **Sunrise of Wonder**
1999 oil on canvas 98x27
MT

St Francis

From a very early age I have been passionate about St Francis of Assisi. I painted scenes from his life on my walls when I was very young. In 1969 Michael and I and the then Vicar of Sancreed, Stuart Barrie went to the Friary in Dorset and made our commitment as companions of the Anglican order known as the Society of St Francis. This has formed the basis of a daily prayer life ever since. I made a TV programme about St Francis and the Franciscans called 'A Painter in Search of St Francis' which was produced by John Bartlett.
I am passionate about St Francis' 'Canticle of Brother Sun' and could visualise him composing this on Lelant beach, where all the elements in the canticle are to be found: Brother Sun, Sister Moon, Sister Water and even on occasions Brother Fire. It was very difficult to paint because I didn't want to put St Francis in a habit and make him into a friar: I wanted him to be Everyman. Every seer and visionary is Everyman and so in the end I painted him naked. It seemed to work because by painting him naked he is outside time. I loved doing that.

The Canticle of Brother Sun
an extract

All praise to Thee, my Lord, for all creation
And first, my Lord, for Brother Sun;
Who brings the day; and for the light you give to us through him.

How beautiful he is, how radiant and splendid.
How wonderfully he bears your likeness.

All praise, my Lord, to Thee for Sister Moon and the Stars;
In the heavens you made them,
All bright and precious and fair.

All praise, my Lord for Brothers Wind and Air
And fair or stormy, all the weather's moods,
By which you cherish all that you have made.

All praise to you, my Lord, for Sister Water,
So precious, useful, lowly and pure.

All praise be yours, my Lord, for Brother Fire,
Through whom you brighten up the night.
How bright and beautiful he is!
Full of power and strength.

All praise, my Lord, for Sister Earth, our mother,
Who feeds us in her sovereignty and produces
Fruits and coloured flowers and herbs.

All praise, my Lord, be yours for Sister Death
From whose embrace no mortal can escape.
Happy are those who endure in peace,
By you, most High, they will be crowned.

St Francis of Assisi
trans John Miller

▶ **Canticle of St Francis on Lelant Beach**
2000 oil on canvas 160x120
sc

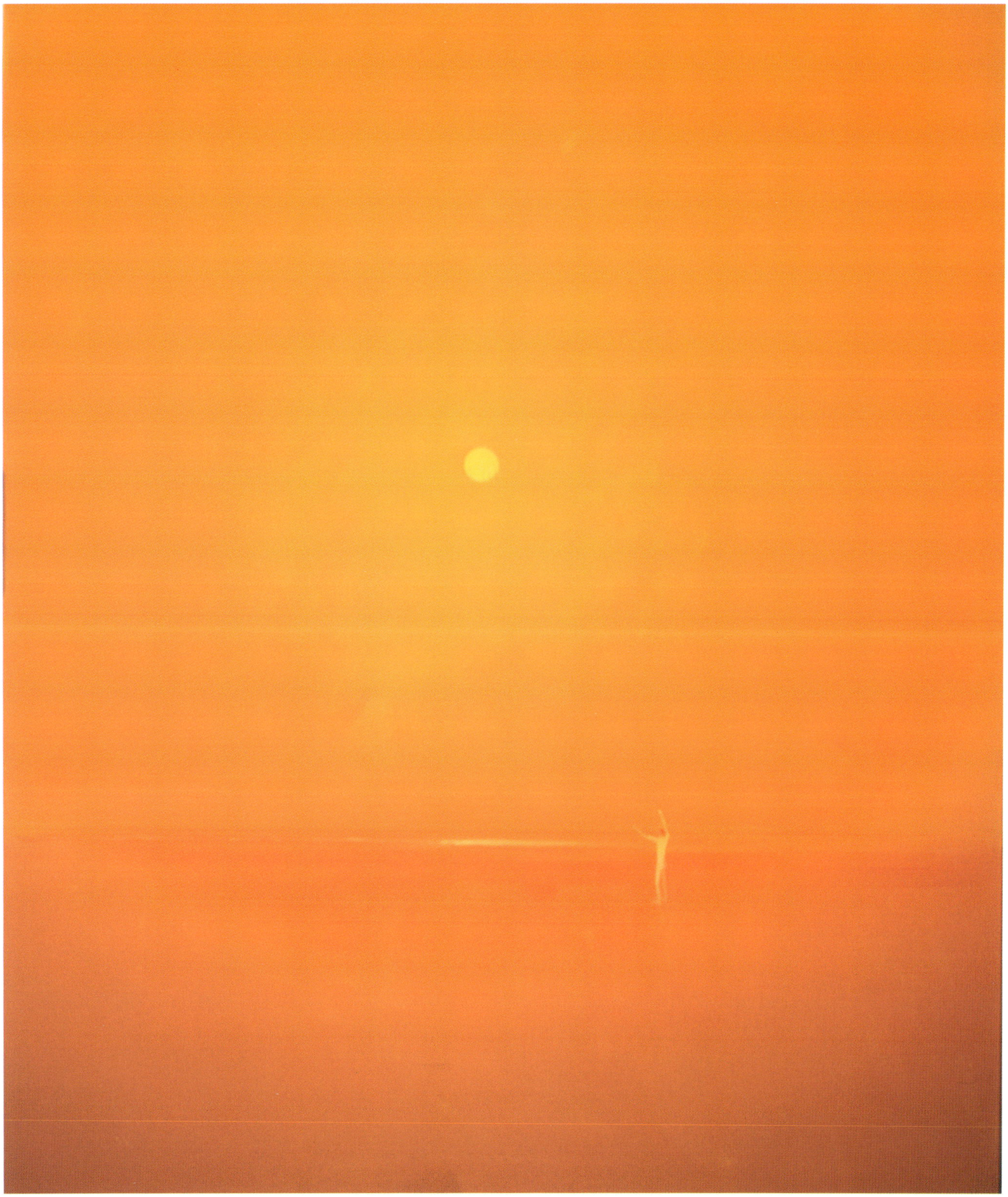

150 Looking at the Open Sea

The 'Canticle of Brother Sun' and the whole notion of creation made me look deeper and deeper into the work. I don't know whether I looked or whether it just led me. I know that when I painted the first black painting it was really quite accidental. I'd been making a painting that wasn't working out and I saw, as I passed through into the studio, jars of French black powder. I thought 'I must really use that.' I made up a mixture with dryers and oil and shook it about and then I just planted it on. Then I began to mix other colours with it and it became wonderful greys and the first big black painting emerged and I knew that was something special – that it represented another movement, another opening of myself to life. Much of this is found in the canticles and in the psalms, for example Psalm 18:

He made darkness his secret place;
His pavilion round about him was dark waters
and thick clouds of the sky.

I've always loved Eliot's 'Four Quartets'. For twenty years I've have been listening to a recording by Sir Alec Guinness with whom I had a few brief encounters – adding, for me, poignancy to the poetry. I was disappointed when Eliot's estate refused permission for some brief quotations in a catalogue of the black paintings. It appears the poet disliked his poetry alongside visual art. 'What about 'Cats'?' asked a BBC interviewer at the time of the exhibition.

▲ **Looking at the Open Sea**
2000 91x86
SC

In 'Four Quartets' there are, as in the psalms, references to the darkness of God and the dark night of the soul by St John of the Cross. That darkness, far from being undesirable, is one to be sought after. When I stand on a dark beach just before dawn it can be as though standing on the threshold of eternity. A recent gift of a three-hundred-and-fifty thousand million year-old ammonite found on the beach at Lyme Regis has added greatly to the wonder of this. We, all of us, have a primitive fear that something will happen when we can't see. We're fearful of our own imaginings. Country people treat the darkness quite naturally. Farm people walk home in the dark, but we see bogies in the dark because we don't see.

If I go for a walk in the dark I experience so many more things because I hear more acutely and feel more acutely. Not all the paintings in this series are dark because not all horizons are dark. Colour is about the way we are when we paint. The dark paintings have their place but now when the sun is rising out of the winter days and the colours are again dancing over the landscape: there is so much more to celebrate.

Or on a primitive Italian Sea
They glide within the grove of spinning smoke
Stunned, as Christ's seamen in Gethsemane
The darkness dragged about them like a cloak.

Charles Causley
'Sailors Asleep in a Cinema'

Selected biographical notes

1931
born In London

1939
educated at St Joseph's College, Beulah Hill

1944
National Savings poster exhibited at Royal Academy

1947
Croydon School of Art for one term

1949
joined the Little Theatre, Derby
National Savings film 'Cycle Tour of the West Country'
Painted seven backgrounds for exhibition at Derby Museum
National Service – commission Royal Army Service Corps – served in Malta

1951
worked in film and TV industry

1952
studied architecture part-time at School of Architecture, Regent Street Polytechnic and articled to Milner and Craze, church architects, London

1958
moved to Cornwall to paint

1960
opened a guesthouse for artists with Michael Truscott on the cliffs at Sennen

1961
elected member of Newlyn Society of Artists

1963
visit to Italy

1964
moved to Sancreed House
elected Chairman, Newlyn Society of Artists to 1965 and 1967-71
elected FRSA

1966
Father died at Sancreed
Consultant designer for Hotels Division of the Rank Organisation. Worked on hotel interiors in Italy, Portugal, England, Ireland and Scotland

1968
designed a supper room in the former kitchen at the Carlton Club, London
accident to right hand. Began to sculpt and model in clay

1969
part-time teaching post at Truro Art School for four years – joint exhibition – John Miller and Michael Iruscott paintings and ceramics at Newlyn Art Gallery
Sancreed Studios produced a catalogue of ceramics and clay cold cast sculptures for sale by post

1973
visit to Cyprus

1974
exhibition at the Orion Gallery, Penzance

1975
visit to Venice with Marika & Robin Hanbury-Tenison
first solo London exhibition at the Anthony Fortesque Gallery

1976
visit to Tuscany

1977
first exhibition at Frost and Reed, Bristol
began to exhibit annually at the Brotherton Gallery, London
painting purchased by Avon City Council

1978
painting 'Penzance over the Hill' purchased by Westward Television and presented to Cornwall County Council

1979
ten historical paintings of St Michael's Mount commissioned by Lord and Lady St Levan and the National Trust – painting of Duchy Farm commissioned by Stoke Climsland Parish Council and given to HRH Prince Charles

1980
visit to Greece and Mykonos with David Cornwell
visit to Jerusalem with David Cornwell
visit to Berlin with David Cornwelll
'Cooking with Vegetables' by Marika Hanbury-Tenison, illustrated by John Miller published by Jonathan Cape
'Cornubia – Land of the Saints' commissioned for Truro Cathedral by the Dean and Chapter and unveiled by HRH Prince Charles

1981
Paraportiani watercolour purchased by Victoria and Albert Museum
painting of the Isles of Scilly commissioned by the Royal Institute of Chartered Surveyors and given as a wedding present to HRH Prince Charles – presented to the Queen Mother in front of 'Cornubia'

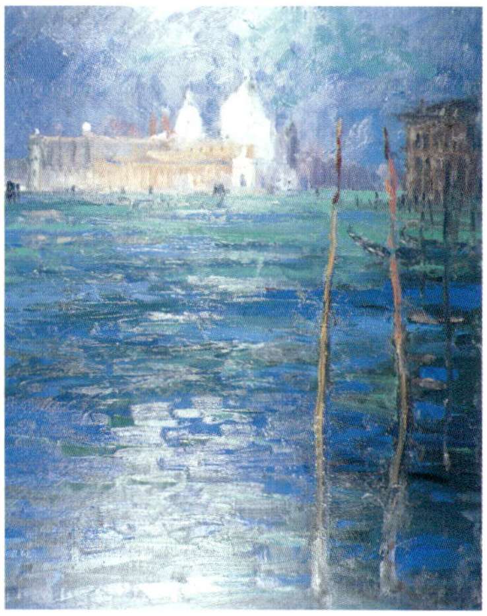

1982
first exhibition at the David Messum Gallery, London

1984
visit to Burgundy with Serenissima Travel before illustrating their brochure

1985
trustee of Passmore Edwards Gallery, Newlyn

1987
crucifix commissioned by Lord and Lady St Levan for the chapel on St Michael's Mount

1989
'Leave Tomorrow Behind' published by Studio Publications
Mother died in Cornwall after a long illness

1991
member of the Truro Cathedral Fabric Advisory Committee – presented to Princess Diana in front of 'Cornubia'
three interior landscape paintings used as covers for books published by Century: 'Living by Zen', 'Introduction to Zen Buddhism' and 'The Miracle of Mindfulness'

1992
'Sketchbook of Cornwall' published and drawings exhibited
painting expedition to Tresco, Isles of Scilly followed by exhibition at the Gallery Tresco
donated painting 'Farm in Mallorca' to St John's Ambulance and exhibited at Portland Gallery

1993
'Looking, Seeing and Drawing' course for the friars at Hilfield Friary of St Francis
'Seaside Sketchbook' published and drawings exhibited
appointed Lay Canon at Truro Cathedral

1994
opened Penzance Arts Club
appeared on Gary Rhodes' BBC TV programme painting 'The Mackerel'
large beach painting 'Penwith Sandspur' on display in the chapel at Royal Devon and Exeter Hospital

1995
visit to Bahamas as guest of Jane and David Cornwell
a celebration of Cornwall in poetry, prose and letters – John Miller and Anna Murphy at Newlyn Art Gallery as part of the Centenary celebrations
moved from Sancreed to Lelant
painting 'Midnight Blue' used as cover image for Robert Fripp's CD entitled 'A Blessing of Tears'
commissioned by Exeter and District Hospice to paint a triptych for the chapel
Vice-president of Hospiscare (Exeter and District)

1997
speaker at dedication of 'Calvary' by Craigie Aitchison in Truro Cathedral

1998
The Halifax 1998 Calendar (Royle Publications Ltd)
acquired St Mary's Studio, Penzance
collection of interior landscapes in Gary Rhodes new restaurant at Dolphin Square, London – 'Rhodes in the Square'

1999
'Simply River' poster commissioned for 'Art on the Underground' to coincide with the opening of the Tate Modern
visit to St Mary's Studio by NADFAS

2000
joined Portland Gallery, London
'A coastal Journey' – IKEA Calendar 2000
Academician South West Academy of Fine and Applied Arts
donated painting 'Clouds over Hayle Estuary' to Redruth branch of Save the Children Fund – used as the cover for their book 'Cornish Connection'
donated painting 'Summer island Beach with yacht passing' to WRVS
painting 'Midsummer beach' used as CD cover image on Chris Rea's 'King of the Beach'
'Another Shade of Blue' published by Truran

2001
exhibited at Portland Gallery stand at ART2001 London Contemporary Art Fair
April commission from Robert Dorrien-Smith for a pair of large Tresco beach paintings for Lucy's birthday
June 14th exhibition at Portland Gallery, London

Solo exhibitions

1961
Newlyn Art Gallery

1962
Yeovil Art Gallery

1963
C'est Ici, Palm Beach USA

1964
Newlyn Art Gallery

1965
Arts Gallery, London

1966
Newlyn Art Gallery

1973
The Framer's Gallery, Penzance

1974
Little Baddow Arts Centre
The Orion Gallery, Penzance
Anthony Lyons Gallery, Surrey

1975
Maidenwell, Cornwall – mounted by Marika and Robin Hanbury-Tenison – proceeds in aid of Survival International
Anthony Fortesque Galleries, London

1976
Newlyn Orion Gallery

1977
The Festival Gallery, Bath
Frost and Reed, Bristol
Brotherton Gallery, London

1978
Newlyn Orion – major retrospective
Brotherton Gallery

1979
John Makepeace Workshops, Parnham House, Dorset
Brotherton Gallery

1980
Brotherton Gallery – illustrations to 'Cooking with Vegetables'
Frost and Reed
Brotherton Gallery

1981
Grosvenor Gallery, Vancouver, Canada
Brotherton Gallery

1982 - 99
David Messum Gallery, London

1990
Selective Eye Gallery, Jersey

1992
Penlee House, Penzance – watercolours from 'Sketchbook of Cornwall'
Selective Eye Gallery
Gallery Tresco, Isles of Scilly
Salisbury Festival – 'Englishman Abroad'

1993
Queens Hotel, Penzance – gouaches from 'Seaside Sketchbook'

1994
Camborne School of Mines – 'Paintings'

1995
Truro Cathedral – mini retrospective

2000
White Gallery, Hove
Innocent Fine Art, Bristol
Joined Portland Gallery
Royal Cornwall Museum – 'Looking at the Open Sea'

2001
Exeter Phoenix – 'Looking at the Open Sea'
Exeter Healthcare Arts – Royal Devon and Exeter Hospital – 'Sunrise of Wonder' touring exhibition to hospitals until 2003
Portland Gallery, London - 'Seeing is Believing'

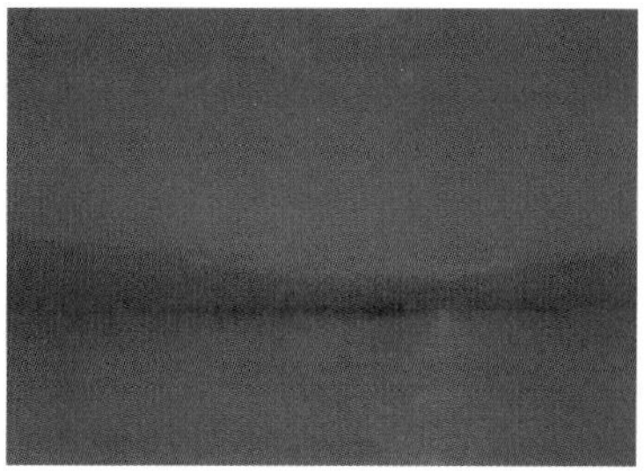

Principal group exhibitions

1962
RWS Galleries, London

1962-72
Newlyn Art Gallery

1963
Ostend, Belgium

1970
Fowey Art Gallery

1971
Plymouth City Art Gallery

1975 Little Baddow Hall Arts Centre
The British Season, Grosvenor Galleries, London

1977
City Hall, Truro Westward Open Art Exhibition
Mitch Morse Gallery, New York
Galerie Am See, Bederkesa, Germany – Joan Gilchrist, Rose Hilton, John Miller

1978
Newlyn Orion Gallery – Summer Exhibition

1980 Rooksmoor Gallery, Gloucester – works on paper – Miller, Moore, Pasmore

1981 Green College, Oxford – British Artists – Contemporary Work

1984
Newlyn Orion Gallery – 'Happy Returns'

1987
Newlyn Orion Gallery – 'Looking West' – touring exhibition
Exeter University – 'Charles Causley Tribute' – touring exhibition

1989
Falmouth Art Gallery – 'Homes and Gardens of Cornwall'
Christies, London at Harewood House – in aid of Survival International
County Hall, Truro – 'A Century of Art in Cornwall' – CCC Centenary

1992
Royal West of England Academy – 'Artists from Cornwall'
Royal Albert Memorial Museum, Exeter – 'Contemporary Icons'
Cuxhaven, Germany – 'The Penwith Art Experience'

1993
Newlyn Orion Gallery – work selected personally by Richard Demarco
JRH Fine Arts – International Los Angeles Art Fair

1994
Royal Cornwall Museum, Truro – 18 of Cornwall's leading artists

1996
Great Atlantic Map Works, St Just – 40 years of art in St Just
Royal Cornwall Museum – 'Art for Healing'
New Millennium Gallery, St Ives – 'Another View'

1997
Penzance Arts Club – 'Quality of Light'

1998
Alpha House Gallery, Sherborne – 'A Matter of Faith'

1999
St Elwyn's Church, Hayle – 'Godrevy'
Royal Cornwall Museum – 'The History of Christianity in Cornwall'

2000 Albany Gallery, Cardiff – 'Cornish Artists'
Belgrave Gallery – 'A View of St Ives'
Upstairs Gallery, Nantucket Island, USA
South West Academy of Fine and Applied Arts

2001
ART2001 – London Contemporary Art Fair Business Design Centre
Royal Cornwall Museum – 'St Michael's Mount'
Great Atlantic Map Works, St Just – 'Behind the Canvas'

Public and corporate collections

Avon County Council

Cornwall County Council

Royal Devon and Exeter Hospital

Truro Cathedral

St Michael's Mount

Law Courts, Truro

BUPA - Roding Hospital

The Burton Group

Cunard

Exeter Hospice

Sony, Europe

John Lewis Partnership

Discipline Global Mobile

Rhodes in the Square, Dolphin Square

Penlee House Gallery and Museum

Harlech Television

Groucho Club

Original painting for poster 'Simply River' commissioned for 'Art on the Underground' in London Transport Museum and Gallery, Covent Garden Piazza

Dining Room Suite, Abbey Hotel, Penzance

The Relatives Waiting Room, The Emergency Accident Department, The Royal Devon and Exeter Hospital (Womford)

Books

1989
Leave Tomorrow Behind
The Studio Fine Art Publications, London

1992
Sketchbook of Cornwall
Sancreed Studios, Cornwall

1993
Seaside Sketchbook
Sancreed Studios, Cornwall

2000
Another Shade of Blue
Truran, Cornwall

Book illustrations

1954
Mary's Shrine of the Holy House Walsingham
A Hope Patten CSA, Cambridge

1965
Sailors' Songs and Shanties
Michael Hurd Oxford University Press

1966
Soldiers' Songs and Marches
Michael Hurd Oxford University Press

1968
An Outline History of European Music
Michael Hurd Novello & Co Ltd

1973
The Timeless Land, the creative spirit in Cornwall Denys val Baker Adam & Dart

1980
Cooking with Vegetables
Marika Hanbury-Tenison Jonathan Cape

1985
Serenissima Travel brochure

1996
Drawing Towards the End of a Century
Newlyn Art Gallery

1999
About St Michael's Mount
Bossiney Books, Cornwall

Address Book Penzance Arts Club

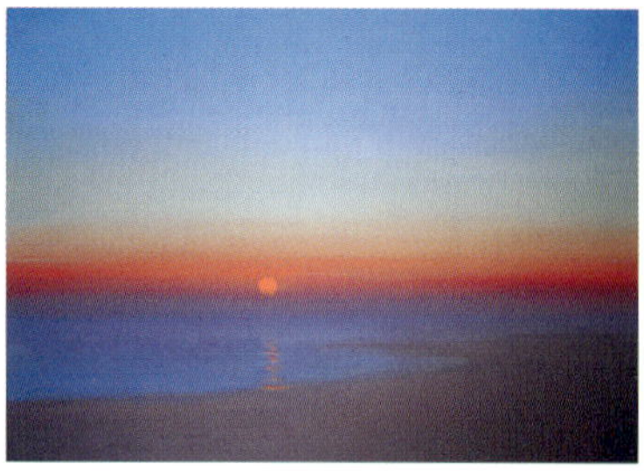

Jackets & magazine covers

1976
Leisure Painter
Cover artist July issue 'March Morning'

1978
Leisure Painter
Cover artist February issue 'West Country Fishing Boats'

1984
Night at the Carn
AL Rowse
William Kimber

1986
Stories from Trenarren
AL Rowse
William Kimber

1987
Reader's Digest
Cover artist July issue 'White Dome and Geraniums'

1988
Arts Review
Cover artist July issue 'Planters Chair in the Poolroom, Sancreed'

1989
Reader's Digest
Cover artist August issue 'From the Studio Door'

1990
Reader's Digest
Cover artist August issue 'Bougainvillaea'

Arts Review
Cover artist November issue 'Mauve and Blue'

1991
Leading Edge
Cover artist Summer issue 4 'Cadmium Orange'

The Miracle of Mindfulness
Thich Naat Hanh Rider

An Introduction to Zen Buddhism
DT Suzuki
Rider – Random Century Group Ltd

Living by Zen
DT Suzuki
Rider – Random Century Group Ltd

1993
For the Time Being
Michael Fisher SSF Gracewing

1996
When Words Fail
David Shearlock Canterbury Press

Christina Rossetti
Everyman's Poetry JM Dent, London

Offshore Finance Handbook
Sue Stuart Lily Publications

1999
The Open Secret (Second edition)
Tony Parsons Connections

2000
Remembering Blue
Connie May Fowler Bantam Press

Cornish Connection
Save the Children Fund, Redruth Branch

2001
From Now to Eternity Margaret Laird
Religious & Moral Education Press

Articles and features

1967
The Cornish Review Autumn issue No 7
Denys val Baker

1976
Leisure Painter 'Sources of Inspiration' April, May, June & July issues

1978
Leisure Painter 'Painting with Oil Colours' January, February and March issues

1981
Time Out Sarah Kent on the opening of 'An Experience with Light'

1983
Woman and Home February issue 'New Horizons' Lesley-Ann Jones

1988
Kindred Spirit Spring Vol1 No2 Interview by Tony Parsons

Arts Review 15th July issue 'Seeing Beauty for the First Time' Max Wykes-Joyce

1989
Harpers and Queen December issue
Jennifer's Diary

The Sunday Times Colour Magazine
24th September 'Upstart' Alison Beckett

The West Cornwall Experience 'Artistic dimensions' Douglas Williams

1990
London Portrait November issue
'The Mind's Eye' Emma Burn

Arts Review Profile:
'John Miller' Frank Ruhrmund

Homes and Gardens December issue
'Miller's Retreat' Joanna Laidlaw

Dictionary of 20th Century Painters and Sculptors Frances Spalding First edition

Dictionary of British Art VI
Antique Collectors' Club Publications

1991
Leading Edge Summer issue 4 'Artist and Mystic' Tony Roeber and Julie Pinson

1993
Eighty from the Eighties Sue Monro
Photograph by Ashley Peters
Rainyday Publications

1994
Gardens Illustrated June/July issue
'Miller's Tale' Kirsty Fergusson

What's On Inside Cornwall October/November issue 'Painting the Blues' Felicity Whitehead

1995
100 Years in Newlyn Diary of a Gallery
Melissa Hardie Patten Press

1996
Another View – Art in St Ives Marion Whybrow

1999
Arts & Crafts – South West Guide July/August issue 'Seeing without looking' Glyn Macey

1999
The History of Christianity in Cornwall
Royal Institution of Cornwall

2000
Cornwall For Ever Cornwall Heritage Trust

Hello! magazine 11th July John Miller photographed at the White Gallery, Hove with Jean Shrimpton, who opened the exhibition, and Gary Rhodes

Art and Christianity Enquiry Bulletin October issue No 24 'John Miller' Stephen Laird

Cornish Connection October Save the Children Fund, Redruth branch

Western Morning News 2nd June Profile
Frank Ruhrmund

2001
Exeter Express and Echo 5th March Profile
David Marston

Behind the Canvas Sarah Brittain & Simon Cook

Radio and television
since moving to Cornwall

1981
'Made in the West' ITV Produced by Kevin Crooks. Programme received bronze medal for TSW

1986
'A Breath of Fresh Air' TSW and Channel 4 TV play about the Newlyn School painters. Miller played Frank Bramley with Nanette Newman as Elizabeth Forbes and Michael Culver as Stanhope Forbes.
Produced by Kevin Crooks

'Midweek' with Libby Purvis on BBC radio

'Highway' with Sir Harry Secombe ITV

'Record Choice' with Ted Gundry Radio Cornwall 11th June

1987
'At home with . . .' Tim Hubbard BBC Radio Cornwall

'Looking West' exhibition Spotlight South West September

'A Painter in Search of St. Francis' on ITV
Two half-hour programmes written and narrated by John Miller. Produced by John Bartlett 13th and 20th December

1990
'Inspiration' with Kate Figes Kaleidoscope BBC Radio4. Produced by Sally Marmion 31st August

1991
'Dig' with Carolyn Marshall an offbeat gardening programme on Channel 4 9th May

'Songs of Praise' with Pam Rhodes
BBC1 27th October

1994
'Rhodes around Britain' with chef Gary Rhodes 5th July

1996
'Time of My Life' with Dennis Cornish
Westcountry Television 21st October

1998
Radio Cornwall interview by Dan Rivers following collection of 'Interior Landscapes' in Gary Rhodes new restaurant 'Rhodes in the Square' June

1999
'Postards' a series of early morning homilies recorded by The Rev'd Chris McQuillen-Wright Pirate FM Radio

'Collectors' Lot' with Jethro
Channel Four 30th November

2000
'Testament', half-hour programme produced and directed by Jill Husband
Carlton Broadcasting 12th November

'So you want to be an artist?' at Kitley House by Wildcard Film and Television Ltd
3rd December with Alan Cotton, Ken Howard, Graham Ovenden and Annie Ovenden

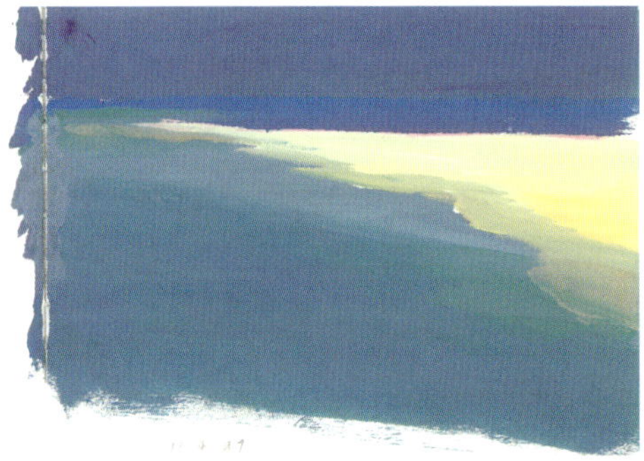

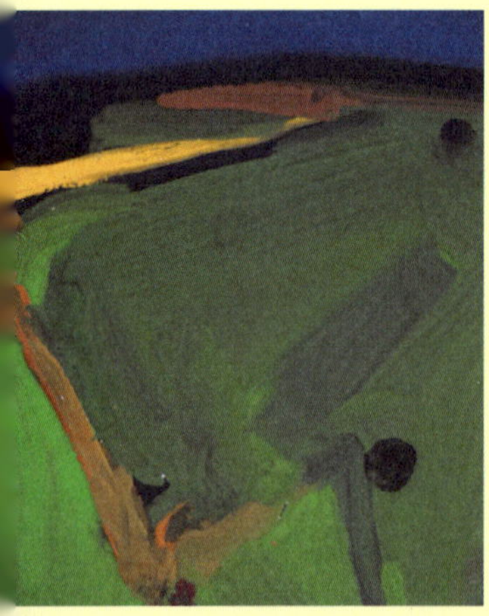